Diamond Street

The Hidden World of Hatton Garden

RACHEL LICHTENSTEIN

D0489887

PENGUIN BOOKS

PENGUIN BOOKS

Published by the Penguin Group
Penguin Books Ltd, 80 Strand, London WC2R ORL, England
Penguin Group (USA) Inc., 375 Hudson Street, New York, New York 10014, USA
Penguin Group (Canada), 90 Eglinton Avenue East, Suite 700, Toronto, Ontario, Canada M4P 2Y3
(a division of Pearson Penguin Canada Inc.)
Penguin Ireland, 25 St Stephen's Green, Dublin 2, Ireland
(a division of Penguin Books Ltd)
Penguin Group (Australia), 707 Collins Street, Melbourne, Victoria 3008, Australia
(a division of Pearson Australia Group Pty Ltd)
Penguin Books India Pvt Ltd, 11 Community Centre,
Panchsheel Park, New Delhi – 110 017, India
Penguin Group (NZ), 67 Apollo Drive, Rosedale, Auckland 0632, New Zealand
(a division of Pearson New Zealand Ltd)
Penguin Books (South Africa) (Pty) Ltd, Block D, Rosebank Office Park,
181 Jan Smuts Avenue, Parktown North, Gauteng 2193, South Africa

Penguin Books Ltd, Registered Offices: 80 Strand, London WC2R ORL, England

www.penguin.com

First published by Hamish Hamilton 2012
Published in Penguin Books 2013
001

Copyright © Rachel Lichtenstein, 2012
All rights reserved

The moral right of the author has been asserted

Every effort has been made to trace copyright holders and to obtain their permission for the use of copyright material. The publisher apologizes for any errors or omissions and would be grateful to be notified of any corrections that should be incorporated in future editions of this book

Typeset by Palimpsest Book Production Limited, Falkirk, Stirlingshire
Printed in Great Britain by Clays Ltd, St Ives plc

ISBN: 978–0–141–01852–2

www.greenpenguin.co.uk

MIX
Paper from
responsible sources
FSC
www.fsc.org   FSC® C018179

Penguin Books is committed to a sustainable
future for our business, our readers and our planet.
This book is made from Forest Stewardship
Council™ certified paper.

ALWAYS LEARNING   **PEARSON**

This book is dedicated to Dave Harris and Isadore Mitziman

Here had I come with a notebook and a pencil proposing to spend a morning reading, supposing that at the end of the morning I should have transferred the truth to my notebook. But I should need to be a herd of elephants, I thought, and a wilderness of spiders, desperately referring to the animals that are reputed longest lived and most multitudinously eyed, to cope with all this. I should need claws of steel and beak of brass even to penetrate the husk. How shall I ever find the grains of truth embedded in all this mass of paper?

Virginia Woolf, *A Room of One's Own*

Contents

Contents

List of Illustrations

List of Illustrations

Introduction

If it is so that we go through the world shedding phantom semblances
of ourselves to hover about those places we have lived intensely, then
Hatton Garden should surely be full of illustrious shadows.

Howard Marryat and Una Broadbent, *The Romance of Hatton Garden*

Over the years my husband, grandfather, uncles, aunts and parents
have all worked in London's jewellery and diamond quarter, Hatton
Garden. My memories of the place go back to childhood, when I
would accompany my father there on buying trips, searching for
stock to sell at his antique stall in Portobello Market. I remember
following him through narrow entrances near to the shops, up dark
stairwells, to tiny, stuffy rooms on the floors above, to meet with
one of the many dealers in second-hand goods who operated in the
area. Security was tight. Entrance to these rooms was often via
three separate steel doors, each of which had to lock shut before the
next could be opened. Once inside I would sit on a chair in the corner and wait while my father talked business before examining the
items he'd come to see. There was ritual in this process. Heavy,
black velvet-lined cases would be ceremoniously lifted out of the
cool depths of large, green metal safes, before being placed on to a
desk, lit by a bright overhead light. Then my father would slip his
hand into the pocket of his sheepskin coat and pull out his ten-
power jeweller's loupe, which he would expertly hold against one
eye by tightly screwing up that side of his face. Then, slowly, he
would pick up each diamond ring, Victorian cameo brooch, ruby
pendant or other piece of antique jewellery and inspect it at great
length under the white light, sometimes tutting a little if he noticed
an imperfection. After much haggling back and forth a price would

be agreed on and the deal sealed with a handshake and the Yiddish words *mazel und broche* before goods were exchanged for cash. This is the way the flow of business has taken place in Hatton Garden for over a century. It is a secret, private, hidden world that operates according to a strict set of unspoken internal laws: never screw a partner; and once a deal is done it must be adhered to.

In the mid 1980s, when the antique business was no longer providing a viable income for my father, he began working full time in Hatton Garden, managing the shop of a childhood friend from Essex. I spent my summer breaks from university helping out by working as a runner; collecting jobs for customers from the workshops dotted around the area. While waiting for the finished item, I would stand and watch elderly men at work, hunched over wooden jewellery benches in quiet concentration; welding bands of platinum together with miniature tools, inserting tiny sparkling stones into clawed mounts, cutting deep-blue sapphires into shape with diamond-tipped saws. Most developed their skills over decades, starting as fourteen-year-old apprentices sweeping up the shavings of gold left on the floor at night, before moving on to work at the benches. One of these older craftsmen told me: 'Hatton Garden before the war was a Dickensian-looking place with a patchwork of run-down houses. There would be a setter in one room, a polisher in another, an engraver in another and if you opened a door sometimes a rat would run out. There were no retail shops in Hatton Garden then, the public was not encouraged to go there. It was primarily a place of manufacture and the centre of the world's diamond trade.'

The men in the workshops told me stories about the master craftsmen who once worked in great numbers in Hatton Garden. 'We had one old Jewish chap I used to sit next to, called Lapidus,' said Dave Harris, a former diamond cutter, 'who had been born in Russia in about 1860. He ran away from home and got apprenticed in Germany, earning nothing. He told me he used to lodge in a room with just a bed and a chair and live off bread and water. In the 1900s he moved to Paris and became a master jeweller and in the

1920s he moved to England. His daughter became quite well known on the stage, Lily Lapidus. He was in his late seventies when he came to us. He worked piecework, so his wages never came to more than three pounds a week, but he made the most exquisite pieces of jewellery I'd ever seen, which often took him up to three months to make. The most beautiful thing I saw him produce was a rose-shaped diamond brooch, set in eighteen-carat gold, with enamelled petals, covered in beautifully set precious stones and diamonds, which had been commissioned by a Russian princess.

'In those days every pearl that ended up in a British jewellery shop, every precious stone, every diamond, rough or cut, came through Hatton Garden. All the big brokerage took place there and the craftsmen of Hatton Garden and Paris had the best international reputations in the world for fine, handmade jewellery. Today the majority of the jewellery sold in the street is either cast or imported. A few of the master craftsmen remain, but when they die, their knowledge will be lost. The tradition of passing on skills from one generation to the next in the Garden appears to have stopped.'

Although Hatton Garden is no longer the centre of the world jewellery market, it remains a major player and still houses the largest cluster of jewellery-based businesses in the UK, with over 300 separate companies that support the trade in the immediate area, and nearly sixty retail shops in the street itself. From the Holborn to the Clerkenwell end of the road, rows of jewellery shops line the street on both sides. Another network of hidden spaces exists both above and below these places: heavily guarded underground vaults filled with wholesale stores of gold and silver, workshops where specialist items are painstakingly made to order, small rooms where precious-gem dealers operate and Hasidic diamond merchants sit examining glittering stones, held tightly between silver tweezers.

Hatton Garden is a self-contained place. Everything the business needs is locatable within a square mile: from the London Diamond Bourse, to the gold-bullion dealers, to the suppliers of precious metals, stones, gems and jewels, to the shops that sell the finished products. The majority of people who work there, in all areas of the business,

are still Jewish. Orthodox Jews trade happily with assimilated secular Jews like my father. There are Jewish people working in Hatton Garden today from Israel, Iran, America, Holland, Britain and many other countries, who have links to an international network of jewellery markets in Antwerp, Tel-Aviv, New York, the Far East and other places.

Despite the global nature of the street, there is a distinct village atmosphere. Everyone knows each other, gossip is rife and much like in the former Eastern European *shtetls*, there are plenty of *schlemiels*, *menschen* and other intriguing Jewish characters making up the community.

One of these is Isadore Mitziman, known with affection to all as Mitzy. For over half a century he regularly made weekly rounds to the shops and suppliers in the street, personally dropping off his much sought-after 'specials': French court wedding rings, made by him to order, by pulling lengths of gold thread with a large pair of tongs through different-sized holes on a drawplate until he got the right measurements. Each time the threads were pulled through they had to be quenched and then reheated again. It was hard physical work and Mitzy had tremendous strength in his upper body, although he was nearly lame in his right foot. He worked from a small attic room near to Clerkenwell Green and it seems unlikely that his operation was ever commercially successful. The process involved in making these rings was lengthy, Mitzy was scrupulously honest and never overcharged, raising his prices only by the bare minimum when the value of gold and platinum increased, and he never added on a penny if the quality of the metal declined, causing his rings to crumble and break halfway through the making. His workshop 'was at the top of a steep flight of stairs and very run down, filthy', remembers my father. 'You could barely move in there because there was stuff everywhere: files, papers, ancient equipment, boxes, rolls of gold thread, tools; it probably hadn't been cleaned for decades.'

Mitzy's life story was shrouded in mystery. He always dressed like a tramp, wearing shabby trousers tied up with string and a dirty old mac, but there were rumours he owned millions and lived with a young blonde wife in a large house in Essex. He'd come limping into the shops, energetically dragging one large flat foot behind the other, and sit down with a sigh, wiping his bald head with a stained handkerchief pulled from his pocket. Sometimes he would come into the back of my parents' shop for a cup of tea and tell stories about his time as a flight engineer, assigned to Lancaster bombers during the Second World War. Once he told me how he acquired the legendary eighteenth-century drawplate that he used to make his rings with: 'I bought it in the 1930s from a second-hand wedding ring manufacturer who had gone bankrupt. They had bought it from an antique shop years before. When I examined it I found a date on the back, 1789. This was the period when the French demanded smooth court wedding rings that felt like silk gloves.' The rings Mitzy was making with this drawplate, over 200 years after it was manufactured, had the same profile as eighteenth-century rings once much in demand by French royalty.

Mitzy was well liked and respected by everyone in the community. I often saw him around the area, chatting on the street corners with shop owners, visiting the workshops or gold-bullion dealers. He retired from the Garden some time ago, and no one had seen him for a long time, when I happened to bump into him by chance in 2004 in Brick Lane, arguing with a couple of homeless-looking men outside the Bagel Bakery at the top of the street. He didn't notice me at first. He had a salt-beef sandwich in one hand and a coffee in the other. Hot brown liquid was spilling from his polystyrene cup on to the pavement as his arms waved about in a wild fashion. As I approached, I realized his shouts were in Yiddish. I called his name and he turned towards me, spraying coffee and scraps of salt beef all over his friends as he did so. He came over to where I was standing and shook my hand vigorously and we spent some time talking. I told him about the book on Brick Lane I was writing at the time and he smiled. 'I grew up here,' he said, in his lisping *Yiddishe* accent. 'Not far from where we are now standing.' Then he began to tell me stories from his childhood, covering me in a fine film of spittle as he did so. He told me about the hidden *mikvah* behind the great mosque, his visits to the Russian Steam Baths and tales from Black Lion Yard: 'Those guys in the workshops there used to see the kids down in the street and throw pennies to them,' he said, chuckling and choking at the same time. 'But they'd heat them up first with the flames of the welding torches, then laugh when they tried to pick up the hot coins.' I asked him if he remembered Rodinsky: 'He was one of the Whitechapel Cowboys, I think,' he said. 'You know, the *frummers*, in their big hats and long black coats, that's what we used to call them, the Whitechapel Cowboys. Of course most of them have left here now, but there are still many working in Hatton Garden. Some of them I have known since they were kids.'

Moving on from tales of the East End, he began to talk about Hatton Garden, which he felt to be far more interesting. He knew the territory well, having worked there all his life. He spoke at great speed, his large eyes expanding widely as he talked. He told me that the entire area floats above a labyrinthine network of subterranean spaces: abandoned railway platforms, buried deep underground, decommissioned government bunkers and forgotten rivers. 'It amazes me the entire place doesn't cave in,' he said. 'With the weight of gold and heavy metal above and all those ancient, watery passageways honeycombing the ground underneath.' He told me fragmented stories about chain gangs marching from Hatton Garden to an underground river near Fleet Street, before travelling on to Australia. He spoke of the Diamond Club in the street being used by medical students from Barts for dissecting dead bodies. He recounted stories of highwaymen and daring thefts where jewels were scattered over the pavement, and told tales of abandoned monasteries, extraterrestrial sightings, hauntings and freak fairs. 'Did you know,' he said, grabbing my arm tightly, 'that Hatton Garden was once the site of a medieval palace, surrounded by vast gardens, with fountains, vineyards and orchards?'

Before Mitzy had a chance to tell me more, one of his friends shouted something to him in Yiddish, and with a stamp of his foot

he was back off into the throng, arms akimbo, passionately contrib-
uting to the heated debate. I haven't seen him since, but he did spark
my interest in the wider history of the area, and I resolved, one day,
to find out more.

Diamond Street

The further one probes into the musty old records
the more interesting does the story become.

Howard Marryat and Una Broadbent, *The Romance of Hatton Garden*

Hatton Garden is the fold in the map, a place on the edge of different borderlands that sits on the city fringe, somewhere between Clerkenwell, Holborn and Farringdon. In the *London A–Z* the street is defined as a single, long, straight road, just within the borough of Camden. The southern end intersects with Holborn Circus, a busy roundabout where five other roads meet, and the northern end flows directly into Clerkenwell Road.

I found, however, that after speaking with people who work there today, the geography of the street became more fluid. For them, 'the Garden' describes a wider area, including Hatton Garden itself and a number of surrounding and interconnecting roads, filled with businesses connected to the jewellery trade, which extends to Leather Lane to the west, Farringdon Road to the east.

I wanted to find out if the shifting borders of this place had any relationship to Mitzy's tales of underground rivers, lavish gardens and forgotten palaces. I began my researches by surfing the web. Most of my hits consisted of brief potted histories of the place attached to jewellery shop websites. Many of them, including the Wikipedia entry, claimed Hatton Garden had been a jewellery quarter since medieval times. Others told of a large estate, belonging to the Bishops of Ely, which occupied the land from the twelfth century. I found intriguing fragments of other stories relating to the area: tales of Roman remains, references to medieval soldier monks, Tudor feasts, prisons, rivers and grand mansions.

At this point in my research I had no expert guide to walk me through the history of the district, as Professor Bill Fishman had so generously done for me before in Whitechapel. The story of Hatton Garden is not well known. There are no walking tours of the place and although the wider area has fascinated many great writers – from Shakespeare, Dickens and George Gissing to contemporary authors such as Peter Ackroyd, Iain Sinclair, Sarah Wise and Michael Moorcock – there is not an extensive canon of literature to refer to, as there is with East London.

To uncover the story of Hatton Garden for myself I knew I needed to visit London's libraries and museums and call up from deep underground vaults below the city streets all the archival records I could find relating to the place. My first trip was to the oldest repository of London's history, the Guildhall Library, which is located a short walk away from Hatton Garden, in the financial district of the City, within a square of medieval stone buildings that look entirely out of time with the surrounding architecture of glass and concrete. In the heart of this complex stands the beautiful Gothic Guildhall building, once the administrative and ceremonial centre of the city – the most important secular building of Elizabethan London. The library was originally housed in the Guildhall but in the 1970s the collections were moved to a purpose-built building on the opposite side of the square.

After a thorough security check, I made my way into the library and towards the manuscripts reading room, where I hoped to examine old maps of London and learn more about the early topography of the Hatton Garden area. Luckily for me, the Guildhall's maps expert, Jeremy Smith, was on duty that day. Pleased to have an opportunity to share his extensive knowledge he told me the oldest printed map of the city is known as the Agas map or Civitas Londinium and was probably surveyed between 1570 and 1605. It is generally attributed to a cartographer known as Ralph Agas, although Jeremy said there is no real evidence for this. This map had been based on an earlier copperplate map produced in the 1550s. Only three panels survive from the copperplate map and no original printed version. Before I looked at the Agas map Jeremy suggested

I studied *The City of London from Prehistoric Times*, an atlas of reconstructed maps put together by academics at Oxford University in the late 1980s. 'They used scientific methods of cartography and survey to interpret early medieval records, such as the land register, diary entries, commentaries and various other historical documents, and then laid these findings over skeleton street maps, with control points of known features. This is the closest you can get to examining London before Agas's map.'

The next few hours passed quickly as I pored over the coloured prints in the atlas. The prehistoric map revealed a wild London landscape of wooded valleys and grasslands on either side of an unrecognizably wide River Thames. In the map dated AD 200, the ancient walled Roman city of Londinium sat on the north shore of the Thames, stretching west from the current site of Blackfriars to the Tower of London in the east. Holborn, just outside the city walls, was a place of open fields, uninhabited apart from a few farming cottages.

The dominant feature of the territory around the Hatton Garden area of that period was the River Fleet, once a major tributary to the Thames, which formed a natural boundary between the west of the city and its environs. In Roman times the Fleet was London's second-largest river, fast-flowing and navigable, with a tide mill in its estuary and a width of over 100 feet at its mouth with the Thames at Blackfriars. In this map the river filled the valley, which later became Farringdon and Clerkenwell. Commentaries to the map stated that during the Roman period the banks of the Fleet often burst, turning the surrounding area into floodplains, making the land unsuitable for housing but perfect for growing crops to feed the huge Roman army living in the city near by.

For me, the most familiar element of this antique terrain was a long straight road in the same position as Holborn High Road today. This ancient thoroughfare was originally built over 2,000 years ago as a major Roman route running from east to west of the walled city.

I knew the Romans devoted the roadside beyond the city limits to the dead. I remembered the burial site in Spitalfields, when part of a Roman cemetery had been excavated from behind the market, thought to be the location of Ermine Street, another major Roman road into the capital. In 1995 I installed a large mosaic on top of that site, made with the help of over 100 East London schoolchildren. The mosaic had been commissioned as a temporary measure to stop the development of the land before the dig took place. In 1999 the mosaic was removed and installed on Brick Lane. The Spitalfields site was then boarded up while an archaeological team from the Museum of London unearthed extraordinary treasures there.

I read that elaborate Roman tombs and memorials had also been found during excavations near St Andrew's Church cemetery, which is situated near to the southern exit of Hatton Garden today, making this ancient church a place of burial for over two millennia. The

Museum of London's archaeological department had also uncovered fragmentary traces of Roman burial grounds around Holborn Viaduct and nearby Fleet Street. I decided to visit the Museum of London straight away, to see if I could find out more about these archaeological finds.

After a short walk, across the labyrinthine Barbican estate, I reached the museum, home to the world's largest collection of urban history. Located on an island roundabout, surrounded by busy roads, the museum overlooks fragments of the original Roman walls of the city.

The first gallery showed how the Thames has shaped the London region, sculpting the landscape over time, as changing sea levels and

advancing and retreating ice sheets constantly changed the route of the river. In a large glass case sat a magnificent display of artefacts recovered from the river bed: shards of bronze swords, fragile pieces of bone, horn, pottery and flint – the fragmented evidence of thousands of years of human habitation along the banks of the Thames.

In the next gallery I discovered that in places such as Holborn, on the city boundaries, there were probably small British communities living in native-style roundhouses, built of wood, straw and mud. No traces of them remain. I was fascinated by the exhibits on display, the recovered relics of Roman times: marble idols of gods and goddesses and the gold coins retrieved from among the bones; payment for Charon, the Hades ferryman, for safe passage across the river of the dead on the long journey to the underworld. The last display case in this gallery was filled with objects excavated from the site behind Spitalfields Market: a sarcophagus containing the skeletal remains of a noble Roman lady, fine fragments of silk as fragile as a butterfly's wing, jet hairpins and a perfectly intact opal-green glass phial.

An exhibit in the Tudor Gallery stated that Cheapside, not Hatton Garden, was London's oldest gold and silverware quarter. Once known as Goldsmith's Row, the street had over fifty-two goldsmiths by the late fifteenth century. A quote from Andrea Trevisano's description of London, *c.* 1498, describes Cheapside as: 'So rich and full of silver vessels, great and small, that in Milan, Rome, Venice and Florence I do not think there would be found so many.' On display was a selection of jewellery from the Cheapside Hoard, which had been discovered when workmen digging at a building site on Goldsmith's Row in 1912 drove a pickaxe through a decaying wooden chest buried under the floorboards of a crumbling Tudor house they had been employed to demolish. Hundreds of pieces of early-seventeenth-century jewellery spilled on to the floor. The treasure was split between a few museums but the bulk of it went to the Museum of London. In velvet-lined cabinets, miniature scent bottles covered in fine enamel sat beside delicate neck chains, their intricate filigree work revealing the great skill of London's jewellers and craftsmen during that time.

In a dark corner of the gallery, standing vertically in a bulletproof-glass case in low light, was perhaps the most precious artefact in the museum: one of the three original surviving copperplates of the oldest map of London estimated to date from 1550. The reverse side of the plate had been painted on, probably after being thrown away by the printer. Some details on the copperplate had been worn away by the hundreds of ink impressions that must have been made from it but the quality of the engravings that remained was extraordinary. Still visible were details such as the feathers on the archer's arrows in Moor Fields and the severed limbs of traitors, spiked on to poles on the turrets of Moor Gate.

After spending a few hours looking at the rest of the galleries I returned to the front desk to attempt to find out more about Roman Hatton Garden. The information assistant gave me the details of the Museum of London's archaeological department, who had undertaken the excavations near to the street. I contacted Jon Chandler, the archaeologist who had written the report on the dig. He invited me to meet him to discuss their extraordinary finds.

2

An Apprentice

The dealers in gems are apparently quite careless with their goods. They trust each other implicitly, passing the stones to and fro with familiarity and trustfulness born of long practice. No guard seems to be kept on their treasures. This carelessness of course is only apparent, as the outsider would soon find were he to assume membership of a trade in which every man knows his neighbours.

George R. Sims, *Living London*

'You must speak to Dave Harris,' said my father. 'He is the only person I can think of who will have pre-war memories of the street. He must be in his nineties by now. He's been working in Hatton Garden for most of his life and only retired recently. Up until a few years ago he used to come into the shop to see me, shouting "Hello, boy!" in his great booming voice, before clapping me on the back with a huge hand and hurling himself into a chair. He always called me "boy", even though I was in my sixties by then. He is such a great big hearty bear of a man, always so enthusiastic, upbeat and warm, a very honourable character. He knew your uncles and grandfather too. When Grandpa's shop in East London went bust and he started dealing in second-hand jewellery, he would come up to Hatton Garden with the stock he bought from Brick Lane Market and Cuttler Street and sell it in the cafés here. That's where he met Dave; must have been the early 1950s.'

When he opened the front door to his neatly kept flat in Pinner, Dave Harris, although bent double and leaning heavily on a walking stick, still towered above me. After pinching my cheeks and asking after the family, the elderly Hatton Garden dealer thrust a large tumbler of whisky in one of my hands and a plate of smoked-salmon sandwiches in the other, before leading me over to the sofa to sit down and talk.

'I have spent nearly seventy years working in Hatton Garden,' he said, in a rich, gravelly voice, while eyeballing me intently. 'Anyone that knows me there will let me poke my head in their safe and think nothing of it. You have to be honest in this trade. You always get a rogue one here or there but not often. Because once you have a bad name in the street, you're finished. There are three "I"s in this business: integrity, intelligence and industry. You have to work hard to get on.'

He talked for some time about his love of the jewellery business, which he called 'a good, respectable line of work' with 'great camaraderie between all the different factors of the trade'. He felt things had changed in the street since the Second World War: 'Before then people always tried to help each other out, it was one lovely business. Afterwards the atmosphere was different, but still the greatest thing in Hatton Garden is trust.'

Born in East London in 1919 to Jewish parents, Dave left school early after his father died, leaving five children. At the age of thirteen, he started working in the fur trade in the city but six months later he was laid off. The year was 1932, towards the end of the Depression, a time when even seasonal jobs were hard to come by. Luckily, he had an uncle working in a diamond firm in Charles Street (now Greville Street) who managed to arrange an apprenticeship for him.

'A number of my schoolfriends were working in Hatton Garden then and we used to walk to work and back each day. Most of the East London apprentices lived at home with their mothers. They were saving their money to buy a house. The big ambition was to buy a new property in Canvey Island, which was being developed at the time. Only £300 for a brand-new house.'

He described Hatton Garden in the 1930s as a run-down place, full of manufacturing workshops and offices: 'The big offices

belonged to the diamond dealers, the smaller ones were for the brokers, who carried the goods around for the dealers, visiting the
workshops and the Bourse, that is how trade is done, even to this
day. The big brokers were merchants, or sightholders for De Beers.
All the world's rough diamonds were once sorted in Hatton Garden
because of De Beers.

'The houses down the Clerkenwell end were the original seventeenth-
century buildings but they were all falling down, crumbling and full
of rats. Clerkenwell was the silversmith place; Hatton Garden was
gold, platinum and diamonds. The only jewellery shop I remember
being on Hatton Garden was S. H. Harris but they sold exclusively
to the trade. The general public only started coming to Hatton Garden when the shops arrived in the late 1950s, early 1960s; before then
they went to Black Lion Yard, that was the main place.

'My main memory of Hatton Garden during the 1930s was of
seeing deals being conducted on the street. You would see men huddled together in clusters on the pavement, heads together,
magnifying glass out, examining some tiny object, usually a rough
diamond. This was dangerous and in my opinion showy. Many conducted their business in the small kosher restaurants that were once
scattered around Hatton Garden, catering for the large Jewish and
Orthodox population that worked there. There were still remnants
of Little Italy in the area as well, with many good Italian cafés and
delis near by, but very few Italians went into the jewellery trade.
Back then most of the dealers, workshop owners, traders and brokers were Jewish.

'The biggest people in Hatton Garden when I started were the
Italian barometer makers Negretti & Zambra, who had a large
building down the end of Hatton Garden by Holborn Circus. They
funded the Italian Church. I remember watching the Italians making ice cream in the street in their barrows, and we used to go to
Terroni's all the time, which had the most fantastic food, but like
many they have been forced out, the rents are too high.

'Leather Lane in the 1930s was only opened at lunchtimes but you
could get bargains down there, really good stuff. Today it's rubbish.

It was a real old English market: sweets, chocolate, all cut price, magicians doing tricks. After the war it was one of the only places you could buy melons.'

Dave served his apprenticeship in a cramped, underground jewellery workshop, with twenty-eight other men and boys: 'During the first year, being the last one in, I would do the donkey work, all the fetching and carrying, making the tea, sweeping up. The others would pull my leg, sending me on wild goose chases for a diamond magnet or elbow grease, things like that.

'One of our apprentices working in the workshop became one of the best craftsmen in the trade. He was an orphan, who was terribly bullied by some of the other workers, but it made him into a man. My boss, the governor, dressed in a dark jacket and striped trousers. The workers wore overalls or long coats over their clothes. We had a union for jewellers and dental craftsmen; they made agreements with the owners, which were honoured.

'About half of the workforce were Jewish, some were brilliant craftsmen, most were well educated and everyone worked hard. They were all respectable people and became like a family to me. Some of the older ones had been in the First World War. On my first day one of them got a razor-sharp scalpel and drew it right into his leg. I nearly passed out. He had a wooden leg. I didn't know it was his joke for all the new apprentices. Some of the veterans would talk about their experiences, terrible stories, but mostly we didn't talk, we sang, old war songs, a bit of opera maybe but mainly musical-hall songs.'

Dave worked at a round wooden bench with a pin in the middle and a leather skin hanging beneath to catch the gold dust. Underneath was a tray in case any dust escaped the skin. When he started working on a piece of jewellery, the precious metal required to make it was carefully weighed out before and after the job was completed, along with any gold dust collected in the tray and any scrap metal left over.

'If you were short too often, you got the sack. This is one of the reasons the apprentices used to work late. Every night we had racks on the floor, which we'd pick up and shake, then we would sweep up the gold, silver or platinum dust off the floor, and put it in the sweeps. If you went out in the day you had to wash your hands in a bowl of water and then at the end of the day this water was poured into another bowl, with a sacking across the top, and the wet metal dust was all collected. Sometimes a boy like me would take all the collected dust to one of the firms to be melted down. I had to stand there all day, in a room like a furnace, and watch to make sure they didn't nick any of it. Other times I would melt all the sweeps myself and at the end of the year take the lot to Johnson Matthey's and they'd dip into the bucket and get a sample and give us a quote on the barrel.'

During the second year of his apprenticeship he sat next to another man on the bench who taught him how to make the diamond wristwatches and line bracelets the firm were producing at the time. 'The only section in gold was the clasp at the end, which was made from hard white gold. The rest was platinum. Eventually we got some blocks so we could press up parts of the backs of the cases but before then every part of the watches was made by hand. You would start off by getting a block of soft iron and filing it into the perfect shape of the inside of a watch, with all the flanges on it. This would be case-hardened and used as a pressing tool. We had a big lid cake, which was a large piece of lead, and on to this you'd put the iron mould and press a thin piece of platinum on to it and then you'd cut this down. Then the other parts would be domed up and soldered on to the case. A movement bezel would be made the same way, all by hand. Boys did this work; it was very labour intensive to turn out platinum watches, at a price you couldn't believe. The movements, the internal mechanisms of the watches, came from Switzerland; the rest was made by us. When finished, the watches were sent out to a dial writer who'd paint the face and fit the hands on to the movement and then a glasscutter would cut the glass to fit and we'd solder it inside. The diamonds would be inserted by hand too. We had an ordinary Archimedes drill, which we used to drill the holes to place the diamonds in. The workers were all very adept; we had to be. The normal working day in winter was from nine in the morning until seven at night and, in the summer, from eight until six. Every night I took the precious items from the workshop to the nearest safe-deposit facility, which was in Chancery Lane, in a big case strapped on to my arm, so no one could take it from me, and the foreman would come with me as security.'

Much like today, all the different factions of the trade were based in and around Hatton Garden. The watches and bracelets produced in Dave's workshop were sent out to a workshop near by to be polished: 'There was a Jewish family next door, from Belgium, a father and all his daughters, who were very skilled polishers; their workshop had smudges all over the place – polishing is a dirty business. All the little meek apprentices would be lining up to go in and look at the girls and me, and the other boys would go right to the front. There were many Jewish polishers, setters, diamond dealers and cutters who arrived from Antwerp and Amsterdam before and during the war. Their numbers and skills really boosted the trade in

Hatton Garden. Before they arrived hardly any cutting took place in London. The Dutch and Belgium cutters worked in secret, carefully guarding their skills, refusing to let anyone into their workrooms to learn their art. They could charge a great deal, so many came to work in London. India is probably the biggest cutter in the world now although a lot takes place in Israel too. Most manufacturing today takes place in India, Hong Kong, China or other places in the Far East. They can produce goods at half the price that we can make them in England. We can't compete.'

During his apprenticeship years Dave earned the equivalent of two pounds a month in today's money, working a basic forty-nine hours a week, plus overtime. 'We were journeymen, working by the hour. Most of us didn't take holidays, maybe a few days in Southend or Brighton, nobody went abroad, but even the poorest boys seemed happy. The trade, compared to others, particularly back in the East End, paid well. For most it was a job for life, you worked your way up like I did, from apprentice, to workshop fore-man, to running your own business.'

It took him four years at the bench to finish his apprenticeship, then several more working as an improver before he was experienced enough to be considered a fully-fledged craftsman. He became so skilled at his work he once completed a job for the Queen Mother: a watch set in the top of a daffodil made from precious metals. 'The governor sent me out for a daffodil from the market and I copied it absolutely perfectly in platinum and gold. There were emeralds set down the stalk, it was a beautiful piece.'

He described pre-war Hatton Garden as: 'A quarter people went to for good handmade jewellery; there were many artists there then and business was good. Back then whenever women went out, to the theatre or a party, they had to be seen to be wearing jewellery: a pair of earrings, a double clip if it was in fashion, a pearl necklace or a decent ring. They wouldn't wear a paste ring. If you could afford it at all people spent the money on the real thing. The more important you were, the better the jewellery. You were judged by it, so the trade was a thriving industry.'

By 1938 Dave's hours had been reduced, war was coming and people were being laid off. On the first day of the war he signed up to the Air Force, where he stayed for the next seven years: 'We started out in Norway. I have many memories about the war, the loss of colleagues, painful stories. I remember the day France fell, they were trying to bomb all the airfields, then we were sent out to Ireland, the Shetland Islands, Iceland. I became an instructor for a while, before going to India.'

Returning to Hatton Garden in 1946 he found it transformed. 'Holborn had been badly bombed, the place looked more run down than ever, the trade had shrunk, those that were left made things for the black market, people paid cash for jewellery and some did quite well. There was such a shortage of everything, anything you made you could sell, although we were on very low wages and the master craftsmen had gone. The quality of the work being produced deteriorated a great deal but there was a big second-hand market: sovereigns, second hand things.'

Many jewellers and antique dealers, including my own grandfather, started dealing in this stuff and made a good living in the late 1940s and early 1950s. The black market flourished in many trades and if people had cash that they needed to spend they invested in diamonds, gold and antiques. It was a boom time for the dealers.

'After the war, people felt deprived of lovely things, and the antique goods were more affordable. We went from England exporting British jewellery to Germany and they were so pleased to see the things we took over there. The Nazis had sold and taken everything. Beautiful stones came to London in the Victorian era: diamonds, sapphires, emeralds. Wonderful brooches, cameos, necklaces. Most of those extraordinary pieces went abroad.'

From 1948 Dave trained for his gemological diploma at night. After finishing at the workshop he would rush down to the Chelsea School of Arts and Crafts to study. He completed his diploma and stayed on in the workshop until 1952 before setting up his own business dealing in second-hand jewellery with his brother, until they went their separate ways. Since then he has worked for himself. His wife and two sons now run the business.

My father described Dave as 'a real *mensch*, a wonderful, warm-hearted man, he was more than just another dealer, having done business with your grandfather, uncles and then me, because of the family connection he was a great help to me when we first opened our business on Hatton Garden; we regarded him and his family with great warmth and affection.' He was very saddened to learn of his passing, in February 2011.

3
MOLA

Gerarde, the herbalist, had a large physic-garden in Holborn.
The site is uncertain, but we may as well notice it here. He dates his
'Herbal' 'From my house in London, within the suburbs of London,
this first of December, 1597.' He mentions in his famous work many
rare plants which grew well in the garden behind his house.

Walter Thornbury, 'Holborn to Chancery Lane', *Old and New London*

Walking from Old Street tube station up to Eagle Wharf Road, on the
Hackney/Islington borders, I reached the large grey warehouse building that houses MOLA, the Museum of London's Archaeological
Department. After being buzzed through a series of doors I was given
a day pass and asked to wait for Jon Chandler to arrive. A few minutes
later a young man in a sweatshirt and jeans walked into the foyer and
shook my hand vigorously. I followed him down through a number
of underground concrete corridors until we reached a temperature-
controlled storeroom the size of an aircraft hangar, with fifty-foot-high
metal storage units arranged in uniform rows.

Jon had the reference for the dig I was interested in and walked
along the shelves until he found the right location. He turned a large
metal wheel, releasing the locked door, and pulled out a couple of
hefty boxes. 'From what I recall the only artefacts retrieved from the
site were small pieces of bone, a few roof tiles and some post-
Roman pottery,' he said. 'There are some maps and historical data
in the file, which might be helpful. Have a look through and ask
security to come and get me when you've finished.'

I sat at a table and examined the report on the Hatton Garden excavations, which began by describing the natural topography of the site, explaining that the whole of the Hatton Garden area sits on a substantial glacial-river terrace beside the Thames Valley, called the Hackney Gravels. Test pits dug in the area revealed little more than 'layers of dirty brick earth found sitting on top of clayey dump, on top of London clay'. After a number of pits were dug the only site thought to have moderate archaeological potential was on Saffron Hill, near to the Diamond Trading Centre and Bleeding Heart Yard.

The report states there was little archaeological evidence to suggest Holborn Road had been lined with buildings although Roman burial sites had been uncovered alongside it and were believed to be part of the cemetery that spread west of the Roman city along High Holborn. Finds from the dig included part of an inscription from the tomb of G. Pomponius Valens, and a lead cistern with coins of Vespasian. A sculptured Roman tombstone was also found in 1911 in nearby Lamb's Conduit Street, and other Roman burials were uncovered in Gray's Inn Road. In 1913 Roman urns were excavated from Holborn Hill and human burials were recorded to the west of the site, originally thought to be related to the civil wars of the sixteenth and seventeenth centuries, although they may date back to Roman times. Another archaeological brief in 1977 recorded the in-filled bed of the River Bourne, a tributary to the Fleet, located south-west of the site. There was no evidence of prehistoric or Saxon activity in the area.

The boxes contained reports and drawings but none of the artefacts from the dig. I called through to Jon Chandler to see if he could help locate them. After much searching through computer databases it seemed the objects were now off site and not available for viewing but Jon offered to show me the historical report he had written for the Hatton Garden excavations.

Taking the lift up to the bright, airy offices on the first floor, we made our way towards his desk, passing a large map of the geology beneath the streets of London pasted on the wall. 'This is an essential tool for investigations,' said Jon, stopping in front of it. 'Whenever we conduct a dig, we take into account what we call the subsurface topo graphy of the place, not just the modern street levels. It is what is going on underneath that is important for us.' Pointing at various coloured lines on the map, he told me, 'The yellow areas relate to the alluvial floodplains. The Thames wriggles around these floodplains so archaeology remains quite deep under this area. In prehistoric times, before rising sea levels, there were little islands of raised ground in the river where people might have lived, which are all buried under layers of deep alluvium. The orange layer represents the gravel terrace, which is the best ground to live on. To the north of the city all you have is London clay, which is no good for building or farming on and probably remained as deep forest for thousands of years.' He traced the flow of the Fleet on the map with his finger and explained how difficult the submerged river made it to excavate in the area: 'You have this valley coming down with alluvial flood deposits and the floodplain near the river bed, where things of archaeological interest can be many metres down, so to reach the early-prehistoric level in that area you would have to put huge step trenches in, which quickly fill with deep water, so it has not been practical to do much excavating there.'

I asked him about the recent discovery by archaeologists who had dug an exploratory borehole for the Crossrail Station on Charterhouse Street and found human bones, which had been taken away and examined for bubonic plague and anthrax spores. Jon had not worked on the dig but said the bones could have posed a biohazard risk, as certain spores can live for centuries and be spread in the air. Tube workers were killed by anthrax spores while working on the Metropolitan line in the nineteenth century. 'The bones could be from a number of different periods,' he said. 'The area you are interested in is so historically rich. They could be Roman, or from a burial ground attached to one of the workhouses that once existed there, or from a fourteenth-century plague pit, but there is no way to tell until they are tested.'

He led me through the spacious open-plan office to his desk and pulled out the report he had written on the Hatton Garden excavations from a large filing cabinet near by. 'Between the end of the Roman period and the middle of the eleventh century the area between the city walls and the River Fleet was abandoned, as was the Roman city,' said Jon. 'The community shifted westward towards the Covent Garden and Strand area and set up a trading emporium called Ludenwic. This continued for several hundred years until the Viking raids forced people back to the Roman city, where they refortified the walls; but your site is quite a distance from this main settlement and I don't think too much went on there during this time. Holborn Road was probably still in use back then but wouldn't have really been maintained. The first building of any

significance in the area was a wooden church, on the site of the present St Andrew's Church. A Westminster Abbey Charter of AD 951 refers to this church, and a later document, dated AD 959, describes the church as "old". Few archaeological features or finds have been discovered to further knowledge of the area during this period. The Domesday Survey of 1086 states that Holborn was a small hamlet of farmers who ploughed the land and kept pigs in the forests. After the Norman Conquest in 1066, the banks of the River Fleet, beyond the settled areas, became a focus for noxious industries such as tanning. A large number of leather fragments and animal bones in wet deposits were found in this area. The Fleet was frequently used for the disposal of butchery waste. Further arch- aeological evidence of medieval activity in the vicinity consists of dumped deposits and rubbish disposal. By the twelfth century the area became the home for a number of monasteries and religious houses, situated pretty much in the countryside. Beyond the settle- ments by the Fleet, the area was a place of open fields, natural springs and meadowlands. I'm not sure about the archaeological excavations that have taken place around these former religious institutions but we can look it up now on the GIS system.'

Swinging round in his swivel chair he turned on the computer on his desk. 'GIS is a fairly new technology,' he said, while waiting for the screen to flicker into life, 'and one of our main tools for writing reports. It's an amazing way to get layers of information about a place, exactly what you are trying to do with your writing project. GIS stands for Geographical Information System and it assists us greatly when producing archaeological desk-based assessments for developers. It is a computer map-based program, with Ordnance Survey mapping and many other layers of information on top of this, such as statuary designations like scheduled monuments, reg- istered parks and gardens, listed buildings, historic battlefields, protected wrecks, as well as information about past archaeological investigations in that area, antiquarian finds and geological informa- tion. The system also geo-references historic maps, stretching them over modern street maps to scale to help us examine the changes that have taken place in these areas over time. At the click of a but- ton you can see all of this data at once.'

Jon's hands flew over the keyboard, zooming into a large map of London on his screen until he located Hatton Garden. A skeletal outline of a contemporary map of the area appeared. To reveal the layers of information he clicked different coded subject areas, listed to the side of the map. 'I can let you flick through for a few minutes,' said Jon. 'The technology has its limits: the maps are only as good as the information gathered and can never tell the full story.'

The first map I looked at showed a jagged green line representing the boundary of the medieval city, over the top of a modern Ordnance Survey map, revealing just how near to the city wall Hatton Garden is. Clicking on the mapping contours of the area, faint, pastel-coloured lines appeared to denote the terrain. The slope of the former Fleet Valley could be clearly seen along with the River Fleet, hidden underneath the city streets today. The click of another button and a sixteenth-century hand-drawn map had been stretched over the modern map, in roughly the same location, clearly showing that the Hatton Garden area had once been a beautiful garden, with a large fountain in the centre surrounded by meadows and orchards. The boundary walls of this estate encircled the same area known as 'the Garden' today. It was as if an invisible perimeter from the past still existed there, constructed from generations of whispered memories about the place.

Later maps showed the gradual development of the area; from open fields, to an ecclesiastical estate, then to a residential street and, finally, to the commercial area it is today. As I clicked the various buttons, one layer of information disappeared, to be quickly replaced by the next. At points the computer could not keep up with my desire for data and the maps would appear one on top of the other, as if they had been torn by hand and haphazardly placed together in a random pile. Soon the image on the screen was covered in brightly coloured dots and lines as I pressed every available category; showing the sites of historical monuments, past archaeological excavations, antiquarian chance finds, Roman rivers, medieval drift geology, ancient boundaries and parishes, Saxon place names and roads. I took a series of photos with my digital camera, frustrated at my inability to decipher the complex image in front of me but determined that over time and through careful research, the story of this part of London would become known to me.

4

Gold

It is such an important time of your life when you get married
and Hatton Garden is a lovely place to go and buy your ring,
which you wear for ever, so it should be a special occasion.
The street is historical, there is a romance to the place, it is
where Londoners have gone for decades for their jewellery.

Angela, Hatton Garden secretary

There is at least one craftsman left in Hatton Garden today who still
uses some of the traditional methods employed by the medieval masters of Cheapside to make his jewellery and beautiful handmade
objects out of gold. His name is Gareth Harris and he is widely
regarded as one of the finest master goldsmiths in London today.

The East London poet Stephen Watts had given me Gareth's contact details a number of years ago when I needed someone to fill in
for me on one of my Whitechapel walks. We had never met but I had
heard lots about the long-time resident of Spitalfields, who like me is
a protégé of Bill Fishman, a walker of the streets of East London.

Gareth has been working for over thirty years, with his business
partner Dennis Smith, from a subterranean workshop in Hatton
Garden, underneath one of the last-remaining seventeenth-century
houses on the street. He invited me to come and meet him there
during his lunch hour.

The tiny entranceway to their building is squeezed between two
retail shops on the street. After pressing the intercom, I entered a dark
hallway, which led behind the shops into the interior of one of the
original Georgian houses of Hatton Garden. In front of me was a

spiralling mahogany staircase, which twisted up a further three floors. The former residential home had been split into numerous small offices and workshops. Behind locked doors, on all the floors of the building, were different businesses connected to the jewellery trade, including polishers, engravers, gem merchants and jewellery repairers.

I found Smith and Harris's goldsmith workshop in the basement of the building, at the bottom of a set of well-worn stone stairs. After I rang the doorbell a heavy, five inch thick metal door eventually creaked open. Standing in front of me, wearing a long leather apron over his work clothes, was a man with shoulder-length light ginger hair, a goatee beard and an unlined, round face that made it impossible to determine his age. He wouldn't have looked out of place in any art school and was not the grey-haired, older craftsman I had expected. Gareth smiled warmly and welcomed me into his cramped working space below.

Excited to finally meet him, I could barely look at Gareth as I entered the industrial workshop. As I had trained as a sculptor, his studio was a wonderland for me. Sculptor's tools in miniature covered the benches of the underground space. The walls were lined with racks filled with Victorian wooden pegs and hammers for bending metal. Wooden benches covered in tiny lathes, mini welders and heavy metal turning and polishing machines filled the room. In the huge fireplace, where the oven of the former house must have once sat, stood a small forge. Above it hung a row of large metal moulds for beating out silver dishes. 'I have always bought tools, since I was an apprentice,' said Gareth, watching as I admired his incredible collection. 'Even when they were half a week's salary I would buy them so I had everything needed for whatever the job was. I have now run out of space to physically store anything else but I can't stop looking for them. Artefacts like this are not easy to find,' he said, picking up a 400-year-old swordsmith's tool, which he still used and described as irreplaceable. 'Sometimes I have been lucky,' he continued. 'I went to an auction once in Birmingham where a huge goldsmiths' company had gone bust and that is where I got these stakes, which are centuries old. We recently used them for hammering silver and gold on to objects and forming metal sheets.'

A tall, slim man came out of a back room and introduced himself as Dennis. Three other men sat at jewellery benches. Gareth put the kettle on and they stopped working, pulled up some chairs and gathered around a small gas heater. Gareth wiped his hands on his apron before clearing some tools off a chair and inviting me to sit down. Tea was made and sandwiches were shared between us. 'I'm glad you like the workshop,' he said, smiling, as I continued to take pleasure in the chaotic surroundings. 'Some people are horrified by the state of this place. They find it problematic, coming down to this mayhem and seeing a callous-handed man in dirty work clothes beating something with a hammer when they have ordered precious objects from us. Many of the things we make end up being pushed across a counter on a purple velvet cushion. Most of our work is made to order to celebrate historic or personal events and it embodies the high need in people to mark something important with something precious. We know we will be the last people to handle many of the objects produced here with bare hands. They go into collections where they will be picked up with white gloves and spoken over in whispered tones before being carefully put back into a glass case. The human element has gone and the thing becomes this precious embodiment of some ideal.'

Gareth told me his fascination with precious metals began when he was a young boy living in Tunbridge Wells. His parents were modernists and everything in their house was brand new. His grandmother lived in Exeter in an old house filled with antiques, which he loved. She had some silver teaspoons with hallmarks on them and he became curious about the little code on their backs. He describes that moment as 'the beginning for me'. He went on to serve an apprenticeship in box-making, which traditionally in the trade is considered the most difficult area of fine metal to work in. In 1975 he enrolled for evening classes in silversmithing at Sir John Cass School of Art in Whitechapel, which is where he met Dennis. Soon afterwards they set up business

together and took on the Hatton Garden premises in 1981. They planned to stay only for two years and then move to a workshop with daylight, but decades later they are still here. 'This workshop is dry and secure and geographically it is in the dead centre of Hatton Garden,' said Gareth, 'and the building is full of other craftspeople, so it's a great place to work. We need to be based here for the bullion dealers and the Assay Office.'

Before they moved in, their building and the one next door had been occupied by a manufacturing silversmithing business called R. Hodd & Son, who had been silversmiths to Queen Victoria and shown their work in the Great Exhibition of 1851. Gareth and Dennis bought their lease from John Terry and Samuel Henell, famous eighteenth-century silversmiths, so there is an unbroken tradition, lasting nearly 200 years, of precious-metal craftsmen in their building. 'There was still one Hodd employee working here when we took over the lease,' said Dennis, 'a polisher called Tom Sadler, who was in his seventies then and had been working here since he was fourteen. When he died the lease was split between this floor and the ground floor, and we took on the basement.'

The workshop came fitted with workbenches, drawbenches, polishing and turning lathes, a forge and various tools. 'We were still bolting equipment to the benches when our first commission came directly from 10 Downing Street,' said Gareth. 'Thatcher had just got in and decided to cut out the middleman, so rather than going directly to Garrard's she sent out an edict saying, "Where do Garrard's get these diplomatic gifts made?" – and they came to us.'

They began as a specialist trade workshop, supplying retailers and other silversmiths with handmade objects in precious metals. Over the years they have become respected designer craftsmen, with a varied client base, which includes prime ministers, city livery companies and the Guildhall. They make military and ceremonial individual pieces, trophies for Ascot, badges of office, maces, finely detailed statues, big ceremonial objects and bespoke requests for private clients. They offer a complete service from design to production, including engraving and polishing.

The most unusual piece they ever made was a life-size solid-gold sculpture of Kate Moss, doing a complicated yoga pose. Commissioned in 2007, by the artist Marc Quinn, Harris and Smith

transformed a plaster cast of the model's body into gold. They bent and hammered forty separate pieces of two-millimetre-thick eighteen-carat gold into shape before fixing the pieces together using TIG (tungsten inert gas) welding, which created a seamless finish. 'When the artist came to see the sculpture,' said Gareth, 'we cleaned up the workshop and draped black velvet to hide the tools and placed a couple of spotlights on the piece, which we sat on the floor as it weighed over fifty kilos. It was the most extraordinary thing to have in this tiny, low-ceilinged place. It took a year to produce and is thought to be the largest man-made gold statue since ancient Egyptian times. It is the biggest gold item to bear the Assay Office London hallmark, which is in the lining of her gold bikini bottoms.' The artwork, called *Siren*, was recently on show in the British Museum.

'We have a personal relationship with many of our clients,' said Dennis. 'We look after several army regiments who are big users of silver, so we have built up relationships with certain soldiers. We make their wedding gifts, christening presents and retirement pieces. Some people have been our customers for twenty years. They come to the workshop for a chat and a cup of tea. Last year we made something for the grandson of a customer. Some of our clients from the guilds like to pop in and see how we are getting on with pieces we are making or they'll come in to get something fixed, the master might be going to an important ceremony and a stone could have fallen out of his badge and we'll fix it for him there and then.'

'I think many people have a new respect for handmade skills in an age when most things are made by machine,' said Gareth, pouring me another cup of strong tea. He talked of long periods of time spent working on something in multiple parts, and then the joy of watching it suddenly come together to make a whole. After decades spent hunched over benches in the near-dark the process of creating a unique piece in precious metal still holds a certain magic for Gareth. 'The final act of polishing changes it into something beautiful,' he said. 'A good polisher can transform a piece.'

Dennis told me about a beautiful cup they had recently designed for a livery company, who then invited them to dinner: 'It was fantastic to see this object we made being held up in this huge room and how thrilled people were with it. I enjoy seeing the pleasure my work gives to others.'

They know many of the other craftsmen working in Hatton Garden, hidden away from the street like they are, in small independent workshops. Although Dennis told me he had just met a diamond dealer who had been in the Garden for thirty years, a few doors down the road, and they had never even seen each other before. 'This is because of the way we work. I don't even go out at lunchtime; I get in at half past seven in the morning and go home at six, and unless I would have seen him walking down Greville Street to the tube our paths wouldn't have crossed. Just the other day I visited a beautiful workshop near here for the first time and inside, sat at benches, were three old men, making gold cases for watches by hand and lathe-turning on the premises, it was so unexpected to see.'

'My parents' experience as retailers in the street is different,' I said. 'They need to visit the workshops and dealers, but if you are manufacturing I imagine you don't necessarily meet many other people working in the street?'

'That's true,' said Gareth. 'Although when you need to find somebody, a specialist, there is a tremendous grapevine here.'

Gareth and Dennis's basement is now the only silversmith and goldsmith workshop left on Hatton Garden. 'The front shops, as we call them, only existed from Greville Street down to Holborn Circus in the early 1980s,' said Gareth. 'The north end of the street was filled with workshops and manufacturers with an infrastructure for supporting heavier industry. Now the only evidence of this is in names, like the Gunmakers, which is a pub near the end of the street named in honour of the inventor of the machine gun, Hiriam Maxim, who lived in Hatton Garden in 1884.' There is a plaque to Maxim above his former house on the corner of Hatton Garden and Clerkenwell Road. He tested his machine gun at a specially built underground firing range in the basement of this property.

A phone call led Dennis away into a small office space to the side. The apprentice and the other craftsmen brushed the crumbs from their clothes, drained the remains of their tea from their mugs and returned to their workbenches. Their lunchtime break was over and there was plenty of work to be finished.

Before I left I asked Gareth about his interest in the history of East London and whether it extended to the area where he worked every day. He described himself as a part-time historian who likes to know what is going on behind the façade of places. He had a deep passion for the history of the Hatton Garden area, which he felt probably started with his first job, with London's oldest-established goldsmiths Barnard & Son. Originally based in the city in 1640, they moved near to Hatton Garden in the late eighteenth century, settling in the Clerkenwell Court House, which Dickens writes about. Gareth described the place as being 'largely unchanged: patterns were stored down in the basement, which still had the cells in place, where condemned prisoners were taken out the back and put in ships on the Fleet for transportation. Sometimes they were marched up Cowcross Street to the Hope pub, where they found out if they had got a reprieve; if not they went on to Newgate to be hanged. Old men who worked there remembered heavy metal rings on the walls for chaining up the prisoners.'

The area's long association with metalworking was another source of historical interest for Gareth. 'In nearby Fetter Lane, in Farringdon, medieval armour was once made by metal craftsmen for the Knights Templar. If you ignore the street signs and imagine walking down the street as a lane you end up at the Temple, where they were based, and you have a run of gunmakers and armour makers along this route. This has been the metalworking side of the city for 1,000 years. The two men who set up Johnson Matthey, the oldest business in Hatton Garden, were brilliant chemists who really understood metals. Johnson was the first person to refine platinum out of gold. On one side of the road in Hatton Garden you have the man who virtually invented platinum and on the other side of the road is someone cutting diamonds. I enjoy the fact that we continue the tradition of skilled, handmade manufacturing, real craft, that once made Hatton Garden famous.'

5

Civitas Londinium

I Iolborn was the old road from Newgate and the Tower to the gallows
at Tyburn. At regular and frequent intervals both sides of the way were
lined and all the windows were covered with curious and often sympa-
thising spectators to see light-fingered gentlemen, murderers, forgers,
and such like, riding to their doom.

John Stow, *A Survey of London*

Back in the Guildhall I studied the medieval map in the reconstructed atlas. On the outskirts of Holborn I could see the church
and estate of the Knights Templar, the swordsmiths' street of Fetter
Lane and the ancient hospital and church of St Bartholomew's.
Medieval Holborn itself was predominantly a rural district, filled
with vineyards, herbal gardens, orchards and pastures attached to
private homes, religious buildings and the Inns of Court. The largest properties on the map were: Gray's Inn and Lincoln's Inn Court,
St Andrew's Church, the Bishop of Lincoln's Palace (built on the site
of the original Knights Templar church), the Bishop of Chichester's
home and the Bishop of Ely's Inn. From the position of the church
of St Andrew's and the River Fleet it was clear that the expansive
gardens and buildings of the Ely estate once occupied the same site
as the present-day Hatton Garden.

The buildings of the Bishop of Ely's Inn included a chapel, a great
hall, cloisters, and a grand gatehouse fronting on to Holborn High
Road, then named Holbourne. Scrope's Inn, a medieval serjeants'
inn, marked on this map roughly where Ely Place is today, was an

ancient house, which was removed around 1498, the site later becoming tenements. The land belonging to the Bishops of Ely included a grandiose garden, laid out in four symmetrical squares, a large orchard, pasture and a strip of land marked as being under cultivation. The bishops' estate was bounded by Holbourne to the north, Lyver Lane (now Leather Lane) to the west, the former River Fleet to the east and roughly where Hatton Wall is today to the south.

Running parallel to the Fleet, in the same location as Saffron Hill today, sat a narrow pathway, winding through open fields, named Gold Lane. I searched through various documents looking for more information about this street, only managing to find one brief mention of the place, in John Stow's *Survey of London* (1598), where he describes it as: 'a filthy passage in the fields, now both sides built with small tenements at the bottom of Oldboorne hill'. One secondary source I came across suggested Gold Lane had been named after a Dutch merchant who once lived on the street. To me it seemed as if the prophetic naming of this dirt track had somehow foretold the future use of that land.

At some point during the medieval period Gold Lane was renamed Saffron Hill probably after fields of crocuses that grew there: a valuable crop planted by the monks for the flower's stamens, which were dried out to produce the spice saffron.

Curious to see how the sixteenth-century Agas map compared to this reconstructed version, I asked Jeremy Smith if I could examine it. He told me the six-foot-long original is too fragile for public viewing but he gladly fetched me a facsimile of the map, which had been split into sections and bound together in one heavy volume.

Exquisite engravings depicting a bird's-eye view of Elizabethan London filled every page in graphic detail. Flicking through the large pages of the map I became mesmerized by the pictorial depiction of the Thames, snaking through the city, busy with nautical traffic; sailing ships and barges full of goods beside drawings of swans the size of rowing boats. The Tower of London, with hand-drawn battlements and bridges, was surrounded by a watery moat and dwarfed by huge figures in a field behind: a woman the size of a tree laying out washing to dry on the ground, and a dog, bigger than a house, running through the grass.

The section entitled 'St Doste in The West and Fleet Streate' contained the information I was looking for. Beautifully drawn in three dimensions, in the same location as on the reconstructed map, was the large walled garden and estate of Ely Place, with an ornamental maze, a kitchen garden, trees and giant hand-drawn cows, munching on the fertile pastureland beside the Fleet and the marked but unnamed Gold Lane.

Using Stow's sixteenth-century *Survey of London* and various other documents found in the Guildhall Collection, such as Walter Thornbury's nineteenth-century *Old and New London*, I tracked the development of Ely Place. Before the late thirteenth century, the Bishops of Ely, who were based in Cambridgeshire, had lodged with the Knights Templar when they needed to be in London.

When relationships soured, the arrangement was terminated and the Ely Bishops needed to have their own city residence, befitting their important status. In 1292, work began on a permanent London house for the bishops after John de Kirby, the Bishop of Ely at the time, left his successors a large house and some land in Holborn. This was developed into a grand estate known as the Bishop of Ely's Inn, Ely Palace and Ely Place.

When Thomas Arundel became the Bishop of Ely, in 1373, Stow states: 'He did not only repaire, but rather new builded, and augmented it [Ely House] with a large Port, gatehouse, or front towards the streete.' Each subsequent bishop added to the estate until by the fifteenth century it included: a large stone gatehouse with a great hall and chambers, a private chapel called St Etheldreda's, stables, several acres of vineyards, pastureland covering fifty-eight acres, cloisters and beautiful walled gardens, famed by medieval chroniclers for the quality of their strawberries and their fields of crocuses.

By the sixteenth century Ely Palace was described as one of 'the most magnificent of metropolitan mansions', like 'a palace in fairy tales', with a great banqueting hall and exquisite architectural detail-

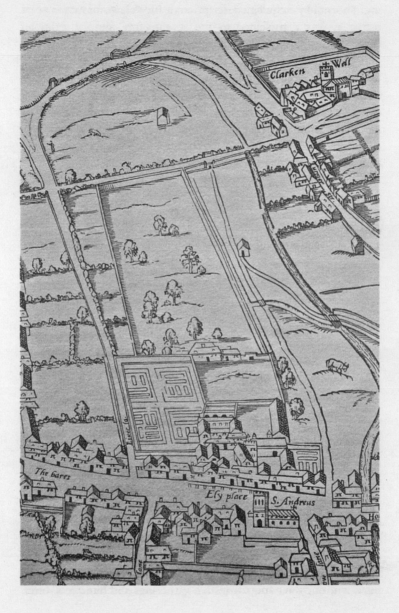

ing. Thornbury includes a description of Ely Palace, about 100 years before it was demolished in the seventeenth century, from an anonymous source. By this time the original grand gatehouse had gone but the great hall was still intact and over seventy feet long, with six fine Gothic windows, an ornamental timber roof and a tiled chequered floor. The cloisters were of a 'great size with a small ornamental garden in the middle'. Above the cloisters were long antique galleries with doors leading off them to various apartments.

Some of these apartments were let out to visiting nobles. The Duke of Lancaster, known as John of Gaunt, lived there after his mansion, the Savoy Palace, was burned to the ground during the Peasants' Revolt of 1381. John of Gaunt had been blamed for his part in encouraging Richard II's heavy-handed enforcement of the third medieval poll tax, which provoked the uprising, led by the rebel Wat Tyler, who was slain at Smithfields shortly after. Shakespeare's *Richard III* has John of Gaunt dying in Ely House. During a famous scene set in the Tower, the Duke of Gloucester sends the Bishop of Ely to fetch some of the 'good strawberries in your garden there'.

The Bishops of Ely, 'in the true spirit of hospitality', states Thornbury, lent out their hall for festive gatherings and banquets, often becoming hosts to the celebrations of the newly elected serjeants of law, as 'no doubt the halls of the Inns of Court were often too small to accommodate the number of guests.'

In 1495 a grand banquet took place at Ely Palace and was attended by Henry VII and his queen, but the 'most splendid of all' the feasts to take place there occurred in November 1531. It was an 'event on an unparalleled scale of magnificence'. The entertainment lasted for five days; Henry VIII and Catherine of Aragon were present but dined 'in two chambers'.

Stow remarked that it would be 'tedious' to set down all 'the preparation of fish, flesh, and other victuals, spent in this feast'; but he mentions the 24 'great beefs', or oxen, 100 'fat muttons', 51 'great veals', 34 'porks', or boars, 91 pigs, a dozen larks and 14 dozen swans that were consumed during the festivities, among many other delicacies.

In 1536, Henry VIII began to dissolve the monasteries and most of the ecclesiastical properties around the country were reclaimed by the State. Before then the Church owned two thirds of the land in Central London. Outside the city walls, in areas such as Holborn and Clerkenwell, nearly all the large estates belonged to the Church. The only sizeable piece of land not occupied by the clergy in the area during the sixteenth century was the open grounds of Smithfield to the west of the River Fleet, which had already been long established by that time as London's central meat market.

Near to Smithfield, bordering the Ely lands, were the ancient priory and hospital of St Bartholomew, the Priory of St John, the Benedictine Nunnery of St Mary's and the Carthusian Monastery of Charterhouse. All these great religious houses were disbanded during the Reformation. The monks of Charterhouse suffered dreadful deaths after refusing to comply with Henry VIII's demands of total allegiance to the State. The prior, John Houghton, was arrested along with other monks. They were imprisoned in the Tower before being bound to carts and dragged by horses to Tyburn Gallows for execution, where they were hanged in their religious habits. While still alive their hearts and intestines were torn out and burned in front of them; then their bodies were beheaded and quartered, before the dismembered parts were displayed across the city. Prior Houghton's decapitated head was spiked over the gates of the Tower. One of his arms was hacked off and nailed to the entrance of Charterhouse. The violent reclamation of the religious houses of Holborn and Clerkenwell changed the quiet, rural landscape of the area for ever.

The Bishops of Ely survived the Reformation by splitting from the Catholic Church and turning the chapel of St Etheldreda's into a Protestant church. The palace also survived the Great Fire but by the mid seventeenth century most of the buildings were in ruins. In John Noorthouck's *A New History of London*, published in 1773, the author describes the buildings of the Ely estate as being 'very old' and comments that 'the expensive state which the large old town mansion required the owners to maintain, has occasioned it in general to be deserted; Ely House is neglected'.

In 1771 the run-down estate was bought back by the Crown and the Bishops of Ely were compensated with a large house in Dover Street, Mayfair. The land and remaining buildings were sold to an architect and property developer called Charles Cole, who demolished the crumbling palace in the following years and erected grand houses over its former site, building a street named Ely Place.

The only part of the medieval estate of Ely Palace to survive today is St Etheldreda's Chapel, situated in the gated, residential cul-de-sac of Ely Place, which runs parallel to Hatton Garden. The easiest way to enter Ely Place is on foot, either through a small gateway that connects Ely Place to the cobbled courtyard of Bleeding Heart Yard, or through a narrow passageway, called Mitre Court, which exits on to Hatton Garden, between nos 8 and 9.

6

Gamagic

Nearly everything we made was in platinum, we only had one gold
ring maker and he made everything by hand. He got paid peanuts and
worked like a dog. He specialized in making five-stone rings. The
quickest way to do it was by making tubing, by drawing gold by hand
through an ancient drawbench, which dated back to the fifteenth
century. When he had five bits of tubing prepared he would cut them
into strips and then solder the five together. Then he'd cut them with
a saw and bend them back into a half-loop and solder them up again.
I did the donkey work for him, milling out thin eighteen-carat
platinum, which he soldered on to the top.

Dave Harris

Gareth Harris put me in touch with a man called Michael, a jewellery repairer who has worked from a small attic workshop in the
same building as Gareth for decades. 'I haven't time to stop and
speak with you,' he told me on the phone, 'unless you are happy to
come up and see me and talk while I work.'

Entering the dark hallway of the Georgian house again, I made
my way towards the grand staircase, noticing a framed poster from
the 1850s hanging there advertising the silversmith workshop that
had once been in the house. It was described as being 'fitted with
drawbenches, polishing and turning lathes, fixtures and tools', as
well as offering spacious accommodation and 'a pump of excellent
spring water'. Gareth told me a spring still exists beneath his workshop: 'Clerkenwell was named after the wells here, natural water
flows underneath this area.'

Climbing three floors up, past the former sleeping and dressing rooms of the house, now converted into jewellery-related small businesses, I breathlessly reached Michael's workshop. A short, older man, with swept-back grey hair, wearing a visor on top of his head, welcomed me into a tiny, square, well-ordered box room. 'I took on these premises in 1973,' he told me. The orange-and-white Formica cabinet, faded, patterned lino and retro fridge suggested the decor inside had remained the same since then.

After making us both a cup of tea, Michael sat down at his wooden jewellery bench beside the window, overlooking Hatton Garden. 'If you look above the shops,' he said, pointing to the buildings opposite, 'these seventeenth-century houses are still much the same. Internally they have been tarted up but some of the original features remain. This building has improved since I started. It used to be a real rat run with no hot water, an old-fashioned toilet with a chain – and the ceiling leaked. To get hold of someone in the basement I used to ring the old servants' bell outside.'

Michael began working in Hatton Garden as an apprentice diamond mounter in 1963, a common career choice for a Jewish boy from Stoke Newington at the time. He described the workshop as 'a real dump' but he stayed for six years, working in terrible conditions before moving on to another workshop in Greville Street: 'There was a silver shop on the corner, where all the apprentices hung around outside and dealers would stand about, buying and selling off each other, looking openly at the stones on the street. That rarely happens now. There used to be few criminal types hanging around but it's the kind of area that draws that kind of person to it.'

Picking up a gold ring from a pile of jobs in front of him, he began sawing through the shank as he talked, moving his visor and its large magnifying lenses into position over his eyes. His hands moved quickly and confidently, cutting through the yellow metal, creating a sharp, clean break. Holding the ring in one hand, he moved the other to a hook beside his bench, where he picked up a small soldering torch, its blue flame already alight. He welded the

broken joint back together and, as the tiny molten scar cooled, he began expertly filing down the join, until the surface of the ring was smooth again. Not a trace of his handiwork remained after it had been polished and placed in a small plastic bag for collection.

'Everyone was Jewish when I started in my workshop, including the governor,' he said. 'Hatton Garden is more multicultural today, with people from India, Mauritius, Greece, all over, and they all seem to work happily together, because they all come with the same aim, to earn a few quid and get through the day. It is still easy to work here if you are observant. There used to be plenty of kosher eateries around here catering for the Orthodox workers but they have all shut down now bar one. This was a good trade to go into if you were a practising Jew. The working week was built around the religious needs of the community. It still is to an extent, the Bourse still shuts on a Friday afternoon and Saturday, also on *yontif*. There was a restaurant called the C & A in the 1960s, where Abigail's is now in Greville Street, and you used to get dealers going in there, buying and selling across the tables in the afternoons. Now it is very different; the Bourse has its own purpose-built premises on Hatton Garden, with extraordinary security precautions to get into the building.' I asked Michael if he knew anyone who could get me inside. He laughed. 'They wouldn't let you in; they don't let anyone in who is not a member. I've never been inside and I've worked here for over fifty years.'

Leaning across his jewellery bench he pointed to 87 Hatton Garden, a white building nearly opposite, which he told me had once been the site of the London Diamond Club for traders in rough diamonds; the Bourse was for dealers in cut diamonds, precious and coloured stones. 'They started around the 1940s, although I think the Diamond Club may have been older. Most of the dealers in rough were Hasidic. I would see them going into the building but it was an incredibly secretive, closed place; little is known about what went on there, it was impossible to get inside. I only ever saw Hasidic older men go in there.'

Steadily tending to the items on the bench, Michael told me

about his working life: 'I do repairs, polishing, stone-setting, resizing; all sorts really. Over the years I've had to adapt as fashions change. There was one time I seemed to do nothing but solder gold charms on to bracelets or set sovereigns in rings. Now most of my work is for the shops, resizing wedding and engagement rings, polishing up stones, making new claw settings, that kind of thing. Trends change a huge amount but the important thing is to always ensure the repairs are of the highest quality, whether I'm working on someone's old watch chain or a diamond ring that costs thousands of pounds.'

As we talked the phone rang many times and Michael stopped briefly, to chat to a colleague, take a new order, organize a delivery. Tiny packages, wrapped in brown paper, arrived through a wooden hatch in the door. 'Repairs,' said the elderly craftsman, as another packet fell on to the table. 'I have plenty of work on at the moment. I should have retired years ago but the thought of not working scares me. I'm determined to keep this workshop on for as long as I'm able to get up the stairs. Most of the old ones like me have passed on.'

I asked him what Hatton Garden looked like when he arrived in the early 1960s: 'Much quieter than today. There were only a few jewellery shops: George's in Greville Street, Fine Jewels, Ullmann's and J & A Jewellers. The shops never really started until City Jewellers opened in 1968, which was the first proper retail shop open to the general public, in my memory. It was all jewellery manufacturing and workshops before then and a few other general shops in the street, like a tobacconists, a sweet shop, a few pubs, an optician's. It was much more of a working place in the 60s, tourists never visited unless they were going to Gamages Department Store, which back then took up the whole square of Hatton Garden, Greville Street and Leather Lane.'

Michael's first visit to Gamages was at the age of eight to purchase a train set: 'I used to take the 643 trolley bus from Stoke Newington and come to Holborn especially to visit Gamages, because they had just the most fantastic toy department in the

whole of London and a brilliant record department. It was a real old-fashioned department store, the like of which you don't see any more. The layout of the place was extraordinary – it was an adventure just to walk around the place. They seemed to sell everything: fishing nets, wheelbarrows, sweets, cars, all sorts, and they had a huge mail-order section. In the toy department were enormous train layouts, with trees, bridges, farms, stations, houses and everything. I was mesmerized by it, watching the trains going round and round. The Meccano displays were incredible. Instead of having a cash register they put the money in a tube, pushed the button and that's where the money went. It was a smashing place for tools. Every year they had a huge exhibition of Lego and trains. A visit to Gamages was a tremendous treat for a small boy.'

Above Gamages, he told me, there was another floor in the building, which was a rabbit warren of little workshops housing people from the jewellery trade. There were many different sections that you reached by walking down tiny corridors, or climbing steep, narrow, wooden staircases. 'When Gamages shut down in 1972 all those people in the workshops were chucked out and the building was knocked down. Many of these craftspeople went to Clerkenwell, which had traditionally been an area for watchmaking and clockmaking. They moved into a big building called Penny Back Chambers in Clerkenwell Green.' Michael was lucky to find his workshop in Hatton Garden as space was hard to come by for individual artisans like himself, even then.

Gamages was flattened and replaced by new shops like WHSmith and Boots. Other shops were built on Holborn High Road and in Hatton Garden, with council flats above.

For nearly a century Gamages had been the primary reason that the general public visited Hatton Garden. The store had begun as a tiny hosiery shop on the corner of Leather Lane and Holborn, opened in 1878 by Arthur Walter Gamage and his business partner, Frank Spain. The frontage was less than five feet wide and the motto over the door read: TALL OAKS FROM LITTLE ACORNS GROW. Arthur Gamage was ambitious. He soon bought his partner out and started

to implement his radical business plan – to sell every type of domestic item imaginable as cheaply as possible. The plan worked, the shop expanded rapidly, spreading into the surrounding properties, which were knocked through to create more floor space, the layout of the interior changing continuously. The building became so large that on occasions a circus ring, with tiered seats for over 300 spectators, was temporarily installed in the basement.

By 1900 the grand Edwardian frontage of the shop, known then as the People's Popular Emporium, stretched from the Prudential Building in Holborn down to the corner of Hatton Garden and from there along Hatton Garden up to Greville Street and down Leather Lane.

Gamages became one of the most popular department stores in London, with the best-loved toy department in the city. Their keenly awaited Christmas catalogue was often 1,000 pages long. Much of the store's business was conducted through mail order, with goods being shipped to any address in the UK or abroad. A 1906 advert for the Gamages Christmas Bazaar claimed it to be 'the grandest exhibition in London', with 'over five acres of floor space', selling 'novelties from all over the world', offering free entertainments, afternoon teas and Christmas displays. Photographs of the period show a fantastical interior, crammed with exotic goods, lit by gaslight and packed with shoppers and excited children.

Looking at the catalogues in the archives gives an insight into the vast array of goods they once stocked. Some of the items listed in their 1912 catalogue include: boot and skirt holders; mosquito nets; motor horns; toboggans; bee-keeping equipment; hammocks; boats; marquee tents; dog kennels; fencing foils; cinematographs; false moustaches; invalid carriages; travelling baths; and clockwork submarines. In the tailoring department, you could order a full frock coat, morning coat, lounge suit or dinner suit, all made to measure, as well as servants' outdoor liveries, for your coachman or footman. The hat section included pith helmets for all climes: 'The Delhi, The Polo or The Gold Coast', along with a large selection of Panama, bowler and silk top hats.

By 1924 Gamages had its own hairdressing salon and a large department selling 'comfort clothing for the motor cyclist', another with 'colonial wear for men'. Masonic regalia could be purchased along with fancy-dress costumes, fur coats, cabin trunks and even rickshaw carts for children. Guns, swords, catapults, knives and knuckledusters were for sale. The store even had a livestock department, selling the usual domestic pets alongside 'ringtail and brown lemurs', mongooses, squirrels and 'a few tame miniature bears for 5/6 each, with their own travelling box'. The largest department sold motorcars, bicycles and motorcycles, with all the paraphernalia that went with them.

Gamagic, one of the most frequently visited departments, sold magic tricks, conjuring cabinets, masks, jumping beans and many other things for the professional or amateur magician. I had recently spoken to Martin Macmillian, whose father, Ron Macmillian, used to run the magic department in Gamages in the 1950s. Martin is the owner of International Magic, a curious, tiny shop on the corner of Leather Lane and Clerkenwell Road. He inherited the business from his father who opened the shop there fifty years ago. He told me that Ron had been a talented magician who started his working life touring music halls and fairs in the UK, then, when he became more well known, he began performing in bigger shows in Europe and America as well. Ron wanted to stop travelling after he had a family so he became the manager of Gamagic, which he called 'the great house for anything magical'. In the 1960s Gamages cut back on their magic department so Ron set up International Magic near by and they have been there ever since. 'We are now the only magic shop in London left on street level,' said Martin proudly.

From Clerkenwell Road, the narrow, red-painted exterior of International Magic, with its box-shaped windows around the door, filled with tricks, wizard hats, wands and games, looks like a façade for a Harry Potter film set, right down to its wonky doorway and period detail. The building dates back to 1902 and originally housed a metal company before Ron took over the premises. I asked Martin if the location of the shop had any relationship to Clerkenwell's long association with magicians, alchemists and occultists. I mentioned Peter Ackroyd's fictional work *The House of Doctor Dee*, where he has the famous Elizabethan conjurer to the Queen and communer with angels living in a house near Clerkenwell Green, although in reality Dee's home was in Mortlake. Martin had not heard these stories. He told me 'the shop is in Clerkenwell because the family lived in East London, so it was near enough to the city for business, easy to get to, and my father knew the area well after spending all those years working at Gamages'.

Inside, the walls of the cramped building are filled with wooden shelves, painted black, overflowing with brightly coloured tricks, books, capes, wigs and every imaginable magic accessory. As I spoke with Martin, a group of off-duty magicians came into the store and gathered around the front desk, exchanging gossip on the latest tricks and the forthcoming magic convention, which is organized by the shop and known as 'Ron's Day' after Martin's father, who started the first convention over forty years ago. 'This shop is a meeting place now for magicians from all over London, all over the world,' said Martin, handing me some leaflets advertising the convention and lectures they run for professional magicians from a room above the Italian Church on Clerkenwell Road. 'We also run beginners' courses in magic from there,' said Martin. 'We are well connected with the Italian community, having worked in the area for so many years.' He started to reminisce about the local businesses that had closed down since International Magic opened. 'This area was still very Italian when I first started coming here as a child. There were many locally run cafés and delis; most have gone now. Back then you would hear Italian being spoken in the local shops. There was an old-style tobacconist next door to here, a wonderful family-run chemist near by, and a pub called the Leather Bottle in Greville Street, which is now the King of Diamonds. All the staff from Gamages used to get drunk in there.'

7

Ye Olde Mitre and St Etheldreda's

We find a fragment of the old Episcopal residence preserved in, and giving its name to, Mitre Court, which leads from Ely Place to Hatton Garden. Here, worked into the wall of a tavern known as 'The Mitre', is a bishop's mitre, sculpted in stone, 'which probably', Mr Timbs conjectures, 'once adorned Ely Palace, or the precinct gateway'.

Walter Thornbury, 'Ely Place', *Old and New London*

In the middle of the tiny alley of Mitre Court, there is a small, oak-fronted pub called Ye Olde Mitre, with bottle-glass windows, Victorian gas lamps and wooden barrel tables outside.

About three o'clock, one wet September afternoon, I walked into the front bar; a cosy little wood-panelled room, with a fireplace, a few tables and chairs and enough space for about twenty people standing. Apart from a couple of men who looked liked regulars sitting at a small table in the corner I was the only customer. An elderly man, wearing an apron over his work clothes, was busily sweeping the floor behind the bar. I sat on one of the high stools beside him, ordered a drink and started up a conversation with the barman, who introduced himself as John.

'I've been working here since 1985,' said John, 'but I've been drinking in here since 1953 and the place has hardly changed at all as it's a listed building. The Mitre is just a real old-fashioned pub and people come here because there is no music and they can talk without shouting. The only thing that has changed over the years is the customers. This pub used to open really early and the journalists from the *Daily Mirror* building, which was just by Holborn Circus where Sainsbury's is now, used to come in here straight off their night shift. Now most of our customers are pinstripes and lawyers from the Inns of Court up the road. If you'd come at lunchtime you wouldn't be able to get in the door, it's packed. In the evenings it's pretty quiet and at the weekends it's closed. Most people don't know about this place as it's so tucked away. It's the most hidden pub in London,' he said proudly. 'I've had people come in here who've worked in Hatton Garden for years and never even knew about the place. You get others walking up and down Hatton Garden for hours and they just keep missing the tiny entranceway and never find us.'

'It's the oldest boozer in London, isn't it?' said one of the suited men in the corner.

'Second oldest,' said the barman. 'I have picked up quite a bit of history about the place over the years. In the evenings you get the tour guides coming in and spinning yarns. The Americans love it here, think they've discovered a bit of secret London. I've heard them say Dr Johnson used to come in here when he was writing his dictionary and Dickens used to meet his mates here, as he lived round the corner in Holborn.'

'It's like stepping back in time, walking into this place,' said the other man in the corner, while pointing at the antique prints on the wall and the beams on the ceiling. 'It looks like something out of a period drama.'

'So do most of the staff,' said his drinking companion, laughing.

'This pub was originally built in 1546,' said the barman, ignoring their banter, 'for the servants of the bishops' palace. It got demolished along with the rest of the palace in the 1700s but it was rebuilt again shortly after.'

'Do us a pork pie and a cheese toastie,' said one of the men in the corner.

'Legendary toasties they are,' said his mate. 'We've been coming here for years because it's a proper old London boozer, with good grub and real ales.'

'We've won awards for our beer,' said John, pointing with pride to certificates above the bar. 'Want another, gentlemen?' The two men nodded. The barman nipped over to their table, took their glasses and refilled them, while calling their food order through to the kitchen area. Resuming his position behind the bar, he began vigorously polishing glasses with a tea towel and continued telling me stories.

'Elizabeth I danced around the maypole here with her boyfriend Sir Christopher Hatton,' he said. 'The Bishop of Ely and Sir Christopher had a wager to see who could get the most land, they was arguing about it for years. Hatton won, so they planted that cherry tree there to mark the boundary between Hatton Garden and Ely Palace.' He led me over towards a corner cabinet near the door where the petrified remains of this ancient tree sat behind glass. 'I've been told it used to bloom until the last century,' he said, before launching into the tale of Christopher Hatton: 'He was an aristocrat from Northamptonshire, very handsome and a really good dancer. Lots of people say he was the queen's boyfriend. She gave him Ely House.

He wanted to live there, as it was the most beautiful building in the sixteenth century, with big gardens full of roses, orchards and fountains. The bishops wouldn't agree to it at first but then Queen Bess said she'd unfrock them, so in 1576 he moved in. The bishops were allowed to live in one of the apartments and walk in the gardens and gather twenty baskets of roses a year. All the rent Hatton had to pay was one red rose at midsummer, ten loads of hay and ten pounds a year. He spent thousands of pounds of the queen's money doing up the palace. Then he built a huge mansion over the grounds called Hatton House. The queen got annoyed and said he had to pay the money back to her. He died at his big mansion in 1591 of a broken heart because he loved Queen Bess so much and she wanted all that money back and he didn't have it. She went to Hatton House herself and fed him soup with her own hands but he was a goner. He never married. His nephew's widow, Lady Elizabeth Hatton, who was very beautiful, inherited his house and had loads of boyfriends and one of them killed her in Bleeding Heart Yard, which was once part of Hatton's estate. One night, Lady Hatton threw a big party at her mansion and all night long she was dancing away with this stranger, who had a hunchback and a clawed hand. At midnight she disappeared. The following morning she was found murdered with her heart still beating, lying in a pool of blood. Killed by the Devil himself.'

'He knows all the stories about this place,' said one of the men at the table, nodding in the direction of the knowledgeable barman.

'See that chair over there,' said the barman, pointing to the corner near the fireplace, 'that film *Snatch*, about the gangsters, was filmed in here, and Mike Reid sat in that chair when they done the diamond deal.'

'Do you get many of the Hatton Garden diamond dealers coming in here?' I asked.

'Nah, they're all *frummers*, ain't they?' he said. 'Don't go to pubs. You used to get crooks running down Mitre Court from Hatton Garden into Ely Place though. The police wasn't allowed down the alley because it came under Cambridge laws until quite recent.

When there was a robbery in Hatton Garden they used to run into Ely Place as they knew the London police couldn't go in there. All they could do was surround them and wait for the police to come up from Cambridge; but when Camden took the area back that all changed. That law goes back to the Middle Ages when the part of Cambridgeshire known as the Isle of Ely was under the authority of the Bishops of Ely. So Ely Place really was a part of Cambridgeshire. There used to be a beadle on the gates with a big hat with a tassel on and a big long coat. I used to see him all the time, as he was a regular at the pub. Until recently the lamps were all gas-lit and he used to light them every night. He had his own little lodge in Ely Place and was the only law of these streets. The gates used to close every night at ten in the evening and all through the night until six in the morning; the watchmen used to call out the hours: 'Ten o'clock and all is well . . . Eleven o'clock and all is well.'

'There used to be a convent round the corner, a monastery, a hospital and a dungeon. When the gates were closed and the monks from the palace went out after time they had to climb back in over the roof,

61

which was made of tin, and that's how you got the saying "on a hot tin roof". Henry VIII and all them all used to stay at Ely Palace, probably used to come to this pub. He stayed there with Catherine of Aragon once for a party that lasted five days and they ate swans stuffed with other birds, and oxen and sparrows and loads of stuff like that. Another thing: there was a prison underneath Holborn Viaduct round the corner and they used to tie the prisoners to the railings and drown them in the Fleet. Some people have heard the wails of the drowning prisoners walking round here. There used to be barges going up and down the Fleet, near where Saffron Hill is now, and that's where they had the hideouts of Fagin, next to the river. It was a horrible right rough slum area round here in Dickens's time.'

The door to the front bar swung open and a customer walked in.

'Yes, governor, what can I get you?' said John, moving swiftly into position behind the bar.

I left him to serve and wandered into the larger back room; another wood-panelled and carpeted space, the walls of which were covered in pictures and documents relating to the history of the area. There was a copy of the Agas map, prints of some old deeds, an etching of Ely Palace on a grassy lawn surrounded by trees, and an advert placed in a local paper, dated 1837, for a new landlord to lease Ye Olde Mitre 'at the low rent of fifty pounds a year'. Back then the property had a 'capital double-fronted bar, a bar parlour and a coffee room' on the ground floor along with an 'excellent lofty cellarage and cool vault' in the basement.

As I stood looking at the prints, John appeared in the back room. 'See that snug over there?' he said, pointing to a small, enclosed area. 'It's called Ye Olde Closet. It's supposed to be haunted. The last landlord here sat in there one night and the door just slammed shut by itself and he saw dark shadows in the corner, but maybe he was just drunk.' He led me upstairs to another bar area, with a little nook called the Bishop's Room, which had its own resident spirit. 'You get all the ghost hunters coming in here,' he said.

I told him about the secret tunnels I had read about, which are thought to still exist underneath Ye Olde Mitre, leading under Hatton Garden and to St Etheldreda's Chapel. They had been discovered years ago, when the floor of the pub had been taken up for some building work and an underground passage was found beneath the pavement in the courtyard of the Mitre.

He did not know about the passage but instead started to talk about the chapel of St Etheldreda's, which he used to visit every year: 'When the choir came up from Cambridgeshire to sing there, until 1978, absolutely magical it was. They had beautiful gardens once, famous for their strawberries, and there used to be a strawberry fayre day every year, with stalls, live music, different people dressed up performing in the street and loads of stuff for kids; it was great but they stopped it two years ago. That church is one of only two buildings in London remaining that were built during the reign of Edward I; the other is Westminster Hall. A tour guide told me that.' As I left the pub he came outside and watched me walk along the narrow alleyway towards Ely Place. 'See that metal post there?' he shouted after me, pointing to a steel pole that dissected the exit of Mitre Court. 'That was put there in the olden days to stop horse riders charging through here.'

Walking out of Mitre Court on to Ely Place gave rise to one of those strange portal moments that occur at certain points in cities, where there is nothing of the contemporary city visible and you feel as if you have stepped into another era. Directly in front of me was a row of perfectly intact, grand Georgian houses, the façades of which looked as if they had barely changed since property developer Charles Cole erected them in the eighteenth century. There were no cars moving along the street, which is gated at Charterhouse and closed to traffic.

Sandwiched between two tall houses, on the west side of Ely Place, sunk far below the current level of the pavement, is the medieval chapel of St Etheldreda's, built between 1250 and 1290. The chapel and palace originally stood on a hill and could be seen for miles around. The topography of this area has changed a great deal over time.

I entered the building through a small open doorway by walking down some worn stone steps. The doorway led into a slender hallway, with a flagstone floor, which looked out on to a little courtyard. In the centre of this corridor was a table, covered in leaflets and information. I put some coins in a box and picked up a guidebook. Walking up another small set of stairs, I passed through a large Gothic entranceway into the chapel itself, which was much bigger than it appeared from the street. There was a sharp drop in temperature as I entered the cool, dark interior and the sounds of the street outside all but disappeared, as if they had been sucked up by the thick stone walls. The only discernible noise inside was of sirens sounding faintly in the distance.

Rows of black wooden pews were gently illuminated by a soft light from the cathedral-sized stained-glass windows at either end of the room, which stretched almost from the floor to the high wooden-beamed ceiling. Battered tapestry prayer cushions were scattered on the pews and the dusty parquet flooring.

I sat for a while at the back of the church and began to flick through the guidebook. Reading it I learned that in a jewelled case to the right of the altar sits a priceless relic: a piece of the hand of St Etheldreda, the patron saint of chastity. Researching this relic further, I discovered it had been dug up on a Sussex farm in a perfect state of preservation, having been hidden there in penal times for protection in a long-forgotten priest-hole. 'Around the hand, which was as white as white, and somewhat of the consistency of ivory, was a lace cuff, which was embroidered.' St Etheldreda was a seventh-century princess of East Anglia, who took a vow of chastity, fled to Ely, became a nun and founded a religious community. Fifteen years after her death her body was removed from its tomb and found to be still intact. She became a saint and over the centuries her popularity grew, especially when her body was removed again, over 400 years after burial, still perfectly preserved. The chapel is dedicated to her memory.

It was peaceful sitting in the empty chapel and I began to imagine the bishops of old coming in there to pray, and to feel how tranquil

the place must have been for hundreds of years. The Bishops of Ely and their large household had sole use of the chapel and the inner gardens of the estate, which were filled with roses, herbs and ornate fountains. The smell of the fragrant flowers and the sound of trickling water must have added to the meditative ambience of the place. Beyond these gardens were acres of land, with orchards, vineyards, kitchen gardens, ponds and terraced lawns, sloping down towards the Fleet, which was filled with salmon then.

It is easy to visualize the past in this ancient place. It is one of those unique buildings in London that appear to hold time in a different way to street time. I was brought back to the present by the appearance of a young couple clad in biker leathers who sat down in a pew a few rows in front of me, whispering urgently to each other about their forthcoming wedding due to take place in the building.

As I sat there, the sun burst through the clouds outside and the chapel was suddenly filled with a mosaic of coloured light that fell on to the stone floor from the large east window in hues of pink, deep yellow and royal blue. I read that this window is the largest Gothic window in London, a replacement of a Victorian copy from the original medieval design, which had been destroyed during the Blitz.

Hanging on the walls of the chapel, on either side of the aisle, were eight life-size statues of English martyrs who refused to take the Oath of Supremacy during the Reformation. One of them is of St John Houghton, the last prior of Charterhouse. The west window depicts the execution of the monks of Charterhouse, mentioned earlier, hanging from gallows at Tyburn for failing to denounce their Catholic faith.

The long history of St Etheldreda's fascinated me, seeming to reflect both the wider history of England as well as the changing demographics of the surrounding area. I learned that in 1620 the building was leased to a Catholic Spanish ambassador called Count Gondomar, who was able to use the chapel for private Catholic services, even though they were still punishable by death at the time in

England, as his ambassadorial status meant that when he was in residence the building was considered to be on Spanish soil. Gondomar had a concealed door built into the back of the chapel for people to come and go unnoticed and mass was conducted in secret many times while he lived in Ely Palace. In 1624 the chapel briefly became an Anglican church before being used, along with the surrounding palace, as a prison and hospital during the English Civil War. When developer Charles Cole bought the chapel in 1772 it reverted back to being an Anglican church, mainly used by the wealthy residents of Ely Place.

In 1820 the building was bought by the National Society for the Education of the Poor, who were trying to convert Irish settlers in the area. In 1829 the Catholic Emancipation Act was passed and for the first time in 300 years it was no longer illegal to say a public Catholic mass. The Rosminian Order bought the chapel in 1873 and spent five years restoring the crypt and upper church back to their original medieval designs. In 1878 St Etheldreda's reopened as the first pre-Reformation church in England to be restored to Catholic worship.

Under the Rosminians the chapel continued to serve the poor living in the area, as the nuns and monks of the order still do today. As I read this I remembered a guide of St Etheldreda's I had come across in the Holborn Library, written in 1902 by the priest there at the time, who described his parish as one of the most poverty-stricken districts of all London, with greater need even than the most deprived neighbourhoods in the East End. He wrote of visiting crumbling tenements in the area and witnessing heart-rending scenes of impoverishment and misery, with large Irish families occupying a single room, their emaciated children huddled together in the dark, starving and desperate.

As I sat thinking about these terrible scenes a group of suited businesswomen came briefly into the chapel, talking loudly among themselves. They walked briskly up and down the aisle and took a few photographs. Their flashlight momentarily illuminated the stone faces of the martyrs on the walls above. The sound of their

stiletto heels clicking on the hard stone floor echoed around the chapel as they left.

I followed them out and down another set of worn steps near by, which led into a dark subterranean crypt beneath the chapel. There was a faint smell of wine when I entered the low-ceilinged room, reminding me of stories about the time when Sir Christopher Hatton was in residence at Ely Palace and the crypt had been used as a tavern. Back then drunken revelries below often interrupted services upstairs. These days the same space is sometimes hired out for events to help fund the upkeep of the building. The group of women from the chapel stood together in the centre of the room, discussing where they would place a plasma screen for a business presentation.

I wandered around the edge of the crypt, looking at statues set in niches in the eight-foot thick stone walls. This part of the building is much older than the rest and is believed to date back to the sixth century. 'A remarkable stone bowl' had been dug up there in the nineteenth century, 'evidently of great antiquity, possibly Roman. It was placed in the porch, and served as a holy water stoup' (*London Journal*, 11 October 1879). There were other mentions of archaeological finds, even a suggestion by the nineteenth-century architect and archaeologist Sir Gilbert Scott that the chalk, flint and mortar portions of the undercroft formed part of the original Romano-Celtic Basilica of London.

The place has a powerful and brooding atmosphere, which became more intense for me when I read that beneath the crypt are the remains of Catholics who died during the tragedy known as the 'Fatal Vespers' which occurred on 5 November 1623 at the French ambassador's house in Blackfriars. Hundreds had gathered there to attend an illegal Catholic service. The floor the worshippers were standing on collapsed and over 100 people were killed. Eighteen were buried in secret underneath St Etheldredra's.

Against the east wall of the crypt, in a glass case, is a scale model of the Ely estate in the fifteenth century, showing the chapel surrounded by manicured gardens and open fields. Attached to the chapel are a number of cloistered buildings and the grand gatehouse, Ely Palace, along with numerous other outbuildings. Seeing this model was the closest I would get to visualizing what the large Ely estate may have physically looked like before the Reformation. Now I felt I needed to try to find a knowledgeable guide to walk with me around the area, to help me understand the lost landscape of the River Fleet, the wide-open fields, monastic priories, gardens and orchards that had once existed in the area for centuries.

8

Ullmann's

Workshops in Hatton Garden after the war were filled with young apprentices from Brick Lane, Stepney, Stoke Newington and Clapton, and most of us walked there and back daily. The wages were low, the workshops were damp and cold, there was no proper ventilation or natural light, and they were rat-infested, very Dickensian-looking, but it was considered a good trade to go into. After serving a five-year apprenticeship you were considered to be qualified. I learned to speak Yiddish while serving my apprenticeship, I had to, most of the dealers and traders back then were from an Eastern European Jewish background, from many different countries, and Yiddish was the common language.

Anonymous interview

After speaking with Michael I wanted to find out if any of the shops he remembered from the 1960s were still in operation in Hatton Garden. On the Internet I came across the website for one of the places he mentioned, Andrew R. Ullmann Ltd, which specializes in antiques and second-hand jewellery, particularly Georgian, Victorian and early-twentieth-century pieces as well as silver and *objets d'art*. The website explained that the family-run jewellery business had been founded in Budapest in 1902 by Joseph Ullmann, the current owner's grandfather. After Nazis looted and destroyed their shop, Joseph's son, Andrew, relocated to 10 Hatton Garden in 1938. His son, Joseph, named after his late Transylvanian-born grandfather, joined the firm twenty years later, taking over when his father died.

Ullmann's had moved, reluctantly, from Hatton Garden to nearby

Greville Street in 2007, after the building they had worked from for nearly seventy years was redeveloped. The new shop retains the old-fashioned character of the previous one, with a window packed full of antique rings, chains, candelabras and silverware, all with hand-written labels attached. Originally catering only to the trade, Ullmann's was one of the antique businesses my grandfather would visit when he made buying trips to Hatton Garden in the 1950s. Although dealers still come to the shop most of their trade is now retail. They are one of the few shops left in the Hatton Garden area specializing in antique jewellery and they also carry out specialist repairs and restoration work.

I paid a visit to Ullmann's early one morning before trading began. The bell rang as I entered the sympathetically lit interior and started making my way past the treasure trove of jewels displayed in the glass-topped cabinets inside: gold lockets, Edwardian pendants, silver teapots, amber necklaces, cameo brooches, old cut-diamond fringe necklaces, cufflinks, tiepins, garnet earrings, many gold, silver and enamel antique pocket watches and chains, silver clocks, boxes and cigarette cases, alongside numerous other beautiful items, and trays and trays of rings. Dark mahogany cases lined the walls, filled with silver antiques, carriage clocks and other fascinating artefacts. Having grown up in a family of antique dealers I felt instantly at home in the place and had to resist the urge to spend hours looking in the crowded cabinets, trying to spot a bargain.

At the back of the shop, sitting at separate desks, busily working away, were two older men who introduced themselves as Joseph Ullmann, the current owner of the business, and his colleague, Jeffrey Pinkus, who has been working for the company since Joseph's father, Andrew, employed him in 1959.

Joseph, a slight, fit-looking man, with grey hair and glasses, dressed casually in slacks, a pale shirt and a V-necked jumper, has been described to me by many others in Hatton Garden as a true gentleman. He shook my hand warmly before showing me an etching on the wall of the former premises of the shop. Beside it was a photograph taken over fifty years ago of his father repairing a piece of jewellery. The two men looked identical. Next to that was another framed photograph of Joseph Ullmann senior, who had founded the business, a regal-looking bald gentleman, with a wide handlebar moustache.

Joseph suggested I speak to Jeffrey, the longest-serving employee in the business, who had come to Hatton Garden as a seventeen-year-old from Stepney Green after the Jewish Board of Guardians

arranged an interview for him: 'They were like a youth employment agency for Jewish boys. They gave you different options, which were mainly cabinetmaking, tailoring, going into the fur trade or becoming an apprentice in Hatton Garden. It was one of the jobs offered to Jewish boys from East London.'

In 1953 Jeffrey started working at a firm based at 1 Hatton Garden, learning the trade, dealing in precious stones and gems, visiting various big jewellery shops in the West End, buying and selling pearls, coloured stones and diamonds. Foreign traders would visit the office, which he was keen to stress was not a shop and not open to the public. The shops came later, apart from a few such as Ullmann's, S. H. Harris and another firm called Landsberg, who are still around the corner. Jeffrey talked about the way business was conducted back then, with deals taking place on the street, or from offices and cafés. He remembered three kosher restaurants in Greville Street: Lox, the Nosherie and the Jewellers' Café. 'Dealers would go in there, have a cup of tea, and the tables would be strewn with jewels. It was perfectly safe, there was no trouble whatsoever. If you shook hands and said good luck, that was it, the deal was done. You used to see an old man walking down the street, about seventy or eighty years old. He'd take out a little bag from his pocket and perhaps have diamonds worth £100,000 in there. That just doesn't happen today, it's all done behind closed doors now; there are guards outside the shops, security is really tight and it's changed the business. People are more nervous now. We can have brokers who take things on sale and return and then just disappear. The trust that was once there between people has gone. Everyone knew and trusted each other in the 50s; there was a different atmosphere, the businesses were long established. Now it is a bit more fly by night; businesses come and go, they open up a shop, they go bankrupt, then disappear. Back then you knew if you were established you could be trusted and there was nothing to worry about.'

Jeffrey described many master craftsmen in the area, doing very fine work in the 1950s. Today few remain. There are plenty of people mounting and setting but 'not making the kind of quality goods they used to. Most of the shops today all sell the same kind of thing. Modern jewellery, the majority of which hasn't been made here. Our shop is different. We sell mainly antique jewellery, candlesticks, silverware, art deco, Fabergé, more unusual pieces. Our biggest seller is engagement rings. We have our own clientele who have been coming to us for years. In ten years I expect the jewellery shops will still be here but now you have office blocks, residential places, a natural health centre and cafés. Hatton Garden is not just a jewellery street any more.'

While we had been talking Joseph had been working away quietly in the background, a jeweller's loupe placed tightly against his eye as he examined a ring. 'My son and daughter both work in the shop now,' he said proudly. 'They are the fourth generation to be working in the business. My granddaughter helps out too. Five generations of the same family working here – most of the businesses in this street used to be like this but not so much any more. We are now the oldest-established shop in the Garden.'

The old-fashioned bell on the door rang again and an attractive young woman, wearing jeans and a blue shirt, her hair in a long plaited ponytail, came bouncing in and Joseph introduced me to his eighteen-year-old granddaughter, Amelia, who started working in the shop part-time a couple of years ago. 'It's fun,' she said cheerily, 'I love working with the family, it's a really nice atmosphere, with my grandfather, aunts and uncles all here, the shop has always been part of the family.' Her mother is the only one of Joseph's six children who has not worked in the business. Jeffrey is the only member of staff outside of the family, although he feels like family now, having been there for over fifty years.

Amelia spoke to me about the wide range of people she has met since working in her grandfather's shop – from lords to artists. 'Most of the shops on Hatton Garden mainly sell engagement or wedding rings to young couples but people come in here for all sorts of things, stranger items, slightly quirky jewellery, we have many eccentric characters in here, people from all backgrounds.'

We talked about growing up in a family of antique dealers, the games we had both played as children, handling old objects, trying to guess the stories behind them, the magic elements of the trade, the extraordinary artefacts that had passed briefly through our hands before being sold on. Amelia had a particular fascination with the huge collection of charm bracelets in the shop: 'You can't help but think about the people who gathered all these charms over their whole lives,

which often reflect their interests as well as the special occasions they have celebrated, and are then handed down to other members of the family before eventually ending up here to be sold on to someone

else.' Every day she is picking up new bits of information from her grandfather about the antiques they sell and although she is aware there is so much to learn, she is glad he is passing his knowledge on.

Joseph politely interrupted our conversation to remind Amelia she had a ring to pick up from a workshop. She left the shop and made her way on to Hatton Garden. I spent some time talking to Joseph about my grandfather, whom he remembered trading with in the 1960s, along with my uncles and then later my father. Before he had a chance to tell me more, the first customer of the morning came through the door and Joseph leaped up to serve him, while I quietly slipped away.

9

Fons Clericorum

The legends and traditions of this most ancient and interesting
district of London all cluster round St. John's Gate (the old south
gate of the priory of St. John of Jerusalem), and the old crypt of
St. John's Church, relics of old religion and of ancient glory.

Walter Thornbury, 'Clerkenwell', *Old and New London*

I found it impossible to find a guide who had specialist knowledge
of the pre-Reformation Ely Palace but one of my friends, a Blue
Badge tour guide of the City, put me in touch with his colleague
Adele Leffman, who is an expert on the history of Clerkenwell. She
kindly agreed to guide me around the area and suggested walking
the perimeter of the medieval Priory of St John of Jerusalem – the
English headquarters of the monastic Order of the Knights Hospitallers – founded in the eleventh century, on the eastern banks of the
Fleet Valley, 200 years before the original development of Ely Palace. 'There is also Charterhouse, the nunnery of St Mary's and St
Bartholomew's in the immediate area,' she said on the phone, 'but
St John's was the largest and the oldest.' I hoped that learning about
these other great monastic institutions, which sat on the other side
of the River Fleet to Ely Palace for centuries before the Dissolution,
would give me an insight into medieval life inside the Ely estate.

I arranged to meet Adele outside Farringdon tube station on a
wet November afternoon. Standing in the rain beside the news-
stand, looking for a petite woman in her late sixties, I eventually
noticed a dark-haired lady in a raincoat, with bright eye make-up
and an Alice band in her hair, waiting patiently beside the ticket

office, tapping a folded umbrella on the floor. 'Rachel?' she said, smiling as I walked towards her. 'I was expecting someone older.'

We stood in the foyer of the station for some time, chatting about our children and our mutual passion for the history of the area. I felt instantly at ease with Adele, who reminded me of one of my elderly Jewish aunts. 'It is generous of you to share your knowledge and anecdotes with me,' I said as we moved towards the exit, 'this material must have taken you years to gather.'

'These facts are all in the public domain if you know where to look for them,' replied Adele briskly, while leading me gently outside, keen to get walking, bursting with stories to tell.

Out on the street, she directed my gaze up towards Farringdon Road and asked me to imagine the River Fleet flowing there as we walked. She explained that the monasteries and Ely Palace were based in the Fleet Valley, because it was near to the city and next to the river, which would have been wide, clean and fast-flowing during most of the medieval period, providing fresh fish to these institutions, power for the mills and fertile grounds for growing crops and putting cattle to pasture.

We huddled together under my umbrella out of the rain and examined a battered photocopy of the Clerkenwell section of the Agas map I had brought with me. Adele showed me the position of the priories on the map. Ely Palace was the only estate of any real size during the medieval period on the other side of the Fleet. She explained that these large estates needed huge plots of land to sustain them. St John's, the largest, was once so enormous the monks had to move around on horseback just to cover the grounds. Along with the complex of buildings attached to the priory were stables and farriers, dairies and cattle sheds, orchards, vineyards, breweries, kitchen gardens and even fish ponds, which they used to farm fish. She told me the monks of St John's also kept bees and sold honey and mead, along with meat, crops, wine and other produce, to the public to supplement their income. This was similar to various accounts I had come across in the archives about the monks of Ely Palace selling fruits such as strawberries and apples and vegetables such as onions, leeks, beans and garlic, for the same reason.

Looking at the map she pointed out a small wooden structure called Cow Bridge, which once crossed over the Fleet roughly where Cowcross Street is today. 'Drovers used that bridge for centuries, leading herds of cattle bound for Smithfield Market,' she said.

From the site of the meat market, away from the flow of pedestrian traffic pouring out of the tube towards Farringdon Road and the City, we headed into Turnmill Street, which winds east from the station and curves along the line of the railway tracks, beside the former river. As we walked across the former priory fields Adele told me there were never more than a dozen monks living at the monastery at one time, who were all prosperous noblemen. Once the monks had been accepted into the priory they took vows of poverty, chastity and obedience, so they left no descendants, meaning the priory inherited all their wealth. This enabled the order to expand their properties around the world and build forts in the Middle East. The order was originally founded by a group of knights in 1099 after the First Crusade captured Jerusalem. They established a hospital there to care for sick pilgrims and the order spread across Europe. The priory in Clerkenwell was established as the English headquarters of the Knights Hospitallers in 1140. 'The monks did little manual work, their main job was to be holy men, to pray and look after the community and to administer herbs to those who were unwell.'

Adele explained that seasonal workers came to the area to look after the farms, orchards and dairies of the monasteries. I imagine the great estate of Ely was sustained in a similar way and expected the small buildings I had noticed on the Agas map, dotted around the grounds of Ely Palace, were also workers' cottages, like those Adele described on the estate of St John's. She spoke in detail about how Clerkenwell developed from being a tiny hamlet into a bustling suburb on the edge of the city as some of these workers settled in Clerkenwell. Shops began to open both for them and to provide the monks with specialist goods, like vellum – the beginning of the long tradition of the book trade in the area.

As we walked, I began to imagine the gentle, rural, medieval landscape she described; with monks on horseback, grazing cows, orchards and lily ponds, and the sounds that must have been prominent here, of church bells, cattle mooing and the creak of slowly turning water wheels.

I had recently examined a MOLA map which detailed the mills, kilns, buildings and cemeteries that had been uncovered during extensive digs in the area in the 1990s, when archaeologists from the Museum of London had unearthed parts of the former priory between Turnmill Street and the River Fleet. They found evidence of vast medieval gardens and late-medieval tenements along with a palatial complex, the home of the military order. Excavations around the priory buildings unearthed skeletons of horses, a cemetery for the monks, fifteenth-century pottery fragments, a link from a gold neck chain, fragments of a painted-glass window, a shoe buckle and a copper-alloy pilgrim badge. In nearby rubbish pits they found the bones of cows, calves, suckling pigs, hares, skylarks, partridges, geese and swans – all evidence of the monks' rich diet.

The archaeologists concluded that before the arrival of the monasteries, the area had been predominately open land, although they found evidence of earlier human activity: an oyster shell, chalk fragments and butchered animal bones. Below this level were soil horizons and other Roman features, suggesting that a settlement had once existed near by. They also uncovered shards of Saxon pots, bowls, jars and an oval buckle along with a Byzantine gold marriage disc, from the late sixth or seventh century, all dug up close to Farringdon Station.

We stopped on the corner of Turnmill Street and Clerkenwell Road. If we turned left and crossed over the former Fleet River, now Farringdon Road, we would reach the junction of Clerkenwell Road and Hatton Wall, which marks the site of the northern boundary wall of the former Ely estate.

We stood still for a while instead, outside the boarded-up doors of Turnmills Nightclub, where the legendary trade club nights were held throughout the 1990s. The nightclub was the first venue in London to receive a 24-hour licence and kick-started the rave culture of that decade. I spent many happy Saturday nights there, sandwiched within a sweaty, frenetic, mainly gay crowd, grinding away to industrial hard techno until Sunday afternoon, when the doors would open and hundreds of smiling revellers would pour out of the smoky interior into the daylight, covered in bruises, eyes bulging, huddling around the illegal minicabs that gathered outside. The club had recently closed down after someone was shot and killed outside.

Adele told me the site has a long history of public disorder and revelry, although in the times of the monasteries she thought it must have been a lovely place. She explained that three windmills once stood on that spot, next to the river, grinding the grain for the community of monks and agricultural labourers of the priory. After the Dissolution, the entire area collapsed: 'When the monastery and the convent were disbanded the work dried up and people left in droves. Anything of value was taken, buildings were abandoned, the land that had been cultivated by the monks became a wasteland and whoever had the biggest fist could appropriate it. The area became rough, the remaining buildings were used as ad hoc housing and workshops, the place filled with overcrowded rookeries, known for thievery, brothels and all sorts of illegal activity. Turnmill Street turned into a red-light district, where you could get a knee trembler up against the wall for the price of a pint. The taverns there were well known as being places to hire someone to commit murder for you. The street became impenetrable to outsiders, with hidden traps, like concealed cesspits or spiked walkways, which were scattered throughout the many tiny alleyways that once ran off of here. Turnmill Street was commonly referred to as "Little Hell".'

I thought of Peter Ackroyd's theory about Clerkenwell and its 'territorial imperative', an idea that certain places actively guide or determine the lives of those who live within their bounds, through an underlying energy that connects the actions of the past and present. The dark and illicit history of Turnmill Street, from the late sixteenth century until very recently, seems to illustrate this theory perfectly.

Following the course of the lost river, we crossed Clerkenwell Road and walked along the narrow street of Farringdon Lane, stopping outside no. 16, where we saw one of only a few tangible remains of Clerkenwell's monastic past. Behind a glass-fronted window, below the level of the street, sat an ancient-looking brick structure, the remnants of the original Clerk's Well, which had first been recorded in the twelfth century, when it was located in the boundary wall of St Mary's Nunnery. Adele pointed to a spout drawn on the nunnery wall in the Agas map, pouring water into an old stone tank. The fresh spring water was delivered around the rest of the nunnery in pipes made of elm wood. The well, like the river, eventually became filled with rubbish and excrement and lay buried under mounds of earth for centuries before being rediscovered in 1924. There were so many wells and springs along the banks of the Fleet in medieval times that it was often called the River of Wells.

We spoke for some time about the medieval miracle plays, which were once performed beside the River Fleet, on huge moveable wooden platforms known as pageants. Parish clerks felt it was their religious duty to act out stories from the Bible to the mainly illiterate crowds of the general public who went to see this popular and free street theatre. 'They were great social occasions. In 1391 one of these miracle plays lasted for three days and was attended by King Richard II and his court.' Looking at the site of the former riverbank – now a deep trench lined with railway tracks heading into Farringdon Station beside a busy road – it was hard to imagine this colourful spectacle, with clerks in full costume performing religious stories to cheering crowds of thousands.

Before we carried on walking Adele asked me to turn round and look back up towards the City, where we saw a perfect, uninterrupted view of the dome of St Paul's, one of eight protected views of the church. Running beside St Paul's is Cheapside, the first jewellery quarter in London and the former location of the city's principal produce market in medieval times. Adele told me, 'A market had been established there in the thirteenth century and for forty days a year non-nationals and traders from outside the guilds were allowed to sell from there. People came from all over the country, from all over the world, to buy and sell at Cheapside. Spices and silks from the East and the New World exotic foodstuffs such as chocolate, coffee and vanilla were the main attraction. It must have been a wonderful sight.'

Soon after, we turned right into a small side street called Pear Tree Court, part of the old orchard belonging to the nunnery. Near by is Vineyard Walk, another street name that echoes the area's rural past. Vineyards belonging to St Mary's stood on this site for hundreds of years and ancient vines were still rooted in the ground until the eighteenth century.

Apart from one small Georgian terrace, Pear Tree Court is filled with nineteenth century tenement blocks, built by the American philanthropist Samuel Peabody, as affordable apartments for low-paid working people. At the end of Pear Tree Court we turned right into Clerkenwell Close, where the magnificent white stone church of St James sits. Built on the ruins of the nun's chapel, in the style of Wren in the eighteenth century, this church has been a place of Christian worship for over 900 years – another example of Clerkenwell's territorial imperative.

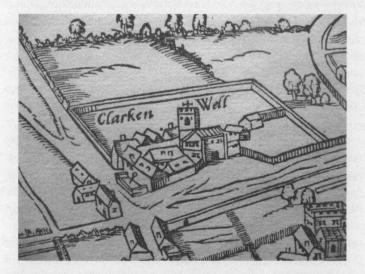

Wet through we stopped for a coffee under the cover of a large awning, outside a café overlooking St James. A Japanese woman served us our drinks. Behind us was a young couple speaking to each other in German. 'This has always been a very cosmopolitan area,' said Adele, cupping her hands around her hot mug to warm up. 'First the Romans were here, followed by monks and nuns in the medieval period, most of whom were French. Then came the Huguenots in the seventeenth century, who were mainly French or Dutch, and later Italian and Irish refugees arrived in Clerkenwell seeking work, followed by many Jewish people, who came to the area because of the diamond trade.'

She told me Huguenot clockmakers and instrument makers were the first skilled workers to arrive in the area. They settled in Clerkenwell because of its position, just outside the city walls, which meant they did not have to belong to a guild to trade from there. Adele explained that during that period of time, you could sell your goods within the city only if you were a guild member, apart from during the forty days at Cheapside mentioned earlier: 'The guilds were formed in medieval times to keep standards of manufacture high in all trades and crafts. There were butchers' guilds, fan-makers' guilds, clockmakers' and goldsmiths' guilds, along with many others. To join you had to serve a seven-year apprenticeship, or if your father had been a member you could buy your way in at vast expense. So Clerkenwell and areas like Hatton Garden developed into commercial areas, with huge influxes of foreign-born skilled craftsmen settling there and selling their goods directly from their workshops, at a much cheaper price than the goods made by the guilds. People started to come to the area to buy directly from them, with shops opening up beside the workshops.'

As we finished our drinks the sun started to come out and Adele stood up, eager to continue. We walked along Clerkenwell Close, past some beautiful Georgian houses, built on land where Old Newcastle House once stood – the former mansion belonging to the Duke of Cavendish, which had been erected over the ruins of the nunnery buildings after the Dissolution. The garden contained six acres of the southern cloister, including part of the cemetery. 'Henry VIII gave much of the Church's former lands to Tudor nobles like Cavendish and many grand houses sprang up on these sites in the late sixteenth century,' said Adele. 'When the area began to deteriorate, the nobles' descendants moved away and the duke's home was split into apartments, then separate rooms. Soon most of Clerkenwell became an overcrowded, undesirable place to live.' By the nineteenth century Clerkenwell was densely populated with craftspeople and artisans employed in small workshops devoted to trades such as watchmaking, jewellery, optical and mathematical instruments, bookbinding, locksmiths, printing and cabinetmaking. The same trades listed in the earliest post office records in 1840 for the first shops that opened up on the ground floors of the former grand houses of Hatton Garden.

We took a brief detour along St James's Walk to the site of a former sixteenth-century palace, which became Bridewell Prison in 1615. The motto above the entrance had been LOOK ON AND DESPAIR, ALL YE WHO ENTER HERE. A century later, another building was erected alongside it named the New Prison. These two institutions were rebuilt in the nineteenth century into one larger facility called the Clerkenwell House of Detention, or Clerkenwell Prison. Like the monasteries, by law prisons had to be outside the city walls. Along with Bridewell (Clerkenwell) Prison, Ludgate, Newgate, Coldbath and the Fleet Prison were all positioned beyond the city boundary.

In 1890 Clerkenwell Prison was demolished, apart from a great network of underground passages and cells below the building, which had been used for centuries to house and torture prisoners. During the Second World War these subterranean tunnels were used as air-raid shelters and later opened as a grisly tourist attraction. Several episodes of the reality show *Most Haunted* have been filmed in the cells, which are said to be 'crowded with ghosts'. Above them now sits a gated community of loft apartments. 'I wonder if the residents here see the irony,' said Adele, pointing to the iron railings and CCTV cameras around the perimeter of the building.

I followed Adele towards Clerkenwell Green, where I imagined the horses and cattle belonging to the monks would have once grazed. 'Picture this place as the last lap of a long journey for traders from the

East coming into the city,' said Adele. 'The monks used to give safe passage across these fields to these weary travellers. The Hospitallers' churches were all sanctuaries, lights were always kept burning in them. The monks would take in anyone who needed protection. They'd wave a torch from the priory to light the way and give them a bed and breakfast. At first light they were woken up with a meal and a "God be with you" and off they went. When the monks left, the area became a no man's land that was dangerous to cross, where highwaymen and ruffians could attack travellers. For centuries this site has also been a place of protest, used by Wat Tyler, the leader of the Peasants' Revolt in the fourteenth century.'

We briefly entered the Marx Memorial Library; a pastel-coloured Georgian building on the Green, dedicated to working-class history, Marxism and Socialism. 'It opened in 1933,' said Adele. 'Many radical organizations used to meet here, there was a publishing house based inside and Lenin used the place as an office when he was exiled in London in 1902. Before then it was a charity school and a coffee house.' Recent excavations there uncovered underground tunnels below the basement of the building that once led into the former nunnery of St Mary's but they were never opened to the public.

We moved on to St John's Square and stood in front of the rebuilt parish church of the ancient priory. 'The crypt is from the twelfth century and one of the oldest remnants of the medieval period in this area,' explained Adele. 'The rest of the church was rebuilt in the eighteenth century.' She pointed out a circular row of cobblestones embedded into the ground in front of the church, which outlined the location of the original building. 'The twelfth-century church was built like the Templar churches, in the style of the round church in Jerusalem,' she said, 'leaving no corners for the devil to hide in.'

Crossing back over Clerkenwell Road we turned left and then right into Britton Street, the site of sixteenth-century gin distilleries, which had been built alongside the banks of the Fleet by Dutch migrants. 'The fact they were here means the water must have been very pure then. It wasn't in the rest of London though.

The drinking water generally in the city was so bad that children were given gin to drink instead.' She stopped outside the former Booth's Gin Factory and pointed out a sculptural frieze, showing the brewing process and the juniper trees, which once grew there in abundance.

There were more Georgian houses further down the street, with attic windows reminiscent of the weavers' lofts in Spitalfields. 'These top floors were used by workers making small parts for clocks and watches,' said Adele. 'Like the weavers they were paid piecemeal and ruined their eyesight working till the last rays of the setting sun to make enough to live on.'

We passed the Jerusalem Tavern – a nineteenth-century re-creation of an eighteenth-century pub named after the Priory of St John and Jerusalem. I followed Adele up a narrow alleyway called St John's Path, there was just about enough space for us to walk side by side. 'Many little streets like this were rebuilt after the Great Fire on old plans,' she said, 'places like this still give you a sense of the city before 1666.' Exiting the walkway we entered a cobbled courtyard. Turning right at the top of St John's Lane, we saw a huge medieval stone gateway, with battlements and latticed windows, straddling both sides of the road, which Adele told me once led into the inner sanctum of the Priory of St John.

The gateway was not original. It had been rebuilt in the Georgian period, in the style of the sixteenth-century building, from engravings by seventeenth-century artist Wenceslaus Holler. 'It is thought to be a very accurate replica of the second gate, which was erected in in 1504 by Prior Dowcra,' Adele told me. 'The original monastery was burned to the ground in 1381, during the Peasants' Revolt, by Wat Tyler and his mob. The peasants attacked many monasteries around the city as their wealth had attracted much resentment over the years. The priory burned for several days, the mob preventing all attempts to put out the flames. It took over a century before the monastery was rebuilt. The second building was much grander than the first and was said to resemble a palace, with spires, ornate gardens, a beautiful church, a high steeple and very fine workmanship throughout. If you look carefully at the stonework you can see that some of the stones are much older than the others and probably date back to the medieval period. After the Dissolution the building was literally taken apart. Henry VIII took all the treasure from inside and used the remaining buildings to store his hunting tents. The building itself, which was made of beautiful Kentish Ragstone, got taken down to build other houses. Protector Somerset blew up the priory tower and used the stone to make Somerset House in the Strand. Only ruins would have remained when the gateway was reconstructed in the eighteenth century.'

One of the first uses of the new building was as a coffee house. It was owned for a short while by William Hogarth's father, who was a Latin teacher. In 1707 he was sent to the largest and oldest of the prisons built alongside the Fleet River – the Fleet Prison. He spent five years there after getting into terrible debt when his coffee-house business failed. This may have been because he insisted his customers speak only in Latin while drinking in his establishment.

In 1731 rooms above the gatehouse became the offices of the first modern periodical, the *Gentleman's Magazine*, founded by Edward Cave, who wrote under the pseudonym 'Sylvanus Urban'. The iconic illustration of St John's Gate on the front of each issue made the monastery gate famous throughout eighteenth-century London. Dr Johnson worked at the magazine and frequented the coffee house below, which later in the eighteenth century became the original Old Jerusalem Tavern.

The building was bought back by the revived Order of St John in 1874, and gradually converted to serve as the headquarters of the organization and its offshoot, the St John Ambulance Brigade – the strongest example yet of Clerkenwell's territorial imperative.

We went inside to see the recently opened museum, which tells the history of St John's Gate and the Order of St John – a story spanning more than 900 years. 'The Knights Hospitallers were initially male nurses who went on the crusades to look after the poor,' said Adele. 'They were trained in the art of warfare but could not attack, only fight to save life and protect the Christian brothers. After the

Dissolution the Catholic Order of St John was disbanded but later revived as an Anglican order, which eventually became the St John Ambulance Brigade who developed in Victorian times from the idea of the nursing warrior monks of the Order of St John.' History had come full circle somehow.

I spent some time looking at the elegantly designed new galleries, packed with rare manuscripts, paintings and artefacts, hoping to find more about a story I had recently come across in Walter Thornbury's *Old and New London* about Templar and Hospitaller knights returning from the crusades of 1247 and presenting King Henry III with a beautiful crystalline vase, containing a phial of the blood of Christ collected during his crucifixion. There was no data about this relic, but I spent a long time looking at the other exhibits on display, learning more about the international history of the order and the development of the St John Ambulance Brigade.

I could not find any information about the relationship between the former priory of St John and the Palace of Ely but I imagined that before the Dissolution the inhabitants of these two great institutions would have once been good neighbours. Maybe the monks from both houses would exchange fruit and vegetables with each other when they had a bumper crop, or meet on Friday nights for a supper of fried fish, or exchange stories of who caught the largest salmon in the Fleet – the life-giving river that enabled the development of these religious estates.

10

Mrs Cohen's Kosher Café

In Hatton Garden we see the dealer in precious stones. Behind one
of the most prosaic exteriors in this famous street, in studied seclusion,
is the Diamond Merchants' Club. A glance inside reveals Dutchmen
and Jews in large numbers, so much so that the physiognomy
of these races is said to characterize the diamond merchant.

George R. Sims, *Living London*

An email arrived in my in-box from a woman whose father had
been one of the founding members of the London Diamond
Bourse. Happy to share her memories, Mrs S invited me to her sea-
side home in Essex. 'My entire life, growing up in the house of a
diamond dealer, security was everything. My father drilled it into us
to never discuss what he did for a living. He was extremely secretive
about his work. Even now, although he has been dead since 1989, I
still find it hard to talk about this,' said the lady on the phone, who
did not want to be named.

As I made my way up the dark stairwell of the block of flats
where she lives, I noted many *mezuzahs* fixed to the doorposts in her
building. A trim woman wearing trainers and a beige velour track-
suit, who I imagined to be in her early seventies, opened the front
door and led me through to a small, carpeted front room overlooking the estuary. A large, patterned three-piece suite and a tall dark
wooden sideboard, filled with books and family photographs, took
up most of the floor space. Long, mustard-coloured velvet curtains
were half drawn over the full-length French windows.

Mrs S sat in one of the armchairs and invited me to sit opposite her. She turned on an overhead standard lamp, illuminating a pile of photographs and papers on a small side table next to her. 'This is a picture of my father, Emanuel, taken in Regent's Park in about 1950,' she said, passing me a faded photograph of a broad-shouldered, middle-aged man with a solemn expression, wearing a black trilby, leather gloves and a long, wool overcoat. 'He always dressed smartly when he went out,' she said, 'he was a very proud man.'

We sat and talked for some time about her father, who had been born in Hungary in 1898 in the run-down Jewish quarter of Budapest, living in a tiny flat with his mother and five siblings; his father had never been around. At the age of twelve, Emanuel left school and began working, 'mostly in low-paid manual jobs', before being called up during the First World War. After being wounded by shrapnel he left the army in 1919 and fled to Vienna, along with thousands of other poverty-stricken Jewish refugees from Hungary, Bohemia and Galicia.

The *Ostjuden*, Eastern Jews, lived in the worst slum areas of the city and were often the victims of anti-Semitic attacks. Most worked as pedlars or craftsmen but Emanuel managed to find a placement as an apprentice diamond cutter: 'The conditions there were appalling, he barely had enough to eat and lived in a hovel, but he finished his apprenticeship and somehow saved enough to start dealing in a few small stones. During this time he became very involved in left-wing politics.'

On 15 March 1938 Hitler entered the city, greeted by huge flag-waving, cheering crowds of Austrians. Vienna became part of the German Reich and Jews were soon excluded from economic, cultural and social life; their homes and shops were attacked, they were chased through the streets, forced to scrub the pavements, and made to wear the yellow star.

Of the many coordinated attacks that occurred during Kristallnacht – 9–10 November 1938 – in Germany and Austria, the Jews of Vienna experienced the most violent pogrom. Mobs of Nazis, SA Stormtroopers and local civilians rampaged through the streets,

torching over ninety synagogues to the ground, destroying Jewish businesses, ransacking homes. Twenty-seven members of the Viennese Jewish community were killed. Thousands across the country were arrested and deported to concentration camps. Only those who promised to emigrate immediately, leaving their property behind, were released from arrest.

In 1939 Emanuel arrived in London, but the details of his flight are unknown. 'He never talked about it apart from to say he came with nothing and that his entire family perished.' He was forty-three years old. He had no English, money, or friends. Like many Austrian, German, Belgian and Hungarian Jewish diamond cutters, polishers and dealers, he started to carve out a living for himself in London's rapidly expanding jewellery quarter of Hatton Garden. It is possible he had some connection with other dealers in the Garden; someone in the community from Vienna may have helped him get started.

Mrs S thinks he was a founding member of 'the Club' or 'the Bourse', which was originally based at Mrs Cohen's Kosher Café on the corner of Greville Street and Leather Lane. Many of the other founding members were Jewish diamond traders from Antwerp, who fled the Nazi occupation of Belgium in May 1940. They made their way to either London or New York, with whatever tools and stock they could carry, and began trading from the café. From 1945 onwards a huge influx of other Jewish refugees arrived from war-torn Europe along with survivors from concentration camps. The London Diamond Bourse website states that: 'As many of these had lost all their possessions and, in the cases of younger ones, missed their education, they started as diamond brokers with the help of those already established dealers.'

Mrs S remembered going with her father to Mrs Cohen's as a child: 'It was filled with smoke and the sound of Yiddish, everyone sounded like they were arguing all the time; I found it hard to believe any business could be conducted in these circumstances. My father must have fitted in there. The place was full of refugees from Belgium, Austria, Germany and Hungary. Some must have managed to keep hold of a few stones and start dealing. There were a few

Russian dealers too, who had arrived in the area much earlier and were more established. I only remember seeing men in there, all dressed similarly to my father. There were a few Orthodox dealers but most were politicized, secular Jews like my father. The main languages spoken were Yiddish and German. The men sat around the tables, drinking coffee, smoking, playing cards or chess, it was a very noisy, very smoky, very male place. How any work was achieved in this environment I have no idea. To me it looked like a group of men arguing and having fun. Somehow, among all this, major business deals were conducted daily.'

Dave Harris had also spoken about the early days of the Diamond Bourse, describing the café, which was practically next door to where he worked, in very similar ways to Mrs S. He told me: 'They had on the door there a very tough, old, retired Jewish policeman from the 1900s; he was a rough old thing. You could only go into the place if you were known, so there was minimal security. Occasionally robberies did happen: one dealer had his pocket picked in the place; he had a parcel of fine diamonds worth over £10,000, a fortune before the war.'

For the most part there was great mutual respect and trust between the dealers, most of whom were refugees who had escaped Nazi-occupied Europe. Alone in a strange country, they must have found solace with each other at Mrs Cohen's. Relationships formed during that time were as solid as the rocks that passed across the tables. 'My father had friends there who were like family to him,' said Mrs S; 'they shared so much history and tragedy. They operated through an unspoken code of ethics that was never broken.'

Emanuel never had an office in Hatton Garden: 'He just did his business at the Bourse and bought his stock home, which is why he had to be so secretive about it. That was how things were done then. Of course it would never happen now. Back then many of the men walking towards the café had thousands of pounds' worth of stones in their pockets, wrapped up in paper packages. My father kept his in a small tobacco tin, which was attached to the inside of his trousers with a metal chain.'

Moving over to the sofa Mrs S showed me her father's tools, which she had laid out on a tin tray for me to inspect. She picked up a tiny paper packet, with the words REAL PEARLS 'A' written on the front in biro in her father's own hand. 'This is the special paper always used to wrap diamonds in,' she told me, as she carefully unfolded the delicate package to reveal a thin layer of tissue paper inside, where the stones would have sat. She showed me the particular way the paper would have been folded, thrice over and back on itself, the edges bent up so that even the tiniest stone could not escape.

As I carefully picked up her father's tools, she reminisced about seeing him use them: 'Those tweezers are so precise,' she said, as I examined the exquisitely made silver instrument, as sharp as a knife; 'he could hold even the smallest rose diamond in them. It makes me nostalgic looking at these objects, remembering seeing my father, sat at the kitchen table, opening up parcels of sparkling stones, poking around with his tweezers, picking up diamonds, looking at them through his jeweller's loupe, inspecting their colour, checking for flaws, blemishes, tutting if he saw any, smiling if the goods were fine, while deciding on who to show them to and how he could get the best price, strike the right deal. He measured the size of the stones with his diamond gauge,' she said, extracting a flat silver tool out of a crumbling leather wallet. 'After inspection the stones would be placed in tiny silver scales to determine their carat weight and then carefully folded away, in small batches, inside their paper packets again. Sometimes he had packets of rose diamonds, so small they were almost impossible to see with the naked eye. Diamond powder would be shaken into a separate packet and sold on to the polishers, who mixed it with oil and used it to polish up rough diamonds.'

At home, when Mrs S's mother cleaned, Emanuel would tip the contents from the dustpan on to a piece of newspaper on the table and go through it with a razor, checking for any lost diamonds. The insides of shoes were checked, even the turn-ups of trousers. 'He never had any insurance and he never trusted authority.' The diamond business after the war suited Emanuel; there was no paper trail then and no receipts: business operated on trust alone.

Diamond dealing back then sounded like an almost underworld operation, with packages exchanged across smoky tables in dark cafés and back offices, dealers trusting payment would come later. The only insurance in the business was the knowledge that if you were even suspected of any bad dealing, you were finished. Within a couple of hours everyone would know about it. Because of this dealers had to be scrupulously honest, and the entire international diamond business still operates according to a strict set of unspoken rules, codes and ethics of behaviour. Break them and you are out.

'He always called it "the Club", rather than "the Bourse",' said Mrs S. 'Most days he would go straight there, meet a few people, make a few calls, do some running around, trying to sell his goods, supplying diamonds to the offices, workshops, brokers and dealers. Sometimes he bought antique jewellery and broke up the pieces to sell the stones.'

Emanuel retired at sixty-five and sold off all his stock. 'We never had any luxuries at home. All the money he made was ploughed back into the business. I bought my mother her first iron a few years before she died. Both of my parents had great determination – they had overcome so many difficulties – but I sensed they never quite overcame their past. They were not as happy as other people.' Emanuel lived to the age of ninety-one.

As I sat, cautiously handling his beautifully made and well-worn tools, I thought back to the watchmaking and jewellery tools I had gathered from my grandfather's house after he died: the jeweller's loupe in its leather case, the tiny brass screwdrivers, gold weights, miniature welders, polishing wheels, minuscule saws. Much like Emanuel's collection, all of these tools could have easily fitted into the pocket of an overcoat. Portable, mobile objects. Items that could be quickly transported, hidden, kept on one's person. Like the diamonds that some merchants managed to escape with from war-torn Europe, sewn into the hems of their clothes. Like the ritual artefacts of the Jewish religion: *tefillin*, prayer shawl, *yarmulke*, spice box, candlestick.

II

Hatton Garden

History and colour and passion can pack a street, leaving but a few
echoes to be collected by the curious. Yet the same ordinary-looking
street, apparently deserted by all its glories, can hold as much potential
riches and splendour as any street of its size in the whole world.

John Pudney, *Hatton Garden*

A librarian at the British Museum Reading Room showed me a catalogue of maps, plans and views of London, collected by the
Victorian Frederick Crace. He described the collection as an essential archive for anyone wanting to trace the gradual development of
the metropolis. 'It was Crace's ambition to illustrate every building
of note in this great city,' the librarian told me. 'If an image of Hatton House exists it will be in this catalogue.'

Searching through the yellowing pages for an image of the mansion
that Sir Christopher Hatton had allegedly built over the gardens of the
Bishop of Ely's Palace, I found listings of engravings depicting other
events and places in the area: pictures of Wat Tyler being slain at
Smithfield, sketches of St Bartholomew's Hospital and the neighbouring Cloth Fair, views of decrepit houses in the slums of Saffron Hill
and Clerkenwell, etchings of the Fleet Prison, St Andrew's Church, the
Priory of St John and Jerusalem and many engravings of Ely Palace,
but not a single picture of the Hatton House mansion.

At the London Metropolitan Archives (LMA) I trawled through
Collage, an online image database, which contains over 30,000 digi-
tized works of art from collections at the City of London Libraries
and the Guildhall Art Gallery and, again, drew a blank.

Returning to the Guildhall's maps of London (which had recently merged with collections at LMA), I studied Faithorne and Newcourt's survey, dated 1658 – an updated version of the Agas map – which shows that by the seventeenth century a wall had been built around the former pastureland attached to Ely Palace, the orchards landscaped into fashionable gardens, with a large fountain in the centre surrounded by box hedges. The only building of any size on the estate was still named Ely Palace, fronting on to Holborne High Road.

In Thornbury's *Old and New London* it is stated that after Hatton moved into Ely Palace in 1576 he spent thousands of pounds 'building and repairing the gatehouse', but there is no mention of a new mansion being erected on the site. I began to suspect that the mansion of Hatton House never existed as a separate building, it was just the name given by Sir Christopher Hatton to the revamped Ely Palace of old.

A vast paper trail of evidence remains in numerous archives, documenting the lengthy legal battles that continued after Hatton's death in 1591 over the ownership of Ely Palace. The Bishops of Ely never gave up their fight to win the property back from the Hattons but, in 1654, the courts ruled that Lord Christopher Hatton III would inherit the land and the decaying mansion. Hatton III leased his estate to a property developer called Robert Smith, who then sublet it to Robert Johnson, who planned to construct one of the first purpose-built residential estates for the upper-middle classes in London on the site. Building work began soon after but it took years for the plans to be fully approved. On 7 June 1659 diarist John Evelyn wrote, 'Ye foundations laying for a streete and buildings in Hatton Garden, designed for a little towne, lately an ample garden.' Work stopped for a while in 1660, after Bishop Matthew Wren of Ely (Sir Christopher Wren's uncle and the last Bishop of Ely to live in Ely Palace) was freed from the Tower, where he had been imprisoned for eighteen years after trying to reinstate Catholic worship in his churches. Returning to his former home he found Ely Palace half demolished and the

Holborne

former palace gardens and orchards turned into a building site. He tried different legal routes to stop the development of the Hatton Garden estate but succeeded only in slowing it down; the estate took a further thirty-five years to complete.

By 1665 Ely House had been completely demolished along with all the other buildings on the estate, apart from St Etheldreda's Chapel. Georgian, Wren-style houses were slowly built over the foundations, constructed in part from the burned-out timbers gathered after the Great Fire. Gradually the grounds were carved up into new streets.

In the Museum of London gallery dedicated to the Great Fire of 1666 there is a map on display called *A Plan of the City and Liberties of London after the dreadful conflagration in the year 1666*, which shows how close the fire came to destroying the partially developed Hatton Garden estate. The flames crossed Holborn Bridge and the River Fleet and burned out between Fleet Street and Fetter Lane, just before Ely Palace and Smithfield. Everything south of this was obliterated.

On this map the Fleet is still visible, Ely Palace has disappeared and the new street of Hatton Garden can be seen laid out over part of the former palace gardens, along with some of the new buildings of the Hatton Garden estate, progressing up towards Hatton Wall. Behind these buildings a section of Hatton Garden was still open ground, awaiting development.

Ogilby and Morgan's map of the City of London, dated 1676, is thought to be the first accurate map of the capital, although Jeremy Smith told me there are many errors of scale. On this map the roads of Hatton Street (Hatton Garden), Cross Street, Saffron Hill and Grevile Street (now Greville Street) had all been constructed. Hatton Street is a wide road filled with plots for large houses as far north as Cross Street. Benjamin Cole (no relation to the architect Charles Cole who built Ely Place in 1772) bought the remaining land on the Hatton Garden estate in 1679 and built grand houses on the empty plots to attract the gentry.

In the Camden Local History Library I examined a facsimile of a detailed survey of the completed Hatton Garden estate, made in 1694, by property developer, builder and carpenter Abraham Arlidge (reprinted by the London Topographical Society in 1983). Lord

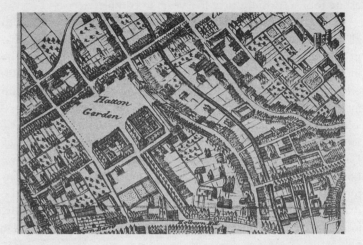

Hatton III, who remained the landlord of the estate, commissioned this decorative hand-drawn map. All 372 houses built on the Hatton Garden estate are depicted on this survey, with the surnames of each tenant written on to the buildings. Most are very English-sounding names, such as Hodson, Manning, Badger, Edwards, Squib, Simkins and Smith. Written over seven properties from Holborn Road up to Old Mitre Court (then known as Ely Passage) is the name of Gelfthorp, possibly a Dutch or Flemish tapestry maker or silk merchant. Arlidge himself also owned the leasehold to many properties on the new estate.

Reading a detailed examination of Arlidge's survey (by Penelope Hunting, *London Topographical Record*, Vol. XXV, publication no. 132, Chapter VI), I learned that each house had a large garden, its own coach house and stables, a basement, and an attic for the servants. Inside, the houses were fitted with oak staircases and had marble fireplaces in every room. Externally they had grand, carved wooden entranceways, casement windows and decorative iron balconies.

In Cross Street and Little and Great Kirby Street the houses were not as large, and along Hatton Wall and Leather Lane even smaller buildings were erected between breweries and alleyways. The vacant land behind the estate became filled with yards, warehouses and stables. Blocking the Bishop of Ely's northern exit out of Ely Palace was a yard and stables marked as 'Arlidge's Yard', now known as Bleeding Heart Yard.

Having been lost for centuries, in the 1920s Arlidge's survey was discovered along with a number of deeds and documents in the attic of 42 Hatton Garden by Mr Howard Marryat, a lawyer and part-time historian who lived in the building at the time. In the seventeenth century Arlidge had occupied the same address. Marryat became fascinated with Arlidge's crumbling original survey: 'a richly illuminated document on vellum coloured in different inks'. The gardens were painted in green, the roads were yellow and the map was decorated in gold leaf.

After studying the survey Marryat began searching through the deeds of his house, 'voluminous documents, covering thirty-five square feet of parchment, weighing as much as a man can carry'. He discovered a family Bible belonging to previous tenants, which recorded their history, including pathetic notes from the mother about the deaths of her children and the old-fashioned remedies she used while they were ill. Marryat conducted an early form of oral history, speaking with other residents of the street, whose memories stretched back to the 1890s when most of the original seventeenth-century buildings on Hatton Garden were still intact.

In 1930, together with the seventeenth- and eighteenth-century historical expert, Miss Una Broadbent, they published a book of little more than 100 pages documenting their research. It was called *The Romance of Hatton Garden*. Inside this long-out-of-print green leather-bound volume, they describe the houses that were built on the new estate as neither 'common place nor palatial'. They imagined that during the days of the Great Fire, Hatton Garden, which was still being developed at the time, would have:

been piling up with goods of every kind, among which the owners sat stupefied, clutching incongruous oddments, caught up, often at the very last moment, from their threatened homes. It was like one of those pitiful open-air encampments of air-raid refugees in the worst days of the war, save for the medley of priceless tapestries and pictures, plate, books, silks, that there had been no time to store in chests for transport, showing in places marks of fire and water: treasure of some of the richest houses in the world.

Writing in 1930 they say of the street, 'There is fortunately no need to describe it in detail, since so many of the original houses remain, outwardly little modified by succeeding owners.' Pre-war Hatton Garden had been filled with 'Georgian façades and canopied door-ways'. Most have long since disappeared, and Marryat's memories of visiting these houses, along with a few early photographs in the archives, are now the only documentation I could find of the former seventeenth-century homes of Hatton Street.

Marryat and Broadbent described how the level of the roadway had risen considerably 'since the earliest houses in Hatton Garden were built and the seventeenth-century ground floors are now below the street'. They mention the original oak floors of these houses, which were made of ships' timbers, and had 'a romance of their own before Hatton Garden was even thought of'. Searching inside some of the houses they found old lead cisterns, 'weighing as much as a ton', 'cast of metal containing a large amount of silver . . . with wonderful designs incorporated into the moulding, coats of arms, busts, emblems, initials and dates going back to 1680'. They describe a building called Hatton House, which was not the original mansion of the first Sir Christopher Hatton but rather a grand private house, built by the last Lord Hatton in the seventeenth century in Cross Street off Hatton Garden. In the eighteenth century Hatton House was used as a chapel by the disciples of Emanuel Swedenborg, a mystic and philosopher who lived for many years at nearby Cold-bath Fields, where he died in 1772. It remained a place of worship, under the name of the Jerusalem Chapel, until it was demolished in the nineteenth century. In the British Library I found a document on the theological writings of Swedenborg, written by the minister of the New Jerusalem Temple, from Hatton Garden, in 1802.

Comparing Arlidge's survey with an Ordnance Survey map from 1920, Marryat and Broadbent wrote, 'All the existing streets and alleys have remained unchanged . . . though some courts have been built over,' as had the gardens, apart from no. 51, which they visited, and saw an 'ivy walled' garden, 'brilliant with flowers', and a mulberry tree, 'a relic perhaps of a Jacobean cult, flourishing there in the last piece of ground in the street still used as a garden, adjoining the old police court'. The last example of the 'vanished fruitfulness of the district'.

Inside this book there is a photograph of a group of artefacts excavated from the garden of 28 Hatton Garden; pieces of an eighteenth-century Wedgwood jug, handmade glass bottles and clay pipes.

Using Marryat's book, Arlidge's survey, parish records and other secondary sources and documents I tried to find out more about some of the early residents of seventeenth-century Hatton Street. Among the first to live in the new houses were physicians and doctors, along with lawyers and barristers working in the nearby Inns of Court. Samuel Pepys mentions visiting Thomas Hollier, a sur-

PLATE VIII.

Measured drawing of portion of doorway.

THE LAST OF HATTON GARDEN, THE ONLY PIECE OF GROUND
ON THE ESTATE STILL MAINTAINED AS A GARDEN.

geon 'for scald heads' from St Thomas's Hospital, in his diary on Wednesday 13 March 1666, 'in his house in Hatton Garden'.

On 23 August 1673, John Evelyn visited Paradise House in the street and described 'a roome in Hatton Garden furnished with the representation of all sorts of animals, handsomely painted on board or cloth'. In 1680 Sir Christopher Wren's assistant Edward Woodroffe leased Paradise House for his daughters.

In the British Library I examined a pamphlet, published in 1673 by a Dr Jones, which he called his 'book of cures'. Jones described himself as 'an English physician', who lived at 'a corner house in Hatton Garden, three doors down from the sign of the Golden Ball, almost against Baldwin's garden gate, at the upper corner near the sign of the George'. He tells his readers he will visit his country house in the summer and be back in Hatton Garden in November. 'In my absence I will leave my cordial-pill in pots, sealed with my own seal.'

In 1667 a playhouse called the Nursery opened in Hatton Garden, with a school and theatre for training young actors. Dr George Bates, personal physician to Oliver Cromwell and Charles I, died in his home in Hatton Garden in 1668. Francis Poyntz, a famous Flemish tapestry maker, who made hangings for Hampton Court, was living in Hatton Garden in 1678. The painter Thomas Gainsborough hired rooms at 67 Hatton Garden in 1743, which he used as his first artist's studio. John Flamsteed, the first astronomer royal of England, lived in the area in the eighteenth century, and the celebrated printer William Bowyer lived in nearby Kirby Street.

The historian John Strype, in his *Survey of the Cities of London and Westminster* (published in 1720 as an updated version of John Stow's *Survey of London* from 1598), described Hatton Garden as 'spacious' and 'very gracefully built, and well inhabited by the gentry'. In the Camden Local History Library I looked at early poor-rate vestry records for the Liberty of Saffron Hill, Hatton Garden and Ely Rents dated 1726, which state the amount of tax that was collected from wealthier residents in the area to 'pay for the wages of the scavengers, rakers and other officers employed in cleansing the streets, lanes, alleys and other public places and carrying away the ashes, dirt and filth' from the neighbourhood. Names of residents and landlords from properties in the area are listed with the amount of tax paid in shillings, which was determined by the value of their property, much like the Council Tax today. In Jack Adam's Alley, a small side street off Saffron Hill, no rates were collected; the residents were 'all poor'. In Hatton Garden poor rates for that year ranged from one shilling to eighteen, with an average amount of ten shillings. The amount collected from the 282 households listed in the street totals £176. The average amount collected from most of the neighbouring streets is just less than fifty shillings, making it clear how wealthy the residents of Hatton Garden were at the time compared to their neighbours. After hours of trawling through these records I decided there was little more of great interest apart from a long list of flamboyant and long-forgotten names of former house owners: Subino Freeman, Widow Horman, Madam Ely, Zackery Gibson, Rich Ball, Fisher Tenet, Lady Child.

In 1761 Hatton Garden was mentioned in *London and Its Environs* as 'a broad, straight and long street, in which the houses are pretty and lofty . . . and the street must be reckoned amongst the finest in the city'. Surrounding the grand houses in Hatton Garden and Greville Street was a maze of little backstreets, alleys and courts, home to some of the poorest people in the city. Looking at a single page of deaths in 1770 for the Parish of St Andrew's, I counted eighteen people who had died in either the Gray's Inn, Saffron Hill or Shoe Lane workhouses. I felt a genuine sadness when I read in the records for April 1797 that William Cropley, Catherine Ansell, Sophia Grifs and Mary Waalls had been buried at St Andrew's on the same day in one mass paupers' grave, after dying at very young ages in the nearby Saffron Hill workhouse.

Crime leaked into the gentile street of Hatton Garden from the surrounding neighbourhood. Violent robberies happened there, long before diamonds arrived in the area. On Sunday 29 December 1778, in what became known as the 'great robbery in Hatton Garden', a gang of twenty thieves arrived at a house, forced the occupants into an inner room at pistol point and ransacked the place. A member of the household escaped and raised a cry of 'Thieves!' and the robbers took to their heels, but they were captured two days later trying to get rid of their booty. In the mid eighteenth century, the 'extraordinary robbery of Mr Campbell, the banker's clerk' took place in Hatton Garden. A criminal gang staked out his house for six weeks, renting the building opposite, watching the bank clerk's every move. The leader of the gang dressed as a clergyman to gain access to the house. During the robbery Mr Campbell was abducted and cruelly treated by 'swindlers, who tied him hand and foot with chains to the copper grate to starve him to death and said if he made the least noise they would blow his brains out'.

At the London Metropolitan Archives I tried to find out more about the early residents of the street by joining the many patient researchers who sit for hours daily at the microfiche booths, searching through reels of often badly photographed and deteriorating records, looking for the names of distant relatives, ancient burial sites, demolished addresses. In the St Andrew's parish register for burials from 1768 to 1785, I found the names of former eighteenth-century Hatton Garden residents who had been laid to rest in the churchyard: Robert Greenway, Esq., 1784; Walter Copper, 1769; Mary Pickering, 1770; etcetera. The 1781 records for christenings from the same parish revealed the names of former residents of Hatton Street who had been christened at St Andrew's: Ellen, daughter of Francis and Catherine Thornborough; John, son of Joseph and Elizabeth Baker; James, son of James and Elizabeth Bachelor – a brief summoning of the dead.

There are seventeenth- and eighteenth-century London directories which I hoped could tell me more about early residents of the area, but they are of course organized via lists of surnames, instead of street names, making them notoriously difficult documents to extract information from about a place. The helpful staff at the archives encouraged me to push my search further. 'You can look through wills, rate books, livery company, parish and land tax records and find out more,' they said enthusiastically. If I had the time to wade through miles and miles of dusty documents I could possibly have found more names and other indecipherable fragments of information but instead I decided to try to find a way of looking inside the original Georgian houses of Hatton Garden.

The only document I came across that allowed a brief glimpse of an early interior was a catalogue for an exhibit called *The Panelled Room of Hatton Garden*, published by the Victoria and Albert Museum in 1920. This room had been extracted intact from no. 26 in 1907 before the house was demolished, then exhibited in the Palace of Decorative Art at the Franco-British Exhibition in 1908 and presented to the museum in 1912. The panelled dining room, installed in the first half of the eighteenth century and photographed *in situ* in Hatton Garden before it was removed, had mahogany doors, moulded plaster cornices, decorative shields, elaborate gilded foliage carvings, carved wooden cornices and pinewood panelling, which would have originally been painted in

hues of olive green and duck-egg blue. When the room was first brought to the museum the surface of the panelling was covered with 'paint added, layer upon layer, for nearly 200 years, so that neither shape of mouldings nor crispness of carving could be seen'. The original room would have had 'paintings and sconces on the walls and curtains of velvet or damask hanging at the window'. I contacted the V&A, hoping to see this room for myself, but sadly it is now packed up in a crate and stored below the streets of South Kensington. In 1851 nos 26 and 27 Hatton Garden became the home of the City Orthopaedic Hospital, with a purpose-built operating theatre and an early X-ray department. The hospital closed down in 1907.

12

Mitziman

It [Hatton Garden] is also Little Jerusalem in England's green and
pleasant land, and Yiddish, the lingua franca of Jewry, can be heard on all
sides. But more and more can be distinguished the rapid-fire speech of
modern Hebrew spoken by young Israelis who come to trade for the
growing diamond industry of their own country.

T. J. Clogger, 'The Diamond Garden' from unnamed, undated
newspaper, Holborn Local History Library

I never gave up searching for Mitzy, asking everyone I met in Hatton
Garden for information about him. Conflicting reports came back:
he had emigrated to Israel; he was still working alone in an attic
room somewhere near Holborn Viaduct; he had become ultra religious and was living in Stamford Hill, studying all day in the back
room of a Hasidic synagogue.

My father had last seen him about five years ago walking down
Hatton Garden in his scruffy old clothes and an incongruous-looking
pair of bright white trainers, which he had bought after his old shoes
had literally fallen apart. By then he was crippled with arthritis, practically bent double. A week later he visited my father's shop to drop
off some rings. The trainers had been blacked up with boot polish, as
he didn't think they matched the rest of his outfit. 'He looked frail,
limping along the street,' said my father, 'but if you shook his hand he
was a powerhouse, barrel-chested, strong as an ox. He had tremendous strength in his upper body from pulling the gold threads through
the drawplate, which was tough physical work.'

One day my husband returned from a day's work in Hatton

Garden with a torn piece of paper. On it was the phone number of Mitzy's carer, which someone had given to him to pass on to me. I called straight away. The man on the other end of the phone sounded guarded at first, revealing nothing about Mitzy's where-abouts. As I spoke further, telling him of my desire to include Mitzy's story in my book, he interrupted me. 'He is dead. I'm Mitzy's younger brother, Frederick. We had been estranged for many years and it was only in the final months of his life that I got to know him again, when he became too poorly to look after himself. I nursed him until he died in 2008 at the age of eighty-five.'

Pleased that someone was interested enough in Mitzy's life to write about him, Frederick invited me to his home in Stanmore, to see some old photographs and talk more about the late Hatton Garden ring maker.

Waiting outside the train station for someone I had never met before, I was relieved when a blue Cadillac pulled into the taxi rank driven by an elderly man who looked so much like Mitzy that I knew straight away it was Frederick. He waved me over and opened the passenger door. I sat in the front seat beside him and listened as he enthusiastically told me about the lecture he had attended earlier that day on black holes. 'You're never too old to keep learning,' he said with a smile. 'Things like this are like an aphrodisiac to me, I'm an active member of the University of the Third Age. You have to keep the mind busy and meet people, talk. I wish poor Isadore had been more social.'

A few minutes later we arrived at his home, a 1960s semi in a quiet, leafy cul-de-sac. Frederick's wife greeted us at the door and went to prepare tea and biscuits. After taking off my shoes, I fol-lowed Frederick up the thickly carpeted stairs to his office on the first floor. The walls of the neat, square room were covered in framed family photographs of weddings, graduations, *bar mitzvahs*. 'I'm a massive Arsenal fan, as you can see,' he said, pointing to a signed red-and-white shirt on the wall. 'I try to never miss a game.' Articulate and bubbly, Frederick talked for some time about his working life as an industrial research chemist. His wife came in with a tray and set it down on a side table.

On his computer desk, Frederick had laid out for me the few photographs he had of Isadore, which were all of him as a young man. One image showed a handsome teenager in an RAF uniform. 'He was such a good ballroom dancer in those days,' said Frederick, looking at the photograph. Another picture was of Frederick, Mitzy, their other brother, Sidney, and their two sisters, all in military uniforms. 'We were a very patriotic family,' he said. 'Our sister Dorothy was in charge of the shelter in Mile End Road during the Blitz. She was a tough girl, one of the first people to go into Belsen when it was liberated, and then she went to Israel when they started the State and has lived there ever since. All the siblings have passed away except me now,' he said with a sigh.

He went on to talk about his parents, who had arrived in East London in 1886 after escaping the pogroms in Russia. They settled in a small apartment on Mile End Road, opposite the People's Palace. 'Things were indescribably hard,' said Frederick, 'we often went without food. Our father worked making suits for a company in the West End but it was seasonal work and there were times when we really had nothing. When the war started we were evacuated for a while. During the war the flat was bombed out and the family moved to Stamford Hill. When the flying bombs began coming over we moved to Clapton Pond.'

Frederick told me that Isadore had started work at fourteen, with a hosiery company, before moving on to a large wholesale and retail company near Brick Lane, which sold 'everything'. Aged seventeen, he joined the air force as a flight engineer and became an engine fitter. 'He always had been good with his hands,' said Frederick. 'He used to mend the gears on our bikes when we were kids. When he came out of the air force he worked for an arms manufacturer in Enfield, where he met someone from Hatton Garden and soon after he started his long career in the jewellery business. Around this time we began to drift apart. He started to work on his own and became an increasing loner. He never married and probably died a virgin. He met a woman

once who he loved and he asked her to marry him but her family didn't think he was suitable. He was very sensitive and this affected him deeply. When she turned him down it broke his heart.'

We sat in silence for a while. An ice-cream van pulled into the close and a group of Asian children quickly gathered around it. 'Different type of neighbour here now,' said Frederick, nodding towards the window. 'Used to be all Jewish when we first lived here in the 60s, but there you go.'

In 1965 Isadore moved with his mother and Sidney into a large house in Barnet. Sidney had a cleaning shop in Sadler's Wells, Mitzy had his workshop in nearby Clerkenwell, and the two of them travelled every day to that area. 'He was happy then, I think,' said Frederick. 'They lived in a big house, with a beautiful garden, and when my mother was alive it was well kept. Isadore loved the garden and grew dahlias and vegetables, which he was very proud of.'

Sidney married late in life and moved away, soon after their mother died, and Mitzy stayed on in the house alone. Frederick lost touch with Isadore for decades. He knows little about the fifty-odd years his brother spent toiling in his small workshop in Clerkenwell, living in Barnet by himself. 'The latter part of his life remains completely undocumented.' When he did meet up with him again and went back to the house Frederick spoke with great sadness about the way Mitzy had chosen to live. It reminded me of visiting David Rodinsky's relatives some years before and their horror at the 'mess and the squalor' of their cousin's Spitalfields garret. Mitzy had been another Rodinsky. A misfit. A Jewish man who never married, who lived with his mother and then, after her death, struggled to cope alone.

'Because he had no wife or children, there was no urgency or incentive to clean up his house,' Frederick surmised. 'When Mother passed away he allowed the house to become far worse than any Dickensian image you might have. "What do I want to bother with it for?" he would say to me. It was absolute chaos. He was a hoarder; he never threw anything out; there was stuff everywhere. The curtains were so rotten they were falling apart. You wouldn't believe how he kept it. When he rode his bicycles he'd put them all in the front room, which became piled up with them, one broken bike on top of another. You could barely get in the front door.

'Classical music was the love of his life. He listened to it all the time, at home and when he worked, he was very knowledgeable about it. He had old broken radios all over that house. He would take them apart, tinker with them, then put them back together again. He did not have any records: he always listened to the radio. He had dozens of radios; most of them were antiques.

'It was a very reclusive life he led, he never had any visitors. He would get up pretty late, go to the garden, tend to his dahlias and then drive down to the workshop in Clerkenwell and never come back before midnight. He worked so hard but never made much money. But he was a very talented craftsman. He had his own gold-mark, which was recognized as his, and when he made his rings he would stamp them with this unique hallmark.'

Mitzy had made my own wedding ring back in 1999. I took it off my finger and looked inside the band, searching for this special mark, which was hard to make out with the naked eye. Frederick opened a drawer beside the desk and passed me a jeweller's loupe, one of the few items he had kept from his brother's workshop. Examining the ring through the powerful lens I could clearly see the letters I M, for Isadore Mitziman, imprinted into the gold next to the engraved date of my wedding.

I told Frederick my parents used to stock Mitzy's wedding rings in their shop, which pleased him a great deal. He seemed surprised when I told him how well thought of Mitzy had been in Hatton Garden. 'I'm so delighted to hear this,' said Frederick. 'Apart from the people he knew there he had no friends.'

In the final years of his life Frederick had started to visit Mitzy in his workshop: 'The owners of the place tried to get him out so they could redevelop the property but he had been there for nearly fifty years and refused to leave. I'm amazed he kept going for as long as he did. His little workroom was right up on the third floor and it became very difficult for him to get up the stairs. He worked in total chaos. His workshop looked like a place from the pre-war period;

he never bought anything new and would always try to mend things, tie them up with a piece of string. All his accounts were made out by hand: even an adding machine would have been too advanced for him. He had so much apparatus in there, for melting, spinning and bending gold, the room was filled to the ceiling with it. Every inch of space was taken up with machinery, papers and boxes piled up everywhere, covered in dust and cobwebs, filthy. Out of this he produced exquisite pieces of jewellery, and he knew where everything was. I'd call him there at one in the morning and he would often still be there in the workshop. He had his satisfaction from listening to his music and from making things and making them well. He predominantly made rings, necklaces and hinged hollow bangles, which took great skill. He was mainly a jobber, setting stones into rings and selling the wedding rings he made to shops and all sorts of people. They were eighteen- and nine-carat rings, in platinum, white and rose gold. He spun the threads of gold to make them, extruding the gold wire through an antique drawplate. He was a great craftsman, so competent, but surrounded by cutthroat businessmen: he was the bottom of the pile. He never reaped the benefit of his labours.

'He bought the gold for his rings himself from the bullion dealers in the Garden, who all liked him very much. Then he would melt it down to get the right consistency. He was very capable and so honest. He called the other ring makers *ganufs*, old thieves, crooks. On occasions I went with him on his rounds, dropping off the things he had made. Everyone seemed very happy with his work. I don't believe there was anyone making wedding rings of such a high quality as his. When he was ill I'd take trays of rings around to the shops to try and sell them for him. I couldn't believe how little he sold them for.

'In the last year of his life he used to say to me, "Why don't you come with me and we'll travel the world?" but by then he was completely unfit to do so. He never once took a holiday. Sometimes he used to go to Brighton or Bournemouth for business, that was the nearest he got to a vacation. He stopped working when he was eighty-four and died a year later. Hatton Garden was his life.'

13

The Liberty of Saffron Hill, Hatton Garden and Ely Rents

All about this foul stream during the eighteenth and nineteenth centuries gathered a maze of narrow streets, courts and alleys, in which lived some of the most desperate characters of the metropolis. The most notorious of these haunts was Chick Lane, better known as West Street, that ran near the end of Field Lane. The Red Lion Tavern, which stood there within the last fifty years, and was a very ancient house, was supposed to have been one of the abodes of the infamous thief-taker, Jonathan Wild. It had sliding panels, secret hiding places and trapdoors opening over the river, convenient for the disposal of murdered victims . . . most of this foul neighbourhood was swept away by the Smithfield improvements . . . and by the Metropolitan Railway.

Henry Barton Baker, *Stories of the Streets of London*

When Sir Christopher Hatton moved into the bishops' estate during Elizabeth I's reign, the land became known as the Liberty of Saffron Hill, Hatton Garden and Ely Rents. After the bishops left, the area remained a 'liberty', meaning there were certain rights of sanctuary connected to the place. The police were not authorized to chase any criminal who crossed over into the region so it developed as a location for all sorts of illegal activity. The police continued to have limited jurisdiction there until the seventeenth century, when the rights of sanctuary in liberties ended, but by then the former orchards, crocus fields and pastures belonging to the bishops had evolved into a notorious rookery of steep alleys crowded with wretched housing, brothels, workhouses, ragged schools and taverns. In John Rocque's 1746 map of Georgian London narrow streets and courts are marked coming off Saffron Hill and Field Lane (the southern end of the street) with names like: Brew House Yard, Fagers Alley, Chick Lane, Bull Head Alley, Blew Ball Alley and Hockley-in-the-hole.

These streets became the centre of the trade in stolen goods, the territory of fences, pimps, pickpockets, villains and immigrants. The most disreputable streets in the Saffron Hill rookery were probably Field Lane, Chick Lane (which ran directly off Field Lane, crossing over the Fleet Ditch and into the sheep pens of Smithfield Market) and Hockley-in-the-hole: the ancient name of a muddy depression on the northern edge of the Ely estate, which used to flood when the banks of the Fleet burst (it was renamed Ray Street in 1774). There was an infamous bear-baiting garden there, mentioned in seventeenth- and eighteenth-century records, where the butchers and drovers of Smithfield gathered together with 'dukes, lords, knights and squires', according to William Pinks in his *History of Clerkenwell*, to watch blood sports: wrestling, sword fights, cock-fights and boxing, as well as bear-baiting. Pinks records 'women boxing on stage' in the eighteenth century on a makeshift platform, 'dressed for purpose in close jackets, short petticoats, Holland drawers, white stockings and pumps', as well as fights between 'mercenary gladiators' and 'infuriated brutes' battling 'with backsword and dagger'. Bears were trained to 'stand on their heads and dance with monkeys on their backs, blind bears were whipped into a violent frenzy or covered in fireworks', and many great wagers were laid on both sides. A 1710 advert for a typical night's entertainment at Hockley-in-the-hole promoted 'a match to be fought by two dogs' along with 'a *green bull* to be baited, which was never baited before, and a bull to be turned loose, with fireworks all over him; also a mad ass to be baited . . . and a dog to be drawn up with fireworks'. In 1709, Pinks states the owner of the bear garden was attacked by one of his own bears, and almost eaten alive.

Today the Coach and Horses pub in Ray Street marks the site of

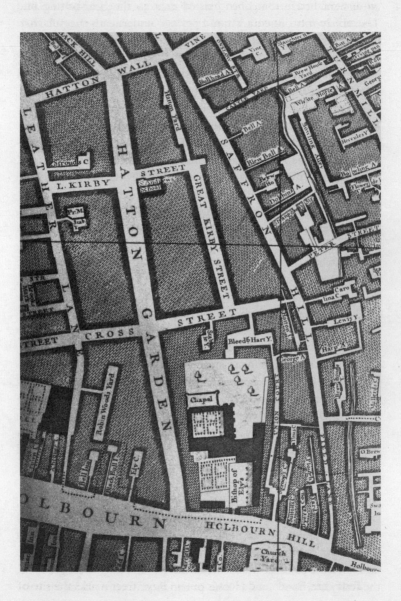

an ancient house that once existed next to the bear-baiting pit. Thornbury mentioned a vaulted passage underneath the pub that led to the banks of the Fleet, he also states that in 1878 a small case was found in this pub, with the name R. Turpin etched on to the lid, along with some old blank keys 'such as thieves wax over to get impressions of locks they wish to open'.

Turpin was also known to frequent the worst of the low-life lodging houses in the area, the Red Lion Inn, which backed on to the remains of the Fleet in Chick Lane (also known as West Street). The pub had been the hangout of many lawless types, including the most infamous criminal of eighteenth-century London, Jonathan Wild (the tavern was often referred to as Jonathan Wild's House) and the legendary highwaymen Jack Sheppard and James Dalton. Pinks describes one of Dalton's robberies near Hatton Garden on 1 December 1730, when the highwayman held up Dr Mead, 'the fashionable physician of Dr Johnstone's time', in Holborn, close to Furnival's Inn:

> The man presented a pistol at the coachman, ordered him to stop, demanded the doctor's watch and money, and told the footman he was a dead man if he dared to jump down. The servant did jump down and cried 'stop thief.' A shopman pursued the highwayman, the latter flashed a pistol at him, but was eventually run down in Leather Lane, taken back to the Black Bull inn, Holborn, and searched. Powder and shot were found in his pockets.

If he had managed to escape, Dalton would probably have made his way to the Red Lion Inn, to hide out for a while. A complex warren of little corridors and hidden stairwells was constructed inside, with dark closets and pivoting panels that concealed secret passages and trapdoors leading directly into the river underneath. A sliding panel opened on to the roof of the next house, 'from which any offender could be in Saffron Hill in a few minutes', according to Pinks. He described the place as 'the resort of thieves, and the lowest grade of the frail sisterhood' and as 'one of the most secure places for robbery and murder'. He tells the story of a chimney sweep called Jones, who hid out in the building for over six weeks. Police repeatedly searched the inn, but Jones was never found; he prevented detection 'by parting off a portion of a cellar with brickwork, well besmeared with soot and dirt'. This cell was later used to rob a sailor, who was 'afterwards flung naked through one of the convenient apertures in the wall into the Fleet'. Many dead bodies were disposed of in this way. When the building was demolished in 1844, it was thought to be over 300 years old.

The reputation of Field Lane was as bad, if not worse, than that of Chick Street. In William Maitland's *The History of London from Its Foundation to the Present Time*, published in 1772, it is described as 'nastily kept, being inhabited by tripe dressers on the east side, by reason of the benefit of the Ditch that runs at the backside of their yards and slaughterhouses to carry away the filth'. Dickens set Fagin's kitchen in Field Lane in *Oliver Twist* (1838). He called it 'a narrow and dismal alley' with 'filthy shops' filled with 'huge bunches of second-hand silk handkerchiefs, of all sizes and patterns', acquired from pickpockets. Nineteenth-century engravings of Field Lane show a place of ramshackle wooden houses, with crumbling exteriors, beside a dirty river, filled with rubbish. An intrepid journalist for the *Builder* visited the Ragged School in Field Lane on 26 March 1853, where he came across over 150 boys and young men asleep on the floor, which had been divided by planks about a foot high into compartments a little larger than a person, each filled with a lodger covered by a rug. At the end of the lane he saw 'houses occupied by doubtful purposes' and a 'witch like figure waiting for business' in a 'dilapidated and unwholesome den'. He entered five coffee shops and described them all as being 'full of misery and vice', with large coke fires burning: 'On the seats, on the tables and under the tables, partly lying over each other like eels in a dish, were men of various ages. In a back room were more lodgers, some of whom at that late hour had just arrived and were cooking their supper.' He defined the lodgers as 'the receivers and assistants of thieves, who no doubt sleep during the day in order to be prepared for night excursions'. In one of the tenements on the street, living in a single room, he found fifteen Irish people, of both sexes and all ages, who had spent the day either begging or selling onions on the street, who told him they had been 'driven from Ireland by sheer distress, and that many fled from certain death at the time of the great famine' (1845–9).

Many poor Italian immigrants lived in the Saffron Hill rookery alongside the Irish. Eighteenth- and nineteenth-century vagrancy orders I came across in the archives were mainly for the removal of 'Irish rogues and vagabonds' living in the Liberty of Saffron Hill, along with single mothers and orphaned children from the area, hinting at the miserable lives of lost communities.

A Victorian edition of *The London Encyclopaedia* depicts Italian women with bright handkerchiefs covering their hair, knocking on doors in Saffron Hill selling recipes for furniture restoration. The street is described as a place 'crammed with open-air markets lined with stalls and barrows of fish, bacon, vegetables and old clothes'.

Organ grinders, young boys selling ice cream, men hawking tortoises, acrobatic toys, nodding dolls and chestnuts would have been common sights there once, making their way among the lodgings and workhouses, taverns and tenement buildings that lined the street.

The Irish and Italian migrants shared many religious and family values and there was intermarriage between the two communities as well as occasional violent clashes. A newspaper report from the *Illustrated London News*, dated 6 August 1853, describes a huge street fight between mobs of Italians and Irish. The Irish were taunted by the Italians on their way to church: 'The result was a terrific riot, the Irish armed with pokers and bludgeons, attacking the Italians, who clasped stiletto knives, stabbing indiscriminately at all who came near them.'

Violence of a different kind took place in the narrow streets and courts running southwards from Turnmill and Cowcross streets, such as Slaughterhouse Yard, Blind Beggar Alley and Sharp's Alley. These mean-sounding alleyways were filled with small workshops whose noxious trades were predominantly connected to the meat market. Catgut workers made strings for violins, burly men skinned the carcasses of horses, sheep and cows from dank, makeshift sheds, whose floors were lined with straw drenched in blood. Tanners soaked raw hides in pits of stale urine or lime. Leftover animal parts – heads, tails, hoofs and eyes – were boiled up in giant vats to make food for dogs and cats. Any discarded fat was then made into soap. Glue makers boiled bones, cutlers turned them into knife handles and buttons. All the remnants – blood, skin, faeces, carcasses, hair and guts – were thrown into the river. The stench must have been poisonous.

There was also an abundance of gin breweries beside the Fleet in the eighteenth century and many illicit gin factories, where people bought home-made gin so strong it was sometimes lethal. William Hogarth's satirical sketch *Beer Street and Gin Lane*, 1751, depicts the streets around Smithfield Market, which the artist knew well, having been born in nearby St Bartholomew's Close. Commissioned in support of a campaign against gin drinking among London's poor, the etching tells the story of the downfall of those addicted to 'mother's ruin'. We see the pawnbroker's balls hanging above the street, a symbol of how addiction to spirits leads to gambling and bankruptcy. The left-hand side of the picture shows an artist and some smartly dressed gentlemen sipping beer, remaining calm and in control in a civilized-looking townscape. On the right, beside the gin drinkers, however, buildings crumble, a gin-sodden mother ignores her baby as it falls to its death from the stairs, and a desperate alcoholic man pawns the last of his belongings for a drink.

Despite being surrounded by such dreadful slums, since its development into a residential street in the late seventeenth century, Hatton Garden managed to remain an oasis of respectability. The wealthy residents of the street were not all immune to the plight of their poor neighbours, however, and from the eighteenth century onwards many philanthropic institutions developed in and around Hatton Garden.

The St Andrew's Church Charity School, housed in the unfinished church at the corner of Hatton Garden and Cross Street, opened in 1721, funded by donations from local residents to provide free education to children from low-income families living in the area. The children started at the school at the age of eight and left when they were fourteen or fifteen. The trustees helped each boy to secure an apprenticeship to train in a city trade and gave each girl an outfit to go into service. The brightest boys were selected to enter the navigational or mathematical school, which had been set up in 1715 in Hatton Garden by a philanthropic barrister called Joseph Neale, 'to instruct youth in the art of navigation to fit them for sea service'. There are still statues of two charity children (identical to those on the tower of St Andrew's Church) wearing their eighteenth-century school uniform outside the building today.

In 1741 master mariner and philanthropist Captain Thomas Coram established the Foundling Hospital at 78 Hatton Garden for 'exposed and deserted young children'. Babies of destitute mothers would be left on the doorstep, with a small token of identification placed upon them – a scrap of fabric, a locket, a button. The mother would keep an identical object in the hope that one day she might be able to reclaim the child. The Hatton Garden house quickly proved to be too small for the number of applicants and the hospital's policy of never turning a child away soon had to be replaced with a harsher lottery system. A permanent location for the institution was found a year later, when a much larger, purpose-built hospital was opened near Bloomsbury Fields, with fifty-six acres of land attached. The hospital moved out of London in the 1920s and the land was partially developed on, although seven acres were kept back and became a children's play area, with a petting zoo, sandpits and a nursery, called Coram Fields, which still exists today and is well used by local children. Adults are only allowed inside if they have a child with them.

In 1819 the Caledonian Asylum opened in Cross Street, Hatton Garden, providing a home and education for up to 120 Scottish children orphaned in the Napoleonic Wars. They were 'clad in full Scottish garb' and played the 'pipes at various festivals'. In 1826 the institution moved to new, larger premises on the Caledonian Road, which was named after the school.

A Miss Hawkins writes in her diary in 1824 that 'Hatton Garden was once an esteemed situation for the gentry; no shops were permitted but at the lower end, and a few parts of the town could vie with it, but this situation, like all others in succession, is ruined by trades and low associations.' I wonder if the 'low associations' she refers to are places such as the Caledonian Asylum or the Female Emigrants' Home, which opened in Hatton Garden in 1853 at 76 Hatton Garden. Its purpose was to temporarily house up to sixty 'distressed gentlewomen' who were educated, often widowed or single and without financial means, and looking for new lives as governesses in the colonies of South Africa, Madagascar, Australia and other places. They were given board and lodging in Hatton Garden, before travelling on to an unknown future abroad.

One of London's most famous institutions, the Royal Free Hospital, started out in 1828 as a small dispensary on the ground floor of 16 Greville Street, off Hatton Garden, called the London General

Institution for the Gratuitous Cure of Malignant Diseases. It was established there by a practising surgeon called William Marsden who became determined to provide free health care for the poor

after being unable to find hospital treatment for an eighteen-year old girl he discovered dying of malnutrition and disease, on the steps of St Andrew's Church. In 1832 Marsden expanded into the upper floors of the Greville Street building, creating a hospital mainly for cholera patients; it was the only hospital in London willing to take them in. In the 1832 epidemic 566 patients were treated there, primarily 'by the administration orally and intravenously of up to four pints of saline', along with uninterrupted bed rest. As a result there were only 135 deaths. In 1835 the hospital became known as 'Free Hospital, Greville Street'; in 1837 Queen Victoria became a patron and changed the name to the Royal Free Hospital. The hospital moved to Gray's Inn Road in 1842.

Victorian social reformers such as Marsden helped to highlight the plight of the poor living in and around the streets off Saffron Hill. As details emerged about the overcrowded conditions, the night refuges, lodging houses, brothels, ragged schools and all-night taverns, public outcry and the need for new roads and housing eventually led to the great slum clearances between 1830 and 1870, which flattened parts of Hatton Garden, Field Lane, Saffron Hill, St Andrew's churchyard and most of the alleyways and narrow lanes making up the rookery.

During the clearances thousands were displaced, but little new housing was created for them and the poorest were forced further east, into the already overpopulated areas of Whitechapel and Aldgate. The warren of courts and passages that once made up the area known as Farringdon Waste disappeared.

As the run-down houses and streets were demolished, concealed secret passages were revealed, leading from one building to another. Small wooden bridges were found, precariously thrown across the ditch, so they could be dumped into the river if necessary. Covered pits were unearthed in the alleyways, filled with excrement, to trap any pursuing police who did not know the territory well.

As the new roads were built the topography of the land changed entirely. Parts of St Andrew's churchyard were carved away, with nearly 1,200 skeletons being relocated to a cemetery in Ilford. Early records refer to the church as being positioned high upon a hill, 'visible for miles around'. It now sits in a depression, five feet below the level of the street.

A new urban landscape was sculpted out of the existing steep hills of the Fleet Valley, designed by the best Victorian engineers of the period during the massive road-development project known as the Holborn Valley Improvement Scheme, which included the construction of Holborn Circus, the new roads of Farringdon Street, Clerkenwell Road, Charterhouse Street and St Andrew's Street, and the magnificent iron bridge-road, Holborn Viaduct.

This enormous structure, which spans Farringdon Road, was one of the most ambitious and expensive engineering projects undertaken in the Victorian era – a showcase for the power of the Industrial Revolution, costing over £2 million to complete. Work started in 1863 and continued for the next six years, as thousands of tons of earth were removed from the steep inclines of Holborn and Snow hills to create a single thoroughfare on one level that stretched across the Fleet Valley, dramatically improving access into the city and alleviating traffic problems.

At the London Metropolitan Archives (LMA), I had been lucky enough to view some extraordinary photographs, not yet in the public domain, of Holborn Viaduct being built. Putting on protective cotton gloves, I carefully took the images out of their acid-free box to photograph them for myself: hundreds of workmen, staring into the camera, tools at rest, stood on the as yet unfinished bridge. Another showed the large tent erected for the celebrations, and another the royal procession, with thousands of people waving flags and handkerchiefs as the Queen passed by.

Holborn Viaduct was opened in 1869 by Queen Victoria during a grand ceremony attended by 'an immense assemblage of people'. The royal procession came down Farringdon Street, stopping beside the bridge, which had been decorated with flags and streamers, and then moving up to the viaduct. Vast crowds were kept back by hordes of police and soldiers. A huge pavilion was erected on the viaduct, while the street was strewn with yellow sand and lined with large banners and seating for the guests of the Corporation of London.

After the viaduct opened it blended quickly into the new cityscape. The lost river, hills and slums of the Liberty of Saffron Hill, Hatton Garden and Ely Rents vanished from living memory, although residual traces of the ancient topography of the area can still be found. The great height from the top of the viaduct to the road below is a measure of the former steepness of Holborn Hill. At Holborn Circus, looking up towards the city, or down towards Smithfield, the slopes of the Fleet Valley are still evident and the street names of Saffron Hill and Hatton Garden retain a faint echo of the earlier uses of that land.

Despite the Holborn Valley improvements, pockets of the former rookery remained. In 1898, when Charles Booth constructed his famous 'poverty map' of London, Hatton Garden is coloured red, denoting a 'middle class, well to do' street, while the parallel street of Leather Lane is dark blue, meaning the residents there

would have been 'very poor' and of 'chronic want'. Patches of dark blue also appear around Saffron Hill and most of the narrow streets on St John's Lane, the site of the former priory. Near Ely Place,

towards the southern end of Saffron Hill, is a single square of black, which Booth used to depict the areas inhabited by the 'lowest class of vicious criminal'.

Hatton Garden continued to be a respectable street although by the nineteenth century it had became a less fashionable residential district as more up-to-date new housing estates were built in the West End. Despite this many lawyers, solicitors, doctors and surgeons continued to live in Hatton Garden, probably because of its convenient location. I came across numerous applications in the archives for licences to conduct lectures on anatomy, botany and chemistry in private houses in the street in the early nineteenth century. One had been granted to John Tauniton, 'for the period of one year, to open a room in his house at 87 Hatton Garden, in 1821, for the purpose of delivering lectures on pathology and surgery'. This was the closest I could get to finding any evidence of Mitzy's story of bodies being dissected in the building that was later to become the Diamond Club, which had also been the home of Sir Moses Montefiore from 1824.

Montefiore was probably, along with his brother-in-law and business partner, Nathan Rothschild, the most famous Jewish person of his time in London. Born into the Italian Sephardic community, he moved to the capital and became an extremely wealthy stockbroker, banker and financier, a true statesman, a diplomat. Sir Moses was a founding member of the Alliance Insurance Company and a director of the Provincial Bank of Ireland. He and Nathan Rothschild together headed a hugely successful banking business.

In 1824 Sir Moses retired at the age of forty and dedicated his wealth and energy to philanthropic pursuits, working to obtain equal rights for the Jews of England and becoming involved in numerous humanitarian projects for Jewish communities internationally, in Russia, Europe and Israel. In 1837 he became the Sheriff of London; he was knighted by Queen Victoria in 1846, became a baron and was the President of the Board of Deputies of British Jews for many years. He was also extremely observant, which makes me wonder if there was a synagogue in Hatton Garden at the time. I'm sure it was no coincidence that the Diamond Club, whose membership was almost entirely Hasidic, moved to the same address a century later.

In the 1830s Sir Moses Montefiore relocated to Ramsgate and purchased a grand estate, where he built a huge house and commissioned the famous British Jewish architect David Mocatta, a pupil of Sir John Soane, to design a private synagogue and tomb for him. I had recently visited this now derelict Grade II listed building while walking my dog with a friend who moved to Ramsgate, although at the time I had not been aware of who had erected the beautiful building, which currently sits in an overgrown park. Next to the synagogue is a large domed tomb, a replica of Rachel's Tomb in Jerusalem, the final resting place of Sir Moses and his wife, Lady Judith Montefiore.

My friends in Ramsgate went to the first Jewish wedding inside Sir Moses Montefiore's private synagogue for fifty years, when a young Jewish couple they knew managed to get special permission to be married in the building in 2007. Privileged to see the interior, my friends told me the abandoned exterior was no indication of the state of the inside of the synagogue, which had been well cared for, and remained pristine and grand. Many Hasidic Jews still visit the building to pray and can often be seen standing together in large groups, *davening* in their long black garbs, beside the crumbling tomb, surrounded by wild woodland, a scene reminiscent of those I had witnessed many times before near the abandoned synagogues of eastern Galicia in Poland.

A few shops had begun to open up in Hatton Garden by the early 1800s, as the fine-precision-instrument makers, clockmakers and watchmakers who had settled in Clerkenwell moved into new premises in the street. From the 1830s Hatton Garden began to really develop commercially, with the establishment of printers, bookmakers and a few jewellers had businesses there. Early records from this period include numerous applications for printing presses to be installed in Hatton Garden. In the LMA I found a handwritten document dated 1834, which set out the terms for George James Dixon during his apprenticeship to wholesale jeweller Frederick Treithy of Hatton Garden. George would earn a total of forty-nine pounds for the full seven years of his term before he learned 'the art of the mystery of a working jeweller'. During this time he was not allowed to 'contract matrimony' or 'play any unlawful games whereby he may have a loss of goods'.

An engraving of Hatton Garden by John Tallis, in his 1840 book *London Street Views*, shows detailed line drawings of the houses on the street, along with the names of some of the businesses on Hatton Garden during that year. Aside from a jeweller's and a number of printers and engravers, there were foreign importers, makers of fancy cabinets, an oil warehouse, booksellers, opticians, pianoforte makers, tailors, looking-glass and artificial-flower manufacturers, floor and cloth manufacturers, gold-chain makers, lathe and tool-makers, chemists, and importers of sponges. At no. 102 was Jacques,

Ivory and Wood Turners, a company that had been making croquet mallets since 1795 alongside stranger items such as false teeth made from hippopotamus ivory. They later became famous as the inventors of table tennis, or ping-pong. No. 79 was the location of Johnson and Cock, Assay Office & Metal Workers. From this engraving it is clear that during the nineteenth century nearly all of the original seventeenth-century buildings on Hatton Garden still survived.

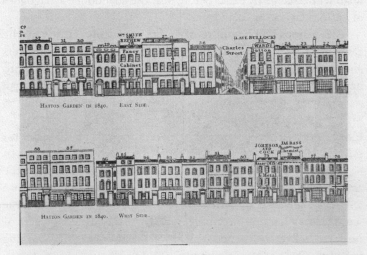

HATTON GARDEN IN 1840.   EAST SIDE.

HATTON GARDEN IN 1840.   WEST SIDE.

Hatton Garden was described in a handbook of London in 1854 as 'a place where many cheap barometers and thermometers produced by Italians could be purchased'. While searching through early London post office directories, I found plenty of evidence of Italian craftsmen being based in Hatton Garden during this time. The London directory for 1850 lists an Italian optician named Pizzala at no. 19 along with a carver and gilder called Ponzini. Italian barometer makers Louis Casella and Ortelli & Primavesi were based at nos 23 and 106. Guanziroli Artificial Florists shared a building with Ortelli. At no. 61 were Loisel & Edan, Italian & French Confectionery Manufacturers. By 1860 there were many more Italians working in the street and no noticeable Jewish names operating in Hatton Garden at that time. The directory for 1860 lists watch and glass manufacturers Benine and Lezard at no. 2, Biancini and Guanziroli Giuseppe manufacturing looking glasses at nos 40 and 106. Optical-glass blower Angelo Tagliabue operated from no. 19, and Bordessa and Batou manufactured mirrors from their workshop at 87 Hatton Garden. Negretti & Zambra were based at 1 Hatton Garden and Louis Casella was working in the same building as a wholesale optician by then.

At the British Library, I came across an 1859 catalogue for Negretti & Zambra, 'Opticians and Meteorological instrument makers, wholesale and export manufacturers of chemical, nautical surveying, mathematical, photographic and philosophical instruments', who were based in large premises at 1 Hatton Garden on the junction with Holborn Circus. They provided instruments to the Royal Observatory at Greenwich and were once the most famous manufacturers in the world of meteorological instruments, thermometers and mercurial barometers, which they continued to make until

1981. Scientific expeditions, whether to the poles or elsewhere, were often equipped with some of Negretti & Zambra's instruments.

Listed inside the catalogue were the instruments they manufactured and sold there, which included chemical apparatus and electromagnetic machines for scientific experimentation: microscopes, telescopes, magic and phantasmagoria lanterns, compasses, globes, orberies, chromeidascopes, anorthoscopes, gyroscopes, barometers, glasses 'specially adapted for fishing, billiards, shooting and riding', mathematical and surveying instruments, theodolites, tide gauges, anemometers and photometers.

The first few pages of the catalogue were filled with drawings of the magic stereoscopes they sold, standing on three-dimensional telescopic stands, handmade in walnut and rosewood with achromatic eyepieces. Beside them a long list of photographic glass slides of 'continental views' they had produced or commissioned of expeditions to Paris, Egypt, the Holy Land, China and other popular tourist sites in Europe, Asia and Africa. In the mid nineteenth century, the three-dimensional images of these landscapes for the stereoscopes would have been comparable, in their technological advancement, to 3D cinema today.

In another catalogue from a private collection I managed to find a blurred drawing of the Hatton Garden premises, showing three floors of merchandise. Comparing the location of the shop to old maps it is clear the original Negretti & Zambra shop sits over the foundations of the former gatehouse to Ely Palace, roughly where the NatWest Bank sits today. This building was destroyed in the Blitz in 1941 and Negretti & Zambra then moved to new premises on Holborn Viaduct.

As I read through the catalogue the jigsaw fragments of my research began to come together and I could now almost visualize Hatton Garden in the 1850s. How impressive it must have been, with the statue of Prince Albert fronting the street, standing on the brand-new Holborn Viaduct, and the imposing window display of Negretti & Zambra; one of the most modern, progressive stores in the metropolis, with its instruments of power, empire, technology, time and science. Further up Hatton Garden were printers, book-shops, importers of foreign goods, opticians, engravers and a few gold-chain makers and jewellers. Diamonds had not yet entered the story, but in a stable, at the back of 79 Hatton Garden, Percival Norton Johnson was starting to refine gold.

14

Farringdon Without

This large ward forms the western extremity of the city of London; and
is bounded on the east by the ward of Farringdon-within, the precinct of
the late priory of St. Bartholomew near Smithfield, and the ward of
Aldersgate; on the north, by the Charter-house, the parish of St. John's
Clerkenwell, and part of St. Andrew's parish without the freedom; on
the west by High-Holborn, and St. Clement's parish in the Strand; and
on the south by the river Thames.

John Noorthouck, *A New History of London:*
Including Westminster and Southwark

In *White Chappell, Scarlet Tracings* Iain Sinclair writes about the
bookstalls along Farringdon Road, where he bought much of his
stock while dealing in books in the 1970s and 1980s. I met with him
at the site of the now vanished market to hear more about the place
and his impressions of the area, which he sees as being 'so important to a particular type of London writing'. He describes
Clerkenwell, Holborn and Farringdon as: 'part of the labyrinth of
old London, one of the real reservoirs of time in the city, connected
to St Paul's, the Old Bailey, the Temple Inn, the Inns of Court and
of course the river. Moorcock invented his London around Bleeding
Heart Yard, which features in *London Bone*, as a partly fictional and
partly real place. He worked in Holborn throughout the 60s, writing Tarzan comics and creating a kind of mythology about the
area. Certain locations obsessed him, like Holborn Viaduct, which
passes over Farringdon Street, then runs south to Ludgate Circus, a
crossroads named after the mythic King Lud, the founder of Lon-

don. He felt the area connects to serial fictions, the Gothic mysteries of buildings and of London, like the Penny Dreadfuls, which were often based around the Fleet Valley, with tales of Sweeney Todd, the demon barber of Fleet Street. Peter Ackroyd was obsessed with Clerkenwell, which features in many of his books. There was a little Italian restaurant on Clerkenwell Green where we all used to meet and have discussions about London writing, when Ackroyd worked near by for the *Spectator*, which had offices near there. This was the mid 1980s, I was still a book dealer but I was writing as well. The area is a powerful part of the metropolis, with Holborn and its connection to old publishing, its sense of hospital enclosures where you get healed, prisons and other enclosures where you get burned, and the mysteries of Hatton Garden, which is a place I never had access to, and remains strange and intriguing.'

Wearing a long black coat, fingerless gloves and a woolly hat, leaning against the last remnants of the Victorian brick wall that once ran from Vine Street all the way along Farringdon Road, Sinclair still looked like a dealer on the hunt. He spoke at length about the daily second-hand book market that existed there from the Victorian era until relatively recently. 'At one time the stalls stretched the length of Farringdon Road but by the time I came to it there was just one guy operating eight big stalls there called George Jeffrey, a slightly balding character, with patches of fluffy hair, who wore a little blue jacket like a barber. He had somehow inherited the right to have these stalls, it was just him – a lone survivor from the group of five or six families who'd once been there.'

Every morning for decades, crowds would gather on the pavement around Jeffrey's stalls, waiting until he decided to remove the giant tarpaulins that covered the books. Standing nonchalantly beside his parked van, slowly pouring tea from a Thermos, the market trader would tease the dealers by looking at his watch every now and then. 'At eleven o'clock precisely Jeffrey would dramatically pull the cloths off the tables and all these vultures would rush in and start heaping up the books, which they stacked up against this wall. They would walk away with just armfuls and armfuls of books.' Tables often collapsed with the weight of people diving on to the stalls, books spilling on to the road, straight into the passing traffic, it was a ferocious daily battle.

'If some innocent turned up and didn't know the rituals and went up to George and tried to buy before the cloth had been removed, George would just very slowly open up the book in front of them and then rip it to pieces. The dealers used to laugh at him, they thought they were getting fantastic bargains, but it was George who was making his fortune. He took off three times a year to Florida to play golf. He was making a lot of money. There was no question of haggling over prices with him, you either took it or left. The range of material was astonishing, he had the remnants of these great libraries. People found manuscripts by Milton and all sorts of very rare books, some of which had been personally inscribed.'

The books were laid out according to their value, starting at five or ten pence, then a pound, and so on until the last stall, where the newer and rarer books would be sold off for twenty pounds or more. Most new books came on a Saturday morning. Iain used to have a stall in Camden Passage and every week he would come to Farringdon Market to buy stock at 'this great scrum'. Over time he got to know many of the strange characters who waited with him on the pavement for Jeffrey to begin the business: 'It was a dealers' and collectors' market, filled with totally crazy, obsessive people. There was one guy that came every day and only bought a single novel by a single writer, something very obscure. He'd take it back to this large house, in St Luke's in Old Street, wrapped in brown paper, and put it on the shelf with the others, and slowly this house just filled up with this huge collection of a single book. A lot of collectors came who were obsessed with things like Jack the Ripper or the Golden Dawn and they would huddle around on the pavement here discussing these things and it always looked like a kind of funeral with these men in their long black coats, waiting for this thing to happen, and the books looked a bit like a covered body laid out.'

The topography of London books, moving continuously around

the city, has many resonances with the jewellery and antiques trade, which operates in a similar way: 'An old Scotsman called Jock would come here every day and scavenge off the stuff on the bottom of the pile that had been rejected by the Saturday people and take the books back on the bus to Hackney to sell at his stall at Kingsland Waste Market. I sometimes bought books off him, which I would take back to Camden Passage where they could be picked up by mid-range dealers in Islington. By the end of the week they could be back in Savile Row and fancy West End shops where American dealers were buying them back out of glass cabinets. From Saturday to the following Friday the books would just flow like a tide or a river across London.'

Jeffrey told Sinclair about a warehouse belonging to his father in Saffron Hill, a magical library, hidden away, that very few people got to see. If you established yourself well enough he would take you there. Sinclair was never invited but told me 'the book trade lived off the idea of secret rooms like this, filled with amazing treasure. It was a terrific way of life. I met John Clute, the science-fiction writer, at Farringdon Market; he used to cycle down there every day and he amassed a fantastic collection of books. Some of the other book dealers were Jewish and many Hasidic diamond dealers used to come and buy books before making their way back up to Hatton Garden.

'There was nowhere else to compare to Farringdon Market. It was a time warp that came out of the Victorian and Edwardian periods, an extension of the market around the yard of St Paul's Cathedral, whose narrow streets were once full of publishers and booksellers. After George died, his son kept up the stalls for a while but he didn't have his father's sense of the place and the whole thing collapsed by the 1990s, after being in the family for generations.'

Pointing further up Farringdon Road, towards Clerkenwell, Iain told me about a workmen's café, 'filled with wooden booths', run by communists, which has since been demolished, where he used to meet other dealers for a coffee and a bacon sandwich after George closed for business, to discuss the purchases of the day and exchange books. He met a doctor there who took him into the London Hospital to show him the Elephant Man's cast.

We started to walk along Farringdon Road, up towards the meat market, following the course of the Fleet beneath our feet. I told Iain about my recent walk with Adele Leffman, who spoke of the written word being introduced to London in that area by scribes who lived in the Clerkenwell monasteries from the eleventh century onwards. The idea fascinated Iain, who talked of three lines of commerce flowing down towards the Thames from that location all responding to the sense of flow from the river: 'Cattle came down one line into Smithfield Market, and then the skins of cattle, in the form of leather-bound books, would return here; and, running in parallel, a line of gold and silver from Hatton Garden.'

We walked briskly, battling against the wind, to the site of the former Slaughterhouse Gallery in the meat market, where our Rodinsky book project began after Iain invited me to make some artwork for the launch of *Lights Out for the Territory* in 1997. He designed the event in the former abattoir with an artist called Paul

Smith, who had been putting on similar sorts of cellar performances, with mixtures of music and literature, on the underground scene in Paris and New York. 'The gallery was the perfect location because of its associations with Farringdon and Smithfield Market and the hospital beyond, and the fact that it was in a subterranean space, where you could sense the Fleet still roaring underneath and hear the tube trains and you were well aware that animals had been kept and slaughtered there.' We looked for the entrance to the former gallery but it had long since disappeared.

It was late morning by the time we made our way through the decorative, brightly painted iron gates of the main market building. There was a sharp drop in temperature as we entered the market complex owing to the many freezer units inside. A few traders remained, packing up. All the stalls had gone but the stench of raw meat hung in the air and a lone man in a blood-spattered apron hosed a river of entrails down a drain. If we had been standing in the same spot around midnight we would have seen long refrigeration lorries, parked around the edges of the market, offloading frozen carcasses, giant hams and blood-soaked boxes of meat on to metal trolleys, manned by porters wheeling the cargo around to the many stalls in the central aisles of the complex. Above the stalls would have hung sides of sheep, pigs and other animals. The market opens for business at three, when customers from restaurants, cafés and hotels flood through the gates to buy meat, fish, poultry, pies and cheeses from the last remaining historical wholesale market in the city. By ten o'clock the whole thing has been swept away.

Once open fields just outside the city walls, the land which has since become Smithfield meat market was used by the Romans, first as a dump and then as a cemetery. By the tenth century a livestock market was regularly taking place there. William Fitzstephen visited the smooth fields in 1174, 'where every Friday there is a celebrated rendezvous of fine horses to be sold, and in another quarter are placed vendibles of the peasant, swine with their deep flanks, and cows and oxen of immense bulk'.

In medieval times jousting tournaments took place at Smithfield;

knights fought to the death in front of cheering crowds, with ladies in grand pavilions, waving handkerchiefs, sitting beside kings and queens. Public duels, political meetings and executions all happened on the waterlogged fields. Criminals were hanged, burned or sometimes drawn and quartered, 'betwixt the horse pool and the river of wels', beside great elm trees (before Tyburn became the popular place of execution). In the sixteenth century, monks and nuns who refused to denounce their Catholic faith were put in cages and roasted alive or burned at the stake there; coin forgers were boiled in vats of oil and, during the reign of Mary I, Protestant martyrs were burned at the stake along with witches and heretics. The land beneath Smithfield is literally saturated in human and animal blood. Slaughterhouses have existed there from at least the Middle Ages, when the fields became the site of London's primary livestock market.

By the Victorian era Smithfield was often referred to as 'Ruffians' Hall'. T. J. Maslen described it in *Suggestions for the Improvement of Our Towns and Houses* (1843) as a place filled with 'cruelty, filth, effluvia, pestilence, impiety, horrid language, danger, disgusting and shuddering sights', where muggings, fights and excessive drinking were the norm and drunken cattle drovers chased stampeding animals through the surrounding streets. There are hundreds of reports in the archives of how cruelly drovers treated livestock, which were driven into the area from miles away, beaten with sticks, then violently forced into crowded pens, before being slaughtered on the spot. Sometimes the frightened animals escaped into nearby houses and businesses, which is where the expression 'a bull in a china shop' comes from.

Dickens describes market morning at Smithfield in 1838 in *Oliver Twist*: 'where the ground was covered nearly ankle deep with filth and mire'. Steam rose from the 'reeking bodies of the cattle', and the busy market was frequented by countrymen, drovers, butchers, hawkers, boys, thieves and 'idlers and vagabonds of every low grade'. The pens were packed with 'sheep; and tied up to posts by the gutter-side were long lines of beasts and oxen three or four deep'. The 'hideous and discordant din that resounded from every corner of the market' included: 'the whistling of drovers, the barking of dogs, the bellowing and plunging of beasts, the bleating of sheep, and the grunting and squeaking of pigs: the cries of hawkers, the shouts, oaths, and quarrelling on all sides, the ringing of bells and roar of voices that issued from every public house'.

Local people had petitioned to have the market removed, for health and safety reasons, but instead a new purpose-built meat market, designed by Sir Horace Jones, was erected on the site in 1868, covering ten acres of land, with a fish and poultry market attached, cold stores, underground storage and access to railway tunnels. This market was once a huge employer of local people, its own self-contained town. Since the Second World War the site has reduced in size after many of the original buildings were damaged in 1945, when a V-2 rocket exploded inside the complex, killing 160 people. But the meat market survives as London's oldest wholesale market in the central area of the metropolis. Many of its buildings are facing demolition and there is a constant threat that the whole business will be relocated outside Central London, like the Billingsgate Fish and New Spitalfields Fruit & Vegetable wholesale markets.

As I walked with Iain through East Poultry, the central avenue of the meat market, we passed the entrance to a cellar café, which opens at three in the morning for traders who breakfast on rump steak, liver and grilled sausage with boiled cabbage and mash. They also visit the pubs on the outskirts of the market, with names like the Cock Tavern and the Butcher's Hook and Cleaver, which also open very early to serve the market traders, along with the butchers, hospital porters, nurses and doctors from Barts, and lawyers and journalists coming off their night shifts; the great mix of Londoners who have been working in the area for centuries.

Turning left on to Charterhouse Street, passing Barts Hospital, we made our way to Cloth Fair, stopping outside a restaurant that was once the home of former poet laureate John Betjeman. 'He lived here because he believed it was the most historic part of old London,' said Iain. 'He wrote a lot of books on London architecture and history from this address.' Directly opposite stood the leafy churchyard of St Bartholomew's, the original location of the Cloth Fair, which later became the riotous Bartholomew Fair, London's wildest annual celebration for hundreds of years.

The Cloth Fair, which took place over three days in September, was founded in the twelfth century to raise funds for the priory. Clothiers and drapers came from all parts of the country, even from Europe, to buy and sell their wares. By the sixteenth century the fair had grown into a much bigger festival, which lasted for two weeks and spread over the churchyard, up to the walls of the hospital and into the meat market. Pens usually used for the sale of cattle and sheep were turned into temporary booths, where puppet shows, snake charmers, fire-eaters, rope-dancers, acrobats, dancing bears, musicians, bare-knuckle boxers and actors performed to huge crowds. Other booths exhibited human freak shows, 'monsters'

collected from around the globe: bearded ladies, two-headed babies, changelings, dwarves, fat men, giants, hermaphrodites and scaly boys. Ben Jonson's play *Bartholomew Fair* of the early seventeenth century was filled with curiosity shows, buffoonery and pickpockets. Pepys visited on 31 August 1661 and was 'troubled' to 'sit among such nasty company'.

By the eighteenth century, Bartholomew Fair had become the most spectacular and raucous event of the London calendar. Maitland described it in his *History of London* as being of 'little other use than for idle youth and loose people to resort to, and spend their money in vanity, and in debaucheries and drunkenness, whoredom and in seeing and hearing things not fit for Christian eyes and ears; many of the houses and booths here serving only to allure men and women to such purposes of impiety'.

The fair attracted people from all over London, across the social divides; thousands attended but as many again protested against it, thinking it to be 'dangerous to life'. Complaints about the noise and lewd behaviour caused the festival to shrink year by year until by 1840 there was nothing left but a few food stalls. In a small way, the anarchic energy of Bartholomew Fair lives on in the area, within the rave culture, which found its first home in venues on the fringes of Smithfield Market.

Walking through the churchyard, with Iain telling me more stories about the great London saturnalia, we entered the Norman interior of St Bartholomew's. Now one of the oldest surviving churches in London, it was once part of a much larger monastic complex, which included the Priory of St Bartholomew's and a hospital.

We wandered around the shadowy, cool interior, talking in whispers, looking at the many altars and monuments in darkly lit niches around the walls. The building is now a mishmash of styles from different centuries, a strange collection of architectures and periods: some parts date back to the twelfth century while others are Victorian. KEEP YOUR EYES FROM TEARS AND SEE THE MARBLE WEEP, I read on a plaque on the wall, a possible reference to floods or plague. We passed many monuments to the dead, including an ancient stone coffin filled with dust and twisted fabric that seemed to have petrified. The strong smell of incense hung in the air.

Behind the altar at the east end of the church, to the left of the Lady Chapel, is Rahere's fifteenth-century tomb: a full-size stone sculpture of the legendary monk, wearing a black cloak, lying on a red-and-gold stone cushion, in a marble bed of Gothic lace stone-work, guarded by carvings of angels and lions, with two priests at his feet. The bones of Rahere are buried underneath. Many believe he was once court jester to Henry I, but Adele told me he was a monk who had had a miraculous recovery from malaria during a pilgrimage to the Holy Land and on his return founded the Augus-tinian Priory of St Bartholomew's in honour of the saint who had rescued him from a winged monster. The church later became known as a place of healing and the sick still visit every year on 24 August, St Bartholomew's Day, hoping for a miracle cure to many ailments.

Standing beside this fantastical effigy, I felt the closest I had come on my investigations into the area to physically touching the medi-eval past. Nowhere else I had been resonated with the energy of the ancient priories quite like St Bartholomew's Church. As I walked with Iain across the graves of the many people buried under the floor of the building, we tried to read the inscriptions but most had been worn away from centuries of feet rubbing over them.

Exiting the churchyard we continued walking down the narrow Cloth Fair, a street of Elizabethan proportions, where you can almost reach out and touch the buildings on both sides simultan-eously. Iain led me to a deserted square at the back of the church called Bartholomew's Close, a place 'associated with relations of John Dee and a circle of alchemists who lived there in the seven-teenth century'. We stood for a while in the centre of the empty cobbled square and listened to the medieval bells of the church ring twelve times, tolling the hour.

As we made our way past the hospital again Iain talked about Sarah Wise's book *The Italian Boy: Murder and Grave-Robbery in 1830s London*,

which mentions the Resurrectionists, who dug up bodies and wheeled them on carts to sell at pubs near Smithfield, from where they would be sold on again to surgeons at Barts for dissection. 'In Conan Doyle's *A Study in Scarlet*, the book begins with a description of Holmes beating a body on a table in the dissecting room of the hospital to see what the effects of bruising are when you hit a corpse, which fits with the idea of sensational fiction, the drama of this area, meat, bodies, slaughter: these themes reoccur again and again here.' Mass graves from the Black Death surround the area, at Charterhouse, Greyfriars and Bunhill Fields.

As if to illustrate Iain's theory we passed a stone plaque to William Wallace embedded into the side wall of the hospital. The Scottish patriot had been hacked to pieces on that spot in 1305. I told Iain about the Mithraic shrine of the dead I had read about, which is believed to have existed on Farringdon Road close to Holborn Bridge. Also near by are the Old Bailey and the site of Newgate Prison, places of so many trials and executions.

Back on Charterhouse Street we stopped outside the window of a large chain pub, piled with old books, a block of stone and a painting of a bishop's mitre. 'Subconsciously the past is resurfacing here,' said Iain, smiling. 'The place seems to naturally respond to the spirit of what has happened here before, but if the market goes the mystery of this region will collapse. I feel lucky to have experienced this area during a particular period of time, before it all disappears. The essence of London is at your fingertips here. I find it impossible not to drift from one street to the next and it's all so astonishingly rich and layered, from here to St Paul's and Fleet Street, where Samuel Pepys grew up, the world of drinkers and newspapers and stories.'

We stopped outside a former cold store known as the Red House, one of many Victorian buildings within the Smithfield complex facing potential demolition. Near by, on Farringdon Road, there used to be a restaurant called Bubs, another place Sinclair would meet his writer friends to discuss the mythology of London. He described a particular afternoon there, with himself, Patrick Wright, Chris Petit and Peter Ackroyd, where 'bottle after bottle was drunk, hours went

by until it was mid afternoon and we were all still eating and drinking and talking and absolutely falling apart. But we had an amazing debate about this area, which we were all so excited about, with its residues of London histories.'

Pleased to be out striding across territory he knows well, revisiting old stomping grounds, Iain moved quickly along Farringdon Road before reaching Holborn Viaduct. He leaped up the winding staircase, ignoring the piss-filled corners, talking at great speed about his passion for the locale. Standing on top of the viaduct, he spoke again about Michael Moorcock, who met the writer Gerald Kersh there and wrote about the place in *Mother London*.

I had watched Iain become obsessed with this overpass back in 1999, after following Rodinsky's walking trails mapped out in his *A–Z*, which led from the scholar's attic home in Princelet Street to Holborn Viaduct. Chris Petit filmed the walk for an Artangel project and I remembered the footage: bleached-out celluloid, bright sunlight bouncing off the lion statues, cutting back to images of Whitechapel and then Holborn again. Iain wondered if Rodinsky had come to the area to visit the Farringdon Road book market; he had many secular books in his collection and would have fitted into the scene Sinclair described, of strange, solitary men in long overcoats walking off to mysterious homes with armfuls of books.

We stood together, looking down on to Farringdon Road below, the memory of the river still flowing underneath ever present, and talked for some time about the elements of the area that resonated with Whitechapel, both being bounded by hospitals, churches, markets and rivers. Both being areas of intensive emigration, shadowing the boundary walls of the Roman city; border places, where illegitimate, particular and peculiar things happened outside a protected zone.

15
Johnson Matthey

When I first visited the Hatton Garden Johnson Matthey
office in 1985 I was struck by the cultural mix in the area, people
out talking in the street, the Hasidic men in full regalia and hearing
Yiddish spoken. I found Hatton Garden a really interesting street,
with manufacturing still taking place in the backstreets, all the small
workshops dotted around, it was a vibrant multicultural, multinational,
friendly, unusual place. You would see people outside their shops,
shaking hands with each other when they met in the morning and
saying goodbye at the end of the day. It had more of a village
atmosphere than you would expect for a street in Central London.

Ian Godwin, Director of Corporate
Communications, Johnson Matthey

In 1812 a twenty-year-old gold assayer called Percival Norton Johnson co-wrote with his father an influential article in the
Philosophical Magazine on extracting palladium from Brazilian
gold: 'The gold is melted with three times its weight in silver,
granulated and parted in nitric acid. The gold so obtained is in a
reasonably pure form and from the solution the silver is separated
using common salt . . .'

In 1817 Johnson set up business as an 'Assayer and Practical Mineral-
ogist' in Leather Lane, adjacent to that of his father and brothers. In
1822 he moved the company to larger premises just around the corner, taking over a converted seventeenth-century house at 79 Hatton
Garden. His uncle, Charles Halsey Johnson, a jeweller and gold
refiner, was already based there at no. 11.

Along with refining and selling silver and gold bullion, Johnson's early concerns were: the scientifically accurate assaying of bullion; the study and development of platinum and chemical tinctures; the preparation of pottery and glass colours; and the extraction of uranium oxide from pitchblende. In his new Hatton Garden premises he continued the experiments with precious metals – particularly those from the platinum group – he had begun while working with his father, another gold assayer who had taught him the trade.

Assayer George Stokes joined Johnson in 1826 and became a partner in 1832 but died suddenly in 1835. Johnson then invited his brother-in-law Thomas Cock to join him. Thomas had worked in George Allen's famous laboratory in Plough Court, one of the first places to purify platinum, and now he helped Johnson prepare platinum in a malleable form. The two scientists experimented in a makeshift laboratory constructed at the back of the house, where they made significant early discoveries in refining sizeable quantities of platinum and manipulating it to make large industrial apparatus. Thomas Cock became Johnson's business partner and their company was named Johnson & Cock in 1837. In Tallis's street view of Hatton Garden dated 1840 'Johnson and Cock' occupy a single Georgian townhouse and describe themselves as an 'Assay Office & Metal Works' (see illustration on p. 139).

From the 1830s onwards more and more jewellery manufacturing began to take place in Hatton Garden, starting with makers of gold chains. The development of Hatton Garden as a jewellery quarter in the early nineteenth century had much to do with Johnson & Cock being based in the street. They were well-respected scientific assayers with an international reputation, who refined and supplied precious metals to the newly emerging jewellery trade that developed around them.

Johnson & Cock sold precious metal bullion from a shop that faced on to Hatton Garden. The laboratory remained at the back and Percival lived on the top floor with his wife, Elizabeth, who gave harp lessons from an attic room to help out with their finances. There was once a garden behind the house but that was eventually built over to accommodate the growing business.

Johnson discovered a more accurate way of assaying precious metals by using a new type of balance held on a piece of string by hand, similar to those used by Victorian apothecaries. This discovery instantly made him an important figure within the international metal market. Standardizing the content of precious metals within bullion boosted the trade and made London the primary metal market but the introduction of a higher degree of accurate assaying was not well received by London's bullion dealers, as they had been able to make higher profits beforehand. Johnson offered to buy all bullion that he had assayed back from them, which meant he had to install a considerable amount of extra refining facilities for melting the many metal bars that were returned. By the 1830s the Hatton Garden parting of precious metals took place in the silver loft on the floor above the refinery, where there were eight sand baths heated by coke fires. Each carried two stoneware parting jars, and the nitrous fumes passed to the ash pits of the fires.

Refining bullion is a dangerous, messy business, involving boiling gold in nitric acid, which produces toxic red fumes, other unpleasant chemical residues and a lot of heat. I can imagine the experimental metallurgists working from their laboratory in an old wooden stable, surrounded by large burning coke fires, brightly coloured smoke and flashes of blue light as they created pure liquid gold.

Johnson & Cock turned gold from mines in Africa into saleable gold bars. They experimented on 'separating gold from jacotinga by amalgamation', creating mercury in useable forms. They discovered ways of separating silver, platinum, rhodium, iridium and palladium from gold. At that time palladium was mainly used for the construction of astronomical, nautical and experimental instruments. I have not come across any evidence for it but I like the idea that Johnson would have provided palladium for Negretti & Zambra at no. 1 Hatton Garden, who manufactured the best of these instruments during that period.

George Matthey, a young scientist from French Huguenot descent,

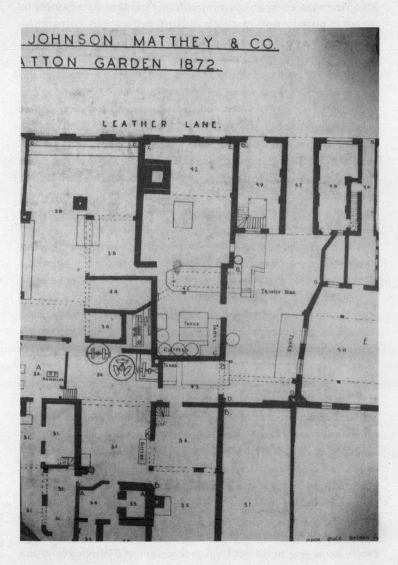

JOHNSON MATTHEY & CO.
ATTON GARDEN 1872.

joined the business as an apprentice in 1837 and became a pioneer in the use of platinum group metals and their applications. He took the company forward technologically, eventually becoming a partner in 1851, when the company was renamed Johnson & Matthey (later shortened to Johnson Matthey). In 1852 they were appointed Official Assayers and Refiners to the Bank of England.

The company had a policy of employing local craftsmen, such as John Harrison, a scientific-instrument maker who had a workshop near by on Kirby Street in the early 1850s. Harrison designed and helped produce sulphuric acid boilers from platinum that were sold on to scientists and industrialists. There is evidence of other similar collaborations with Johnson Matthey and their 'small but enterprising neighbours' in the internal history of the company; a lengthy unpublished document written by former employees.

Johnson Matthey gradually expanded into the surrounding Hatton Garden properties: walls between the adjoining seventeenth-century houses were knocked through, gardens were built over, and stables and yards backing on to Leather Lane, including a Methodist church called Trinity Chapel (where the Christian author of *The Pilgrim's Progress*, John Bunyan, is thought to have preached), were converted into a plant consisting of a melting fire and six refining fires, capable of handling 3,000 ounces of bullion in an hour.

The company handled large amounts of gold and silver, with unrefined gold coming to London from mines in South America and South Africa for refining at Hatton Garden. They struck up a number of lucrative deals internationally to secure supplies of precious metals, including one in 1857 with the Russian government, which had a backlog of Russian Imperial platinum coins, recalled after being poorly produced, making them easy to counterfeit. Vast stocks of valuable platinum lay trapped in the unuseable currency. After fierce competition with French and German assayers, Johnson Matthey won the deal to refine the entire stock. They made a huge profit, managing to extract high percentages of platinum from the coins along with large amounts of a valuable by-product called iridium – a corrosion-resistant silvery-white metal used primarily to tip fountain-pen nibs. The Johnson Matthey Platinum Refinery was situated behind 80 Hatton Garden. It was small and antiquated but able to produce between 1,200 and 1,500 ounces of fine metal per week of a pre-war purity of 99.5 per cent.

THE PULPIT FROM WHICH IT IS SAID BUNYAN PREACHED IN THE SEVENTEENTH CENTURY CHAPEL, WHICH STOOD IN WHAT WAS FORMERLY TRINITY YARD, BEHIND NO. 74 HATTON GARDEN. FROM A PHOTOGRAPH TAKEN BEFORE ITS DEMOLITION.

Johnson retired in 1860, while Matthey, with John Scudamore Sellon, Johnson's nephew by marriage, and Edward Matthey, George's younger brother, continued to take the company forward. They displayed platinum articles in the Great Exhibition of 1851 and in the 1867 Paris International Exhibition, receiving many honours and gold medals. Under George Matthey's direction the company began to refine and fabricate more and more platinum, becoming world leaders in this area.

The income from the firm's refinery and assaying business allowed the experimental chemists to study other metals such as nickel, magnesium and aluminium, which had little commercial or industrial use at the time. They started to develop ways to refine or alloy these materials and to find valuable uses for them, which they would then sell on before turning to another little-known metal to study on a small scale in Hatton Garden. They developed ceramic colours and glazes for pottery and many other chemical and precious-metal-based products. At the beginning of the photographic industry Johnson Matthey provided most of the silver nitrate for Kodak and Ilford; they refined silver into emulsion for developing photographs and for X-rays, mass-producing silver dust to fix memories.

During the First World War the company worked to government orders, refining and supplying metal needed for the war effort, rolling brass and copper, melting down precious-metal objects to create weapons and equipment. The Bank of England restricted the use of gold to essentials only, such as dental fillings. Tons of Russian Imperial gold coins were smuggled into London during the war. In the internal history of the company, there are descriptions of over forty tons' worth of Russian gold arriving in Hatton Garden, in an atmosphere that sounds similar to a Western film. Some sources say these coins were brought in by the Silberfeld brothers, who were Latvian Jews; others claim the bounty, which belonged to the White Russian army, emerged in Istanbul where it was sold on to a Yugoslavian dealer who took it to Johnson Matthey for refining.

Shortly after the First World War ended gold could be legally imported once again and jewellers were allowed to retain their own scraps for reuse. Immediately after the rationing which took place during that war the situation was very difficult for the many goldsmiths, silversmiths and jewellers who had settled in the street by then.

By 1919 the Johnson Matthey Company had opened branches in Birmingham and the US. The core staff stayed at the Hatton Garden main depot, tight-knit small teams of specialist scientists and craftsmen. The descendants of Percival Johnson, George Matthey and Thomas Cock inherited the business and kept building on research with further innovation. Many employees gave long and loyal service to the company with jobs often being handed down through the generations. James Hamlet had been Percival Johnson's assistant when he first set up in Hatton Garden in 1822. Hamlet worked at the firm until 1860; his son took over from him and worked until 1911; his nephew, also called James, took over and worked until 1943, meaning that a member of the same family had been employed by the firm for 121 years.

In 1926, apart from the electrified railways, which owned their own generating station, Johnson Matthey was the largest consumer of electrical power in the London area. By then the firm occupied thirteen Hatton Garden houses – the entire block between Cross Street and Greville Street. Each property had been especially adapted and modified towards a different aspect of the business to suit the needs of the manufacturing and experimentation carried out there. A huge factory sat inside the residential shell of old Hatton Garden town houses with six laboratories spread around the plant. The façade was kept as far as possible intact, but internally three floors of solid concrete were constructed on steel frames to hold the heavy machinery. Between 77 and 78 Hatton Garden a passage was built for trucks filled with precious metal so they could move securely between the buildings.

These ancient seventeenth-century houses, packed with highly volatile and dangerous equipment, flammable chemicals, blasting furnaces and electrical gear were naturally fire hazards. The company maintained its own in-house fire brigade made up of the firm's fitters. The brigade held regular parades on Saturday mornings. In 1932 a 'spectacular' fire broke out at 83 Hatton Garden, in a neighbouring electric-clockmaker's shop, and Johnson Matthey's fire brigade co-operated with the London Fire Brigade to put it out.

If the fans broke down the refinery and sometimes even Leather Lane became filled with choking fog. Many believed there were magical healing properties in this metal smoke. According to the internal history of the company an old Irish doctor who had his practice in the area used to advise his asthmatic and bronchial patients to take a walk in Leather Lane when the fog appeared! Many of the refiners working at the plant seemed to have enjoyed extremely good health and lived to an old age. Their longevity became the source of urban legend, although in reality there were health problems connected to the trade: some of the workers suffered from 'platinum asthma' and had unusual skin pigmentation owing to years of close contact with silver nitrate.

As well as operating their large manufacturing plant at Hatton Garden, Johnson Matthey also sold bullion rod wire, stampings in precious metals, gold and silver sheet metal and other precious metal items directly used by the jewellery industry from a very grand trade counter, which looked: 'a bit like a banking hall, it was very open with big old-fashioned wooden counters and salespeople standing behind serving customers, weighing out gold, selling silver and platinum wires and rods, taking in scrap'. Many of the older craftsmen I had spoken to in Hatton Garden mentioned visiting

Johnson Matthey from the 1930s onwards either to melt down scrap or sweeps, or to purchase precious-metal products they needed for the trade. As mentioned earlier, this is where Dave Harris used to bring buckets full of sweeps from the workshop to be melted down, and he used to give an apple to the Johnson Matthey horse, 'which always seemed to be tied up outside on the street, attached to a cart'.

Hatton Garden 73-83
(Johnson Mattheys)
Feby 1929

The sweeps included the filings and dust left over from making jewellery, offcuts and broken and scrap pieces of precious metal. Even the polishing rags, leather aprons and the floorboards from a jewellery workshop would be melted down for the gold dust embedded within. The melting, recovery and refining of sweeps and scraps took place on the premises, in the refinery at the back of the building, which had large furnaces and other facilities and equipment to turn them into a liquid form, then purify them on site, back into precious metal bullion. The recovered metal would be weighed and customers would be credited for it.

The company continued to develop and expand throughout the first half of the twentieth century, with many new branches opening up in the UK and abroad. When the Second World War started Johnson Matthey became the nation's principal metal suppliers for the war effort again and the manufacturing of jewellery was banned. They refined base metals and produced technical materials, which were used in numerous applications throughout the war. They manufactured parts for radar, aircraft, medical devices and made platinum laboratory apparatus, crucibles, glass chemicals and explosives. They used rhodium plating to protect electrical and radio apparatus, covering items in resistant coating, and they refined silver for silver salts, which made sea water fit to drink, for medicines, surgical treatments, aircraft components and electrical condensers. They also produced the thin films of rolled gold that were placed inside military goggles to stop the glare of the sun.

The Johnson Matthey building on Hatton Garden was badly bombed during the Second World War, and partly out of action for a time, but the refinery was soon repaired and large-scale manufacturing began again after the war. But there were many concerns locally as the thick, acrid smoke pouring out of the building was believed to be polluting the neighbourhood. In 1957 the old refinery and manufacturing section of the Hatton Garden business was demolished, and a huge new factory built in Royston, Hertfordshire. Staff from Johnson Matthey spent days painstakingly combing over the Hatton Garden site, looking to recover any residue of precious metal left in the building after its 135 years as a refinery.

The Hatton Garden building became Johnson Matthey's central office and trade counter, with light-production facilities and equipment for melting scraps and sweeps, which would be purified and turned back into precious metal in a saleable form. The building was refurbished in the late 1970s, including the old trade hall and offices, which, according to Ian Godwin, the company's current Director of Corporate Communications, 'were quite traditional, with lots of wood-panelled rooms. The trade hall still functioned but on a much smaller scale. It eventually moved over the road to 43 Hatton Garden and looked like a modern bank with bulletproof glass screens, under which goods would be passed.

'It was very secure, and jewellers would still bring in their sweeps; the public took in old rings for scrap if they wanted the metal value for it, and when there was a silver-price spike in the early 1980s people queued outside around the block to melt down their old candelabras, silver dinner services and other domestic silver objects. These items would have been weighed, tested, the hallmarks examined, and then Johnson Matthey would have paid cash for them.'

By the 1980s, though, the Hatton Garden building had become a much smaller-scale operation. No manufacturing or melting of the sweeps took place, the trading hall was closed and the building became offices for the company. A modern jewellery operation was opened at 33–44 Hatton Garden but this business was sold on to the Cookson Group in the early 1990s. It still operates there, with a trade counter and the fabrication of gold and silver products for the jewellery industry.

When Johnson Matthey relocated their offices from Hatton Garden to new, larger, purpose-built offices on nearby Farringdon Street a couple of years ago, Ian Godwin told me, 'It was sad to have to move away from the street where the company has had a considerable presence for nearly 200 years but the offices had become too small; we needed more space for our strongly growing global business.'

The Johnson Matthey building remains the largest on Hatton Garden. It is now the home of Grey Advertising along with other media companies.

16

Alma

Little children swarming in and out of courts, which are crowded
with human life, but too insignificant to get into the London directory,
shopkeepers whose names are Luigi and Giuseppe and Biaccio and
Giovanni, may turn to look at you, but only with curiosity, certainly not
with malice. Something of the joy and vivacity and luxurious indolence
of their sunny land has come with these people into the miserable, dingy
streets of their London home. Look at that boy with the red fez and long
black tassel, who lounges against the front door of a squalid cottage.

Unnamed newspaper article,
29 August 1888 (London Metropolitan Archives)

Soon after our walk together, Iain Sinclair invited me to speak with
him at a literary event to launch the paperback edition of his book
Hackney: That Red-Rose Empire. The reading took place at an independent bookshop in Exmouth Market, Clerkenwell Tales. During
the event I talked about my Hatton Garden research, particularly
my investigations into Clerkenwell's Little Italy and my desire to
find someone from that Italian community who had grown up in
the area.

After the talk I was approached by a young woman called Emma,
who told me her mother, aunt and grandparents had all lived there.
We exchanged email addresses and a week later I drove out to visit
her mother, Alma, who lives just outside Redbridge in Essex.

Smiling broadly, Emma opened the door of the small modern
house and led me through into the kitchen where her mother was
making coffee. A short, fair-haired woman, who I estimated to be in

173

her late sixties, stood beside the oven, spooning black powder into a large cafetière. Alma looked up at me with deep-set brown eyes and welcomed me warmly into her home. We stood for a while in the kitchen talking. I commented on the rural view beyond her garden, where I could see a field lined by new houses, stretching into the horizon. Alma opened the French windows at the far end of the room and led me outside. It was a warm summer day. Standing in her beautiful garden, with the sound of the bees buzzing around the flowers and pigeons cooing in the distance, it was hard to believe we were still so near to the borders of London.

Pointing to the green space and homes at the end of her neatly kept lawn she explained that this had once been the site of Claybury Hospital, the place where David Rodinsky's sister was incarcerated in the 1960s and later died. It was a strange feeling to be chasing one story and come across an old familiar one. 'The Claybury Hospital is now a gated estate of very posh houses,' said Alma. 'I used to work there years ago. It was a huge place, with wooden doors that were inches thick. I remember someone being there just because he was blind and had nowhere else to go. There were a lot of underage mothers there at one time too. It was wrong that all these people were lumped together under one roof.'

Moving back into the kitchen Alma told me she had asked her older sister to join us for the interview as she imagined she would remember more. 'She is actually in Clerkenwell right now, helping to clean the Italian Church,' she said. 'She goes every week, has done for years. Even though she moved away from the area decades ago, we are both still very connected to that place.'

Alma picked up the tray with the coffee and cups and led me through to her front room. Before I could set up the recording equipment she began to tell me her story. Born in 1934, to British-born but very Italian parents, Giuseppe and Giovanna Antonioni, Alma and her three sisters lived together in two rooms on the tenth floor of a tenement block in the heart of Little Italy, in Little Gray's Inn Lane: 'We had a front room and a bedroom where we all slept. There was no bathroom and the cooker was on the landing. There were many other Italian families living in our building and in other tenements around the church and off Farringdon and Clerkenwell roads. My mother worked in the kitchens of hotels, like many Italian women in the area. She was a great cook. She used to make ravioli at Christmas and she had this enormous board that she'd roll out the pasta on with a rolling pin that was about two and a half feet long.

'My father was also a great cook. Even though we were poor we always ate well. We didn't have birthday celebrations or presents but we celebrated Christmas and Easter with special food. On Good Friday we had *baccala*, salted cod and salad, ravioli on Christmas Day and Easter. The rest of the time we had pasta and lots of fried food in lard but we had ten flights of stairs to climb so we wore it all off.

'My father worked as an asphalter until his legs got bad and then he used to polish terrazzo for the mosaics. Later he helped a friend making plaster statues. He helped out in the church as well. My uncle, who lived across the road, used to deliver ice with a horse and cart; he had blocks of ice on the back that he delivered to the hotels and he was the only one in the area who had somewhere to keep the ice.

'The organ grinder used to come round, his name was Aggie. When we lived in Gray's Inn Road there was a dairy and stables down the end of the road and he kept his organ there, a barrel organ that he pushed on wheels. It had a handle that he turned and music would come out. We used to see him a lot in the streets playing his organ and we'd always give him something, he was still going around in the 1950s. The knife grinders used to come around and sharpen your knives. There was a dairy near by where you could put money in a slot and get milk out.

'On Back Hill, there were shops selling Italian produce and there was a woman there selling holy pictures and beads and things, but she was murdered, I remember that. Everyone used to be on the street and all the kids played on the street. There wasn't much traffic then and the places we lived were so small you needed to get out to get a bit of air. The sun never seemed to shine; the area was made

up of lots of little cobbled backstreets, the women would congregate outside in groups chatting and all the kids would play. There were lots of street entertainers then. You'd queue outside a cinema and someone would be outside tying themselves up in chains and then wriggling out of them.

'In 1940 my sisters and I were evacuated together to Huntingdon. When we came back the doodlebugs started. My father watched St Paul's burn. The flames rose so high, it really affected him. I remember the air raids; we'd go down into the basement or one of the brick-built shelters outside. Before we were evacuated we'd go down to the tube, to Chancery Lane. My sister would go first with a rolled-up mattress to get a place on the platform. It was packed out – you had to fight for your spot and you had to get up early because people were coming off the trains.

'The area was heavily bombed. We used to play in the bombsites and over the ruins. We were never bombed out but lots of people around us were. Many didn't move back and after the war the Italian community started to disperse. There was nothing to come back to. Many were interned during the war, most of them were just simple country people, they weren't political at all but because they were foreign-born they were interned. There were a lot of Italians who had cafés in the area and the owners tried to give them to someone to look after while they were interned so they had something to come back to. Some people wouldn't give them back. I remember one woman who had about seven or eight children whose husband went down in the *Arandora Star*; there was a lot of tragedy in the Italian community around that time.

'When the bombing got bad again we were evacuated to Wales with my mother and stayed in a miner's house. When we returned, my family moved to Victoria Dwellings on the corner of Clerkenwell and Farringdon roads, where YO! Sushi is now. It was a model tenement block, built to house the poor working-class families in the area, of which there were plenty. There was a mix of English, Irish and Italians living there but most were Italian. We mixed with the others but I felt part of a strong Italian community growing up

in the area. I went regularly to the Italian Church and attended St Peter's Italian school next to the church. It's a ballet school now; it has all gone upmarket there today. I did mix an awful lot with the Irish children and started speaking English when I went to school but I always spoke Italian at home. My parents never really learned much English; they didn't have to, living there.

'The only time I remember being teased about being Italian was when we used to walk to school sometimes and these boys used to call us rat-catchers. It was because we had these little badges on our clothes with RC on them, so if we had an accident and were going to die someone would know we were Roman Catholic and would call a priest to give us the last rites. But we did all mix in together. There were more Italian children than English children in the area so we didn't stick out.

'My parents never moved away from the area. I would have liked to stay living there – it is such a central area – but it was too expensive to stay. Growing up there, everyone was familiar to me. It was like living in a village. Everyone knew me although where we lived was called a slum; most of those buildings have been pulled down now. We were poor but we didn't realize it at the time. Everyone was in the same boat.

'The Italian cafés were not restaurants – they were there for workmen. There were delis although we wouldn't have called them delis, they were grocers that sold Italian goods you couldn't get in other shops, like olive oil, Parmesan cheese and garlic. My mother used to go to Gazzano's on Farringdon Road, which is still there. They used to make their own home-made wine there; food always came first for that community. Terroni's was the other famous deli, right next door to the church. It did great business. My mother swapped her tea coupons with the neighbours during the war and then she went to Terroni's and bought coffee beans, which had to be ground at home. My mother always spoke Italian in the shops but I spoke English. Many others spoke a mixture. If you went to Leather Lane it was called Leather Lana; if you crossed the road they'd say "crossumo la strada".

'Every year during the lively Italian festival, the Sagra, the community really came together: there were stalls all around the place, selling pizza and other Italian food, and for weddings and funerals, people from the community always come back to the Italian Church.

The route of the Italian procession used to be much longer, it went all over the area and all the streets were decorated. Now it's shrinking, it gets smaller every year.

'Hatton Garden was a place I would walk through and look in the shop windows. It was a bit like going to the films, seeing things that were so removed from my lifestyle. I'd look in the windows and just dream. The place hasn't really changed that much, it still looks quite the same, unlike the rest of the area. I do remember Gamages, it was like a fairyland to me, they had enormous dolls there in glass cases, which I wanted so much but could never afford. The toy department was amazing.

'We went shopping in Exmouth Street and Leather Lane and

everyone knew us. There were small shops and daily market stalls there where we'd buy our clothes. We never shopped in the West End. We stayed local for everything. During the war you had to register with a butcher and a dairy, you couldn't wander. The only thing you didn't have to register for was vegetables. You bought everything else with coupons. My mother got most of her rations from a grocer's in Leather Lane. There was another shop in Leather Lane that sold linen. They had those things on the ceiling, on hooks, that shoot across the shop with the change in. It was one of the few shops where you could go in and buy things and pay on the never-never. My mother took me there when I was getting married and ordered me sheets and blankets, which we paid off week by week. When I got married I moved away to Old Street and then East Ham.

But there is still a group of aged Italians living in the area, hanging on to the last remnants of the Italian quarter.'

Later I asked Emma if she had any personal memories of the place. She had not grown up there but had visited her grandmother often at her home in Victoria Dwellings. 'We used to go up on to the roof of the building together and watch the trains going into Farringdon and feed pigeons up there with rice,' she said. 'My grandmother never spoke English but we communicated through food. We used to get ice cream from the van outside and my grandmother would make a well in the middle and pour in a little amaretto, and she always gave us a watered-down glass of wine with dinner. I used to go to Terroni's for her; I remember getting sugared almonds as a treat and the smell of the meats hanging up. I loved visiting that shop and the Italian Church. The priest would always kiss me. They are very friendly there, very community-based, and they do a lot of work for the homeless people and drug addicts in the area.'

17

De Beers

Hatton Garden became the centre of the jewellery trade because of De Beers, who set up their headquarters near Holborn Viaduct in the 1870s, after Barney Barnato and Cecil Rhodes discovered diamond mines in Kimberley, South Africa. All the world's rough diamonds were once sorted by De Beers, mainly coming from South Africa.

Dave Harris

A tight-knit, multicultural community of people work in the many retail shops on Hatton Garden today, selling the jewellery manufactured in the workshops along with stock purchased from around the world. Since shops first began to open up on the street in the 1950s, Hatton Garden has changed from a working area of jewellery manufacture to a street visited by thousands of tourists and customers every year.

On Saturdays, particularly, loved-up couples visit Hatton Garden, spending hours in the arcades, searching for wedding and engagement rings. Single-stone diamonds, known as solitaires, are still the most popular choice for engagement rings, followed by three-stone diamond rings then sapphire-and-diamond rings. 'The part of the job I love the most,' says Adriana, a young woman in her early thirties who has worked in the historic and internationally renowned diamond quarter for the past five years, 'is watching all these people, so happy, as they make one of the most important purchases in their lives. I spend a long time talking to couples about their wedding plans, their honeymoons, where they live, letting them try on many different rings. If people come in wanting a ring we don't have, we can make it up for them, calling around the different workshops to see who has a particular stone. It is all part of the service here, which is why people like to come to Hatton Garden. It is a very old-fashioned place and you feel great when couples leave the shop not just satisfied but happier than they will ever be leaving any shop in their lives. You hope you have sold them something they will cherish every day. Of course it is not always this way, there can be many tensions during a sale as well. She expects him to spend more, he is trying to direct her towards the cheaper rings; sometimes it can be very difficult indeed. You need tact and patience, to let people have time alone to discuss these issues, to remain positive without being too pushy.'

Originally from Portugal, Adriana moved to London at the age of twenty to study geology. After finishing her degree she went on to complete a diploma at the Gemological Institute of America – the world's authority in gemology and jewellery education, where she learned how to grade and identify stones as well as studying the history of diamonds and the trade. She began working a few years ago in one of the retail shops in the street, aiming eventually to become a trader in diamonds or precious stones herself. 'I was told that the ancient Greeks believed diamonds were splinters of stars that fell to earth,' said Adriana. 'There are so many legends and myths about these stones, which have always fascinated humans. Some believed they had supernatural or healing powers. They are millions of years old, formed beneath the earth from incredible pressure. Extraordinary to think they are made from the same stuff as coal!'

In a quiet moment, Adriana took me into the back room of the shop where she worked and told me what she knew about the history of diamonds: 'The first known diamonds were discovered in India over 3,000 years ago in a river bed. Alexander the Great was the person who first brought diamonds to Europe from India. For centuries all the world's diamonds came from Indian mines. Merchants bought them from Arabian caravans, then shipped them to Venice to be cut and polished. They were so scarce only royalty could afford them.

'In the sixteenth century Portugal became the centre of the dia mond trade when a new shipping route was discovered directly from Goa to Lisbon. Many factories cutting, polishing and selling stones were established there. Then the Dutch East India Company found another sea route directly from India to Holland, and Amsterdam became the centre of the world's diamond trade.

'In the eighteenth century a large diamond mine was discovered in Brazil and the Dutch and British East India companies fought for control of this new sea route. In 1867, a new source of diamonds was discovered in South Africa, just as the Brazilian and Indian mines were beginning to run out of them.

'Cecil Rhodes, an English colonial gentleman who moved to South Africa, followed thousands of other prospectors to the newly discovered diamond fields in Kimberley, which were on a former farm belonging to Boer settlers from Holland, called De Beer. Rhodes initially made his money through hiring out a pump, used to suck up water from the many mines in the area, which often flooded. He invested this money in buying shares of other people's mines and, with the help of the Rothschild family, he expanded the company, buying up other smaller mines when the international price of diamonds began to drop due to the vast amount of them found in Kimberley.

In 1880 Rhodes merged with two other huge mining syndicates to form the De Beers Mining Company, which immediately became the largest diamond producers in the world. There was one other big company in the area, which refused at first to sell to De Beers: the Kimberley Central Mine, which had been established by an East End London Jew called Barney Barnato. In 1888 Rhodes and Barnato merged their companies into a cartel called De Beers Consolidated Mines. Rhodes, Barnato and the London-based Rothschild family were all major shareholders in the company, which by the 1890s owned 95 per cent of the world's diamond mines.'

Dave Harris told me De Beers set up their headquarters in London in Charterhouse Street in the 1870s and that this was the reason that Hatton Garden became a jewellery quarter. Adriana could not confirm this so I went back to the archives to research further. Looking through trade directories from the 1870s to 1910, I could not find any presence of De Beers in either Hatton Garden or Charterhouse Street. However, there was clearly a strong connection between the discovery of the diamond fields in Kimberley and the emerging diamond trade in Hatton Garden. In 1875 there were twenty-three diamond merchants. By 1880 there were fifty. I counted nearly seventy brokers, commissioning agents and diamond merchants in 1889. By 1895 there were over 100 diamond merchants and brokers operating from addresses in the street, along with sixteen jewellers all with Jewish-sounding surnames: Joseph, Abrahams, Morris, Hirshborn, Horowitz and Rothschild. Other trades were moving into Hatton Garden to support the emerging diamond industry: cutters, polishers, engravers, dealers in gems, silversmiths, gold beaters, pearl merchants and lapidaries. By 1910 Hatton Garden had firmly established itself as London's diamond and jewellery quarter, with over 200 separate businesses connected to the trade in the street; many of these were merchants and brokers of rough diamonds.

Through further research, and with the help of the archivist at De Beers, I discovered that the reason so many brokers of rough diamonds ended up in Hatton Garden was because of the creation of the London Diamond Syndicate in 1890 by Cecil Rhodes, who invited a group of ten Jewish firms, most of whom were based in Hatton Garden and had family connections with one another, to form a purchasing syndicate. In 1893 De Beers sold their entire production of rough diamonds to the London Diamond Syndicate, who then became the largest distributors of them in the world. The trade boomed: dealers, brokers, cutters, manufacturers and jewellers flocked to Hatton Garden and it quickly became the centre of the world's rough-diamond trade. I couldn't find any evidence of the London Diamond Club opening up in the street by then but I imagine some version of it would have been operating somewhere in Hatton Garden around this time, as a place for the dealers to safely trade with one another. Since the late nineteenth century most leading diamond traders worldwide have had to come to London to buy rough diamonds.

Following the development of De Beers, I learned about the next big figure in the company's history: Ernest Oppenheimer. He was born in Germany but began his working life as a trainee diamond broker for Dunkelsbuhler & Company in Hatton Garden in 1896, at the age of sixteen. His employer sent him out to Kimberley to work as a buyer and he eventually rose to the position of mayor in the town. In 1917 he formed the Anglo American Corporation, primarily to exploit the East Witwatersrand goldfields. The company diversified into diamond mining and bought Consolidated Diamond Mines, which gave Oppenheimer access to the London Syndicate and led to a merger with De Beers, which he became a director of in 1926. Oppenheimer tried to ensure diamond prices remained stable against background economic crises such as the Great Depression, although many accused him of price-fixing, holding back stock and not releasing industrial diamonds for the US war effort during the Second World War.

Oppenheimer became chairman of De Beers in 1929, wresting control from Rhodes following a boardroom battle. He introduced a new business model for De Beers based on the London Syndicate, which later became the Diamond Corporation (1930), which in turn formed the basis for the Central Selling Organization (1934), later renamed the Diamond Trading Company (DTC). All formed to distribute rough diamonds from De Beers mines through one single channel. The DTC's headquarters were situated just around the corner from Hatton Garden, at 17 Charterhouse Street. Since 1934 this building has been the world's central sorting office for rough diamonds, making London the most important rough-diamond centre internationally.

Adriana told me: 'De Beers held a monopoly on the diamond market until fairly recently, controlling supply and demand, keeping stock back when the price of diamonds fell, flooding the market at others. De Beers only sells its rough diamonds to specially selected merchants known as sightholders. The identity of these sightholders is a closely guarded secret. Every five weeks De Beers holds a "sight" where they hand out sealed boxes of mixed diamonds to about 100 sightholders, who buy the boxes of uncut stones without seeing them. The stones have been sorted into the boxes by technicians beforehand. The price, quantity and quality of the diamonds are non-negotiable. The sightholders have to take the good and the bad stones, which they then sort through and sell on to cutters, polishers, private customers and shops throughout the world. I have heard that De Beers will phone up the sightholders and say things like, "There is a bag of diamonds arriving Thursday, deposit $6 million in our account." They don't get a choice, there are huge levels of trust involved on both sides. Most sightholders become very wealthy or are to start with; not just quite wealthy – they need to be multimillionaires, often from large, international diamond-cutting factories. If you question De Beers or pull out of the deal you can lose the privilege of being a sightholder.'

De Beers no longer have complete control of the world's rough-diamond trade but they still have the power to manipulate prices. Along with their South African mines they also own mines in Botswana, Namibia and Canada. They own a number of cutting factories internationally as well as many jewellery shops around the world but their headquarters remains in London at 17 Charterhouse Street, although it will be moving to Botswana in 2013.

De Beers in Charterhouse Street is a notoriously hard building to get into. I tried myself and failed to visit the premises but during her GIA diploma course Adriana went on a field trip there. She described the place as 'fortress-like' and 'filled with security guards'. Her group was taken up to the reception floor where they had to leave all of their belongings. The history of the company was explained to them, along with the story of their extremely successful advertising campaigns: 'Diamonds are forever' and 'Diamonds are a girl's best friend' – two of the most successful slogans of all time. Afterwards they were led into one of the small viewing rooms where clients went to look at diamonds. They were shown some rough diamonds, which Adriana thought 'looked like cloudy bits of soap'.

Underneath the building, they were told, are very deep vaults, containing thousands of uncut diamonds, most of the world's supply.

'De Beers were the sole controller of diamonds in the world,' said Adriana. 'They used to own all the mines but in the 1990s other

mines were discovered in places like Canada, and people began to sell diamonds outside of De Beers, so they no longer have a monopoly. People buy diamonds now from many places, not just from a De Beers sightholder. Many of the diamonds that end up in Hatton Garden may have come from De Beers in Charterhouse originally but before they arrive in the shops they might have travelled all over the world, firstly being sold as rough by the sightholders and then moving on to be cut and polished at centres internationally.

'Of course the more recent history of diamonds and the diamond trade has had bad associations with "conflict" or "blood diamonds", which are the names given to stones that are mined in war-torn areas, or used by rebels and warlords to fund these wars. I am no expert on this subject but from my understanding the international diamond community has had a zero-tolerance policy on conflict diamonds and has developed safeguards to stop these illegal diamonds entering the diamond supply. De Beers claim their diamonds only come from their own mines, so they do not sell on any blood diamonds and most of the diamonds coming into Hatton Garden and the Diamond Bourse still come from De Beers. There are very strict rules in Hatton Garden and in the industry as a whole about purchasing diamonds. Nobody would touch goods from Angola, the Congo, Sierra Leone or the Ivory Coast. All the stones that come into Hatton Garden are very tightly regulated. Everything has to be purchased from legal companies. There is now certification for diamonds from source, so there is a paper trail.'

18

Little Italy

On Sundays Little Italy indulges its love of finery to the full, and the
women, with their bright silk headdresses, large paste beads, and black-
and-gold corsets, are really picturesque as they form gossiping crowds
round the church door. Then the organ grinder comes out with his wide-
brimmed hat and earrings and smokes a cheroot a foot in length.

Anonymous newspaper article, 1898 (London Metropolitan Archives)

Walking along Theobald's Road, past the northern exit of Hatton
Garden and the junction of Gray's Inn Road, I stopped outside the
gated gardens of Gray's Inn Field. It was midday and office workers
were already spreading out on the lush grass inside the walled lawns;
eating sandwiches, smoking, chatting, enjoying the last of the late-
September sun. For most of the day these gardens are reserved for the
lawyers and barristers who practise from near here, but at lunchtime,
for a brief couple of hours, the gates are opened and the general public are allowed into these ancient grounds, to come and relax in one
of the few sizeable green spaces in the area.

Gray's Inn Court, one of the four medieval Inns of Court, has
existed on this site since the fourteenth century, originally providing
accommodation and training for barristers and lawyers. They no
longer house trainee lawyers but the Inns of Court still have the
exclusive right to call men and women to the Bar. Anyone wanting
to become a barrister has to join either Gray's Inn, Lincoln's Inn,
Middle Temple or the Inner Temple. Christopher Hatton studied
law at the Inner Temple, where his graceful dancing, 'fine form' and
'very fine face' impressed Queen Elizabeth, as we have seen.

In the sixteenth century, during the 'golden age' of the Inns, the great halls of these immense institutions became the locations for colourful masques, balls and banquets. Queen Elizabeth I was the patron of Gray's Inn and regularly attended grand social events that took place there. To be seen at court was essential for any young aristocrat. Nobles and country gentlemen sent their sons to study at the Inns. Most had no intention of becoming lawyers. They came to play lutes and cards, and hold wild parties. Late-night revelries often turned into drunken brawls, which spilled out of the confines of the student lodgings and into the surrounding streets, with rowdy gatherings and, further south, river pageants. At Christmas time, the extravagant festivities lasted for days.

Directly opposite the walled gardens of Gray's Inn Field sits the 1960s building of Holborn Library. As I entered the reading room on the ground floor, a strong smell of old hardbacks and disinfectant hit my nostrils, prompting childhood memories of school. The sun was streaming in through the large glass windows, making the room hot and airless. A few people stood around the book stacks, or sat at tables, flicking through the daily papers. Outside the windows, the street was filled with people; rushing around during their lunch break, dashing to meetings, catching buses, stuck in traffic, talking on mobiles, whizzing past on bicycles. Inside, time seemed to stand still, the only audible sound the soft snoring of a young homeless man, fast asleep in a chair next to the crime-novels section.

Passing the main desk I took the lift up to the Camden Local Studies and Archives Centre on the second floor, where I had arranged to meet Tudor Allen, the aptly historically named chief archivist of the centre who has spent the last few years studying, interviewing and researching the history of Clerkenwell's Little Italy. He recently produced an exhibition and a book chronicling the story of the community's origins in the early nineteenth century, through to its height in the years around 1900 and its subsequent decline in the postwar period.

The sparsely furnished study room was empty when I arrived. As

I stood waiting by the front desk, a young man, with a fantastic halo of curly brown hair, dressed in loose slacks and a crumpled shirt, appeared from the archives. I introduced myself and he smiled warmly, while wiping the dust from his hands. 'I've been sorting through some really old maps,' said Tudor, by way of apology; 'let's look at some of the material from the collections before going for a walk.' I followed him through to the reading room, where a few box files and folders sat on a table.

He showed me surveys, drawings and newspaper reports documenting the once-vibrant community of Little Italy. Tracing the boundary of London's Italian quarter with his finger on a map he told me: 'Little Italy once occupied the streets of Saffron Hill, Leather Lane and parts of Hatton Garden, as well as a number of steep cobbled alleyways around Clerkenwell Road.' I was fascinated to see photographs, dating back to the 1900s, of the annual Italian fiesta, which Alma had described. 'Except during wartime the Processione della Madonna del Carmine has taken place every year since 1896,' said Tudor, as we examined extraordinary images of the narrow backstreets of Clerkenwell, decorated with flags, lights and flowers strung across the roads. We looked at engravings of ice-cream sellers, organ grinders, Italian women in traditional costume, hundreds of fading images of a time past.

'Italians had of course been present in London for centuries,' said Tudor, 'many came as merchants in the Middle Ages, but it wasn't until the nineteenth century that they arrived here in large numbers and settled in Clerkenwell. The first wave of Italians to arrive in this area came in the early 1800s. They were comparatively affluent, skilled craftsmen who manufactured thermometers, telescopes, optical instruments and other precision instruments along with looking glasses and picture frames. Many of them settled in Hatton Garden, living above their premises with workshops in the basements and shops on the ground floor.

'Following the Napoleonic Wars many more Italian migrants arrived in the area, driven abroad by terrible economic conditions. Most were poor and unskilled and made their way here on foot, settling in Clerkenwell and nearby Saffron Hill. By 1850, over 1,000 Italians were living in the densely populated, slum-ridden streets, which became known as Little Italy. They were chiefly employed as

organ grinders, makers and sellers of plaster figures, picture frames, looking glasses and scientific instruments. As the community became more established men brought their spouses over. Many worked as domestic servants, made lace or manufactured pasta. Others made money singing, dancing and playing the tambourine or telling fortunes by means of parakeets in cages. To give you an idea of how large the community once was, by 1900 St Peter's School for Italians had nearly 3,000 pupils and there were over 900 itinerant travelling ice-cream sellers living in the area then. Little Italy at its height had its own church, cafés, pubs, schools, clubs, grocers and dance saloons.'

Grabbing his jacket and a stripy scarf from the back of a chair, Tudor led me downstairs and out of the building, to take me for a guided walk around the streets of the former Little Italy. Our first stop was outside the boarded-up shopfront on Clerkenwell Road of Terroni's Italian delicatessen and restaurant, which had operated from that site from 1890 for over 100 years, eventually closing down in 2009 – a sign of the diminishing demand for Italian goods in the area.

As we crossed the busy Clerkenwell Road I moved my microphone closer, trying to capture the sound of Tudor's gentle voice above the din of the constantly moving traffic. He told me the road

had been constructed in 1878, probably by Italian migrants, many of whom worked as asphalters. 'When the road was built it cut straight through the Italian colony, which was well established by then. Many of the tenement houses must have been demolished to make way for the road, but it was advantageous for the central building of the community, St Peter's Church, which had been hidden behind other buildings before then, after its construction in 1863.'

We turned into Leather Lane, where the busy daily market was in full swing. Slaloming our way through the stalls we passed hordes of office workers on their lunch breaks, looking for bargains among the clothes stalls or waiting patiently in line at one of the many hot-food outlets, selling Thai curries, falafels, Mexican burritos and pizzas.

There has been a street market in Leather Lane for over 300 years, making it one of London's oldest markets. The road is first depicted in the Agas map, c. 1570, as a narrow street called Liver (meaning

'very muddy') Lane, running alongside the boundary wall of the
Ely Estate. John Stow described it in his 1598 *Survey of London* as 'a
turning to the fields lately replenished with houses'. In the seventeenth century, Leather Lane, along with Hatton Garden, became a

residential housing estate. In John Strype's updated version of
Stow's survey, published in 1720, he describes the east side of the
lane as being 'best built, having all Brick Houses; and behind them
several Yards for Stables and Coach Houses, which belong to the
Houses in Hatton Street'. Strype mentions a number of taverns in
the street, which grew rapidly over the next few decades.

By the late eighteenth century Leather Lane had become 'a
narrow dirty street, infested with thieves and beggars', filled with
cheap lodging houses and crumbling accommodation. When Italian

migrants arrived in the area in the nineteenth century, many settled in
the run-down streets in and around Leather Lane. Post office directories from the 1860s list organ grinders, Italian plaster-statuette makers,
glass blowers, picture-frame makers and terrazzo and mosaic manufacturers living there. 'Most of the plaster-statuette makers came
from the area around Lucca in Tuscany,' said Tudor, 'where there is
a long tradition of figure-making. In the 1861 census a fifth of the
Italians living in this area were figure makers. They made both religious and secular plaster models, which they would then hawk on
the streets of London.' I could see only one visible remnant of Italian traders left in Leather Lane: a tailor's at the far end of the street,
selling handmade Italian suits.

At the end of Leather Lane we turned left into Greville Street,
walking past a deli selling salt-beef sandwiches, bagels and *latkes*.
Apart from the café, this short section of Greville Street is filled
with jewellery suppliers and small workshops, providing services
for the many shops on Hatton Garden. Turning right, directly into
Hatton Garden, we could see that the wide, tree-lined street was
practically devoid of pedestrians, in sharp contrast to the bustle of

nearby Leather Lane. We made our way to a jewellery retail shop at no. 5, near to Holborn Circus, which Tudor told me had been the site of the first school in Little Italy, established in 1841 by the famous Italian patriot Giuseppe Mazzini. 'He was living in exile in London at the time, with a death sentence on his head for his involvement in an attempt to start a mutiny in the Sardinian army. Mazzini set up the Italian Free School for Workers here to provide education for the poor Italian children living in the neighbourhood (the school later moved to 5 Greville Street). One of the darker sides of Little Italy was child exploitation. There were many young Italian children on the streets begging, after being brought over here from Naples by *padroni*, who promised them a career, singing and playing the organ. They were practically sold into child slavery and often cruelly treated. Their working day could start at nine and last until eleven at night. All their earnings went to the *padroni*. Mazzini started this school to help them and the children of other Italians living in the area. Charles Dickens was a benefactor of the school.'

Passing the site where Gamages once stood, we stopped again on the corner of High Holborn and Leather Lane. 'Gatti and Bolla established a famous restaurant and café here,' said Tudor. 'Gatti was a Swiss Italian who arrived in Little Italy in the 1840s penniless. He started by selling coffee from a barrow on the streets. In 1850 he joined forces with another Italian called Bolla, who was a chocolatier from Castro in south-east Italy. They set up the café and installed a drinking-chocolate machine in the window, which had been imported from Paris and was a real novelty at the time. A few years later Gatti began selling ice cream and that made him a millionaire. He sold the penny ice, a craze in Victorian times, which started with street sellers. Many Italians switched from working as travelling musicians, playing hurdy-gurdies, barrel organs, harps and fiddles, to becoming ice-cream sellers. They would wander around the streets of the city, with their brightly decorated barrows, selling penny ices.'

Dodging couriers on motorbikes we crossed the busy junction of Hatton Garden and Holborn Circus and walked down Charter-

house Street towards Smithfield Market, past the closed gates of Ely Place. About halfway down Charterhouse Street, just past the office of De Beers, we took a sharp left down some stone steps and entered the part of Saffron Hill formerly known as Field Lane. The current street level of Saffron Hill is about six feet below Charterhouse Street although the layout of the place has not changed much since Victorian times. Saffron Hill is now lined by towering office blocks and partly pedestrianized, and its narrowness is the only remaining feature of its less salubrious past, well described in previous chapters.

As we walked through the heart of the former Saffron Hill rookery Tudor told me a story about a fight that had taken place in the bagatelle room of a pub in that area called the Golden Anchor (which no longer exists) between English and Italian customers on Boxing Day in 1864: 'A man was fatally stabbed. The chief suspect was an Italian silverer; he was brought to the dying Englishman, who identified him as the murderer. Negretti, the Hatton Garden barometer maker, who was a respected man, a real pillar of the community, was called to the scene. He wasn't convinced and did some amateur sleuthing himself and discovered the real murderer was the cousin of the falsely accused man. Negretti managed to get a confession from the true murderer and the crime was justly solved.'

Crossing Clerkenwell Road again, we ambled down Herbal Hill, passing the site of St Peter's Catholic School, now a private ballet school. 'The school was attached to the Italian Church next door from 1878 until the 1980s,' said Tudor. 'They employed Italian-speaking staff and Irish teachers too.'

Herbal Hill, with its cobbled road and Victorian cottages, still has a nineteenth-century flavour. The topography and layout of the streets this side of Clerkenwell Road have changed little since the 1830s. Reaching the bottom of Herbal Hill we stood next to the Coach and Horses pub (the site of the former bear-baiting pit of Hockley-in-the-hole), which Tudor told me had once been run by Italians. 'Warner Street and Eyre Street Hill near here are the primary sites of one of the most important events in the annual calendar of Little

Italy – the Sagra, which happens the same day as the procession, when these streets are filled with Italian stalls selling food and drink,' Tudor said. 'The Processione della Madonna del Carmine still happens every year, on the Sunday nearest to the 18th of July, but is very different now as there are few old Italian families still living here. The festival began in 1883. It was the first public Roman Catholic event to take place in London since the Reformation. In the heyday of Little Italy, Saffron Hill was the place where everyone would congregate after the procession. There was a real carnival atmosphere there, with friends and relatives getting together. It was mainly a local event, all the houses would have been decorated and altars to the Madonna were placed in the windows. In a way it was more Italian than Italy, which often happens with migrant communities when they leave their native country.'

We paused for a coffee at Gazzano's on Farringdon Road, which is the oldest Italian-run café and delicatessen still operating in the area. After a quick cappuccino we walked up to Exmouth Market, on the fringes of the former Little Italy, passing stallholders selling different types of street food. A strong smell of home-made Italian sausages was in the air from an outdoor barbecue.

The once-working-class street market is now lined with bars, cafés and boutique shops, catering for a new type of resident who has moved into the area in recent years. We stopped outside the house where Joseph Grimaldi, the father of modern clowning, lived in the early nineteenth century. 'He was the son of an early Italian immigrant who went on stage as a child and had a long career, principally at Sadler's Wells and later Drury Lane,' said Tudor. 'There is an expression in the English Language, "a Joey", meaning "a clown", which comes from his name, Joseph.'

We made our way back down to Eyre St Hill, which had originally been known as Little Bath Street. There was once a Great Bath Street as well, now demolished, which was famous for an incident involving the Darby Sabini gang, formed by six Sabini brothers, with Charles 'Darby' Sabini as the leader, who grew up in Clerkenwell with an Irish mother and an Italian father. Membership to the

79. A Barrel Organ Player, 1884

If you saw my little backyard wot a pretty spot you'ld cry
It's a picture on a sunny summer day
With the turnip tops and cabbages wot people don't buy
I makes it on a Sunday look all gay.
Oh it really is a verry pretty garden
And Chingford to the eastward could be seen
Wiv a ladder and some glasses, you could see to 'Ackney Marshes
If it wasn't for the 'ouses in between
—Words by Edgar Bateman, sung by Gus Elen

gang grew to hundreds, mainly Italians, with many Jewish members too. The gang was notorious in the 1920s for extorting money from race-club bookies. Tudor told me that Graham Greene's *Brighton Rock* has an Italian gangster character in it who was supposedly based on Darby Sabini, who did move to Brighton. During my researches I had come across a story in Heather Shore's *Undiscovered Country: Towards a History of the Criminal Underworld* of a violent November night in 1923 when the Sabini gang clashed with another local gang called the Cortesis in the Fratellanza Club in Great Bath Street. Darby Sabini was attacked, his false teeth knocked out; his brother Harry was shot. Clashes between these so-called Italian razor gangs in the area were not uncommon at the time.

About halfway up the hill we stood outside the premises of Chiappa Organ Builders, which now houses the offices of the contemporary art commissioning body Artangel.

Tudor explained that Giuseppe Chiappa established the firm in the 1860s in Farringdon Road and moved to Eyre Street Hill in 1877, where they made instruments for the many organ grinders of Little Italy. Albert Chiappa, his great-grandson, died recently but a recording was made of him talking about his family business and growing up in Little Italy by Verusca Calabria, a protégé of the well-known oral historian Alan Dein who worked with Tudor on the exhibition about Little Italy at the library. Verusca kindly sent me an extract from this interview she conducted with Albert Chiappa in 2008:

There were three floors and a basement and the factory employed forty to fifty people, making and repairing organs, pinning the barrels, arranging printing and cutting the music for the book organs, which followed on from the barrel organs. At that time we were the biggest mechanical organ company in England, although in that area there were a number of smaller firms making street pianos, where you turned a barrel to make a tune; ten, twelve tunes on a barrel. My great-grandfather had a lot of business with people who installed these penny-in-a-slot pianos in public houses.

They were the forerunner of jukeboxes, when they arrived it cut out the trade.

People came into the factory and hired out a street piano for the day, pushed it down to the West End, collected their money and at night returned it to the factory . . . After the 1920s it was a gradual decline, also the big mechanical organs on the fairgrounds, when records arrived the business soon collapsed.

The organ builders were highly rated craftsmen. The quality of workmanship on the organs, the mechanical side, the tone, the decoration, the carving, they were works of art. On the fairground, there was great demand for the organs.

My family were one of the main employers of organ makers at the time, they moved from barrel organs to book organs, where you could order any tune you liked. In the factory in Eyre Street Hill I have all the music patterns hanging up, there are thousands, different sizes, different tunes, marches, waltzes, overtures, all the popular songs of the day, which was required by the showman who was always trying to attract more business by having the latest tunes.

Work diminished after the 1920s; a lot of workers were made redundant. The basement was cleared out, where all the street pianos were stored, there was no demand for them so the place was let out to printers in the early 1930s. Upstairs we let out parts of the building to pay the rent.

When his exhibition opened Tudor contacted Albert, who helped him locate an original Chiappa-made street piano to play in the library as people came in: 'The guys wheeled it up to the library from Chiappa's yard and stopped on the way outside the Gunmakers Arms in Eyre Street Hill and played it. People were dancing in the street.'

We reached Summers Street, which connects with Eyre Street Hill. Tudor pulled some notes from his bag; copies of the 1871 census, which showed that forty-six Neapolitan organ grinders lived in adjacent houses in Summer Street in that year and sixty organ grinders from Bardi in Palma lived together in three houses.

At the top of the hill we turned left into Clerkenwell Road and stood outside the magnificent Renaissance-style building of St Peter's Church, which is still the focal point for the remaining Italian

community. Outside is a memorial to Italians killed during the tragedy of the *Arandora Star*, mentioned to me by Alma; the ship was torpedoed by a German submarine in July 1940 as it was carrying around 800 Italians from all over Britain who were being deported to internment camps in Canada. Four hundred and seventy-one Italian men lost their lives; many of them were from Little Italy. In June 1940 Mussolini had declared war on Britain and many Italian-born men between the ages of sixteen and sixty were interned as enemy aliens.

Opening the door of the church to look inside, I was quickly waved away. The chapel was packed with mourners for a funeral. Shutting the door quietly I followed Tudor down the steps, moving out of the way as a weeping woman exited the church and leaned heavily against the porch. 'The inside is one of the most highly decorated church interiors in the country,' said Tudor. 'When it opened it was the largest new Catholic church building in England, an indication of the size of the migrant community living here during the nineteenth century. The building is modelled on the San Cristoforo in Rome.'

As we made our way back towards the library, Tudor told me about the Italian Hospital, which opened in the late nineteenth century and provided free medical care for poor migrants. Like many Italian institutions and businesses in the area the hospital closed down during the war. Internment created bad feeling among the community of Little Italy. Many of the Italians who were interned had formerly thought of themselves as British citizens. Women were left alone to cope with businesses and children without any support. The area was also heavily bombed and then, after the disaster of the *Arandora Star*, many Italians just left the area. As others became better off they moved out to less deprived areas of the city. Others who stayed wanted to integrate more. After the war many Italian-sounding names were anglicized: Vittorio became Victor, Pietro Peter. Slowly the community died off, intermarried or moved away.

'One of the last remaining public buildings belonging to the Italian community closed its doors this year,' said Tudor. 'It was originally known as the Society for the Progress of the Italian Working Men's Club in London, and later became the Mazzini Garibaldi Club. It began in 1864 with Mazzini and Garibaldi as the two honorary founders. It was the centre of social life for the Italian men of the community. During the Second World War it was requisitioned as enemy property and didn't reopen until after the war.'

There, with his microphone, to record the old men talking on that last day at the Mazzini Garibaldi Club, was Alan Dein. Later that week Alan emailed me Part 1 of his logging notes, from the five hours of audio recordings he had made at the club:

00:43   Door creaks, climbing up stairs of club . . .
01:12   Where are we, Bruno?
        We're in the main room for recreation, pool table,
        where we all meet once a week, for drinks and to
        chat . . . we left because war came.
        What was it like?
        When I was a kid, it was very quiet . . . a few old boys
        playing cards, barman, nothing much happening.
14:58   It was a place to meet buddies, comrades, socialize, hard
        work to mix with English . . . We were all friends in
        Italian quarter . . . one community, no other place to go
        . . . school was 95 per cent Italian, few Irish . . . mainly
        poor . . . just before war 1938.
17:40   Father owned small café . . . then became an asphalter . . .
19:18   Imagine this place, accordion, packed, youngsters, never
        see that again, wonderful dances up here, everybody
        moved away . . . after war, govt gave us back the prem-
        ises . . . majority of older generation interned, closed
        club down . . . became Soho café owners, all the hard
        work in Clerkenwell . . . little Italy . . . the language,
        English was spoken, my uncle would speak in Italian,
        majority in English, cockney Italian so to speak . . .

Terroni's near the Italian Church, Leather Lane, majority Italian food, father make his own lard and fat, pickle this and that. Used to have baccala, delicacy today, dried cod, polenta . . . make ravioli, pizzoccheri, special taste, eggs, Parmigiano cheese, breadcrumbs, still do now . . .

19

The London Diamond Bourse

Berman went off to the Bourse, but no trading was going on there. In the big hall with its massive gleaming pillars, there was hardly anyone to be seen. The few dealers around, who had not gone away, were unwrapping their parcels of diamonds. The stones caught Berman's eye with their flashing colours of white, red, blue. The dealers showed each other the bargains they had bought and then wrapped them up again. The Club was empty too and only the Shenkl, where the smaller traders dealt, was full of life.

Esther Kreitman, *Diamonds*

The London Diamond Bourse is now located in purpose-built premises in the centre of Hatton Garden, with a diamond trading floor, offices, a bank on the ground floor and a safe-deposit unit in the basement; its position is well known but few people who work in Hatton Garden who are not members have ever been inside. Shrouded in secrecy, the Bourse remains a hidden world that operates like a private members' club, with the security measures of the Bank of England.

With a lot of help, I finally managed to find someone working in the London Diamond Bourse willing to talk to me. My interviewee, a man called Harold, told me on the phone he had been connected to the institution since the 1940s. 'I'm eighty-nine now,' he said, 'so I only work three days a week. It's a social club for me, a way of life, it keeps me young, what else should I do? Wait around for the undertaker to arrive!'

On the day I had arranged to meet Harold, I walked into the

ground floor of the building and picked up a visitor's pass at the front desk. After answering various security questions, I passed through the metal detector and electronic, solid-steel turnstile gates, before waiting for the lift. A number of Orthodox Jewish men, in black suits and trilby hats, walked past, eyeing me suspiciously before I turned towards them, showing my pass.

Security in the street as a whole has tightened over the last few years, partly in response to a heist that occurred in 2003, when diamonds and jewels worth over £1.5 million were stolen from safe-deposit boxes in the basement of another building. The robbery shook the Hatton Garden community to the core, as at first it appeared to have been conducted by a Jewish diamond dealer. The imposter, who went by the names of Goldberg and Ruben, spent months integrating himself into the Orthodox Jewish diamond community, opening up safe-deposit boxes, dressing and acting like the other dealers, slowly gaining their trust until they began to deal with him, buying and selling stones.

One Saturday morning, when the rest of the religious Jewish community of Hatton Garden were at home or attending synagogue, this man entered the building and went down to the safe-deposit boxes in the basement. CCTV footage shows him calmly leaving the vault shortly afterwards, carrying a large black holdall. The robbery was not discovered until the Monday morning when a customer found his strongbox glued shut.

While extremely uncommon there have been historical incidences of crimes like this one. On 21 September 1854, the *Westminster Budget* reported that an 'elegant young man of thirty, with Bond Street references', a dark moustache and a slightly foreign accent, wearing 'lavender kid gloves and other well-fitting appurtenances of civilization', took an office at 70 Hatton Garden, posing as an 'eminently respectable diamond merchant' by the name of T. C. Morris and slowly became an accepted part of the community. Spyzer, a well-known Hatton Garden diamond dealer, visited Morris's office to show him a large batch of stones he had recently acquired in Amsterdam. As soon as the gems had been laid out on the table Spyzer received a heavy blow to the head and awoke shortly afterwards to the strong smell of chloroform. The stones had disappeared, along with T. C. Morris.

Most of the shops along the street have experienced a robbery of some sort. An uncle of mine was held up inside his premises with a gun to his head some years ago. My parents endured a terrifying attack when masked men ran into their shop shouting and screaming before jumping on to the counters, wielding huge sledge-hammers, which they unsuccessfully attempted to smash through the bulletproof-glass tops.

Alongside many other hidden security measures, shop owners, others in the jewellery trade and members of the diamond community have come together in the last few years and hired private security guards, who continuously patrol the street and the area. Rumoured to be ex-SAS, the six-foot-tall musclemen, with their black woollen hats, big boots and large puffa jackets, are deliberately conspicuous. Since they arrived on the street robberies are down, and smash-and-grab crimes have practically disappeared. A network of constant electronic contact exists now between the guards, the shops, the trading floors, vaults and workshops. Anyone or anything looks out of place and everyone in the Garden will know about it in seconds.

Michael, the jewellery repairer, had told me photographs of members of the Diamond Bourse are pasted on the walls. If you are not recognized and do not have an appointment, you will be quickly ejected from the building. As I pressed the lift and made my way up to the trading floor, I was aware all the time of my image appearing on multiple CCTV screens in another part of the building.

Exiting the lift, I walked along a narrow, carpeted corridor with many locked doors coming off it. A thin pale man, with a beard and curled sidelocks, wearing a long black coat and large furry hat, sped hurriedly past, eyeing me quickly up and down as he spoke in rapid Yiddish into a mobile phone held tightly against his ear.

I pressed the intercom at the end of the corridor and a pair of heavy, double doors opened and I stepped into a brightly lit,

sterile-looking anteroom. A few white tables were scattered around, surrounded by straight-backed pale leather chairs. The floor was tiled and smelled faintly of antiseptic. The walls were painted white and decorated with a single poster, with the words YOU ARE BEING WATCHED printed on to it in bold red letters. A couple of dark-suited men, wearing *yarmulkes*, sat huddled together in a corner, talking to each other in Hebrew.

Sitting behind a desk protected by thick bulletproof glass was an elderly male receptionist. I showed him my visitor's pass, while looking directly into the video camera behind him at his request, before telling him the purpose of my visit. 'Harold Karton to reception, Harold Karton to reception,' said the man, leaning forward towards the microphone on a stand in front of him. A few minutes later, another door buzzed open and a very tall dapper-looking older man, in a stylish light grey suit, came up to the reception desk, then dramatically bent over double and kissed me on the hand. 'Lichtenstein, eh?' he said smiling. 'Bloody foreigner.' Winking at me he turned towards his friend at the reception desk and drawled, 'A bridal suite I think for us,' before giving me a sly grin. 'Follow me, Lichtenstein,' he said flirtatiously, as he swiped his card against a flashing red light beside the door he had just entered through.

The heavy door swung open for a few seconds and Harold led me briskly along another carpeted corridor, walking quickly past a huge window, which looked directly on to the trading floor. I just had time to see rows of white desks, all brightly lit by large over-head lights, where diamonds and jewels were exchanged across tables by dealers and brokers from all over the world. The place looked empty when I passed but I could imagine it on a busy after-noon, with dealers sitting opposite each other, trading loudly in many languages, making me think of the scene inside a *yeshiva* I had once visited in Jerusalem, where study partners argued points of Torah and Talmud across a table, as a way of learning and discuss-ing scripture.

I had entered the inner sanctum of the Diamond Bourse, one of the most secure buildings in the whole metropolis, but was not allowed on to the trading floor itself. 'The rules are very strict,' said Harold, 'no visitors in there.'

He led me into a small side room and sat down behind the desk that took up most of the space, leaving just enough room for two swivel chairs. Looking at me intently, through heavy-lidded red-rimmed eyes, he told me he had many stories to tell, but could not divulge the most interesting, in case of the consequences. He smiled impishly but his conversation was guarded. 'Your reputation is everything here and it takes a lifetime to build.'

He described a typical working day at the Bourse: checking his post, making phone calls to jewellers and shops, looking through his stock, asking the other dealers for anything he couldn't get hold of himself. 'I make a lot of calls as the day passes. Much of the time I will meet with buyers who come here to purchase a particular type of stone. If I don't have it I know who specializes in it and go and speak to them and try to sell it on. Also people manufacture jewellery here, you know who does what, the top end of the market or the bottom end. You know who to trade with, you know who specializes in a particular thing. I spend a lot of time here talking with other dealers. There is great camaraderie – I have known most of them for ever; we are like family. I also spend an awful lot of time on the phone, talking to people internationally, selling and buying goods, which are then shipped off around the world. With the development of the Internet methods of trading are changing over the years.'

Picking up a chart from the table he explained that about 100 years ago the Americans introduced scientific grading of diamonds. 'The finest diamonds are completely clear, and are graded as D colour, then in declining order all the way to Z. D to H are qualified as white, but by the time you reach H you are getting colouration in the diamond; K would be very brown or yellow. IF means "flawless", VVS2 "all gradations". In the Bourse we have this set of monthly tables, with the international price of diamonds. Now you can buy them by the grade, like you might buy pork bellies or oil, without even seeing them. So I think the combination of the Internet and buying diamonds in this way is bringing about a change in the way the business is run. I expect there will be a decline in the importance of bourses.'

Reluctant to tell me more about the daily workings of the Bourse, Harold gave a detailed account of how he started his long career in the diamond business: 'In 1936 I became an apprentice diamond mounter for a firm in Charterhouse Street, which had been founded in the early 1900s by a Russian émigré, who had served as an apprentice to Fabergé. The boss seemed to think he was still living under the Tsar and that we were his serfs, the style of management was incredibly strict. I was only fourteen and not very good at the job – standards were very high in those days. The firm made diamond-set earrings, bracelets, brooches and rings, we were all paid a pittance but the craftsmanship was far higher then than it is now. There were millions out of work at the time so the boss had a choice of people queuing up for the job; if you didn't like the way he ran things you'd be fired. My day started by taking the trolleybus from South Tottenham to Holborn. I arrived at the workshop by eight, clocked in and swept up, always being careful to examine the dust for gold, platinum or any precious stones that might have fallen on the floor. Then I cleaned the toilets, making sure plenty of old telephone directories had been torn up, which were used in place of toilet paper. After this, I made tea for the men and then started my errands: collecting metal from the bullion merchants, calling at the engravers and occasionally taking a taxi to Bond Street to deliver goods to the posh shops, always via the back door. After finishing these tasks I returned to the bench, which was circular, with enough room for seven. I sat next to a man called Frank, my mentor, who taught me the trade. At first I performed simple tasks, flattening metal to be mounted into jewellery, then later making the fittings. Eventually I learned how to make the actual pieces. There was another man sharing my workbench called Sydney, who was married, in his thirties with two children and had a house in Chingford. One Saturday he asked me over to his house for lunch. When I arrived I

discovered his wife and kids were visiting the grandparents. Sydney asked me to make myself at home then he popped upstairs and five minutes later came back down. The sight of him petrified me. He was only wearing a bra and panties. I was still very naive and never understood the jokes in the workshop. Without any comment he proceeded to serve lunch, which consisted of eggs and bacon. This was the first time I had eaten bacon as my mother kept a strict kosher home. I left shortly afterwards for the railway station and home, *virgo intacta*. I never told my mum.'

A natural storyteller, Harold continued with tales of his time spent working as a fitter in an aircraft factory during the Second World War before managing to blag his way into the Israeli army, telling them he had served in the Royal Artillery. In 1948 his wife and father tracked him down and, following a meeting with the commander, he was given an honourable discharge and returned to England.

By 1950 Harold was back in Hatton Garden working at a bench in a workshop making and repairing jewellery. 'A man came into the workshop once,' he said, his large eyes getting bigger as he leaned forward in his chair, 'and handed me a three-stone diamond ring which he removed from his finger. It was set in yellow gold and he wanted it reset in a white-gold mount. The next day I got to work and carefully pushed the diamonds out of the ring as they chip very easily. Then I soaked the stones in methylated spirits to clean them. Having removed the grime I examined the stones and to my horror they were paste. I phoned the owner and told him; he called me a liar and accused me of switching the stones. The next day I tore round to my solicitor who asked me where the man had bought the ring. "Haringey race track," I replied. "Go home and forget it," was his response. The owner called about his ring the next day and threatened to sue me, I told him to do so and never heard from him again. A rare example of a solicitor dispensing intelligent advice.'

He went on to tell me about the early days of the Bourse, which during his long time of working in the area had moved around a great deal. 'It started in Mrs Cohen's restaurant, dealing over the tables in Yiddish, which was the prominent language in Hatton Garden when I was young. It is used less now, although a number of the Orthodox dealers do still speak and conduct business in Yiddish. In the early days of the Bourse business felt more cautious. You had to make a walk with your goods from the restaurant to the safe-deposit facilities in Hatton Garden, and I did feel exposed. Dealing used to take place in other cafés as well as pubs and on street corners. All the dealers in rough diamonds operated from the Diamond Club, a separate institution, which opened earlier than the Bourse and was based further down the street at no. 87.

'In the 50s the Bourse moved to the other end of Hatton Garden, to the ground floor of no. 57, on the corner of Clerkenwell Road, near to the place where Hiriam Maxim had his machine-gun workshop. In 1960 it moved again to the first floor of a new building, at 32 Hatton Garden. By 1980 membership had grown to over 700 and there just wasn't enough space for everybody so in 1982 the London Diamond Bourse moved here, to the centre of Hatton Garden, where Gamages once was. It has been on this floor for about five years. In recent years the Diamond Club and the Bourse merged together and now operate from this building. Originally, in the 1940s to 1950s the Diamond Bourse members dealt with polished diamonds and the Club members were dealing with rough diamonds. They were two different branches of the trade. As the rough-diamond trade in London declined, there was less and less cutting and polishing here, but there were more merchants dealing in polished diamonds, precious stones and jewellery, and we welcomed all people involved in the jewellery business, mainly diamond people.

'This Diamond Bourse is a self-contained complex, with links to the bank and safe-deposit facilities in the basement so I can just go downstairs and deposit my goods at the end of the day. We don't sell directly to the public but cater for dealers in the Garden, buying and selling stones for them.

'New technology has improved security, with access cards needed

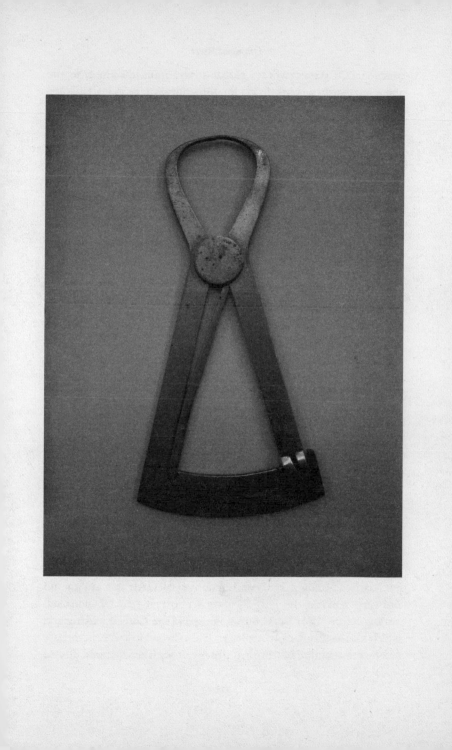

to enter, CCTV everywhere, guards on the door. It is a very secure and easy place to work from for those dealing in diamonds and other precious merchandise. In this building we are well protected: there is fantastic security here and many specialist facilities, like lettable suites, where people can talk privately and examine goods, before they strike a deal. Weighing machines, equipment to test the carat of gold, gauges to measure the size of diamonds are also available for members to use and there are always people around to show goods to, to get a second opinion from.'

Harold told me the primary function of the Bourse was 'to provide a place for dealers of rough and polished diamonds, precious stones and other jewellery items to trade with brokers, from here and abroad. If you join the London Diamond Bourse you instantly become an international member of the World Federation of Diamond Bourses. There are bourses all over the world – Antwerp, Israel, Russia, New York, Bangkok, Singapore, many other places – pretty much all run in the same way, with similar facilities and traditional ways of operating, although each one has its own history. When you visit these other bourses the atmosphere is very similar. The diamond community is very international but still predominantly Jewish. Circumstances over the years have driven Jewish people into the trade.

'Israel is now a major player in the industry. There are over 1,000 diamond companies in Ramat Gan in the Israel Diamond Exchange complex. There are also many Indian dealers with huge diamond offices in Mumbai, where a lot of manufacturing takes place now. Hong Kong, Singapore and Taiwan are more recent diamond-trading centres: a lot of polishing takes place there and manufacturing. Hardly any polishing or manufacturing happens in London now in comparison. New York and London are still important diamond-trading centres, London particularly for rough but Antwerp remains the world's most important general diamond-trading centre. The oldest bourse, known as the 'Club' is in Antwerp, which led the way for all the others. It also began in a café, in the late nineteenth century, before moving many times. The Diamond Bourse in Antwerp is now housed in grand premises on Pelikaanstraat.'

Harold then gave me a copy of a novel first published in 1944 called *Diamonds*, by Esther Kreitman, one of only a few female Yiddish writers of that period, who was the sister of the best-known Yiddish author of all time, Isaac Bashevis Singer. Born in Poland in 1891, Esther 'unwillingly entered an arranged marriage with a diamond cutter, Avrom Kreitman', states the introduction to the book by Heather Valencia, an academic with a special interest in Yiddish who translated the work into English. Professor Valencia thanks Harold in her introduction for his help with historical details and explains that Esther and Avrom were married in Berlin in 1912 before moving to Antwerp in 1914. The Germans invaded the city soon after and the family fled to London. Esther Kreitman based the novel on her own experiences and this little-known story beautifully describes the diamond quarters of both London and Antwerp during the First World War.

The novel begins in Antwerp, focusing on the life of a conceited, wealthy Jewish diamond dealer called Gedaliah Berman, who has his office in Pelikaanstraat and regularly visits the Bourse, which is described as a 'big hall' with 'massive gleaming pillars' where portly diamond merchants strolled around and dealers sat at tables:

> People were talking about everything and anything except business: they were discussing the city, or politics, making jokes and telling stories about mutual acquaintances. Then, as if it were just an afterthought, one of them would produce a parcel of stones. The rest would examine it. Someone else would take out a parcel. There would be a fiery flash, and then another pair of eyes would flash like the diamonds. A blue gleam, a trembling drop of water – and then there was an exchange of '*mazl un brokhe!*'.

At the beginning of the novel, before the German invasion, business is good. Berman sends out carefully selected brokers to distribute packets of his polished diamonds, sometimes he visits those that want to make a large purchase himself:

there were always plenty of people competing for a bargain. You had to look in the other merchant's eyes, and interpret a look or a gesture of his, which indicated he had something to sell. Then you had to be astute, greet each other in a friendly fashion, ask after his health, ask him why he hadn't been round, take his arm as good friends do, and saunter out of the Bourse together for a cup of coffee in a backstreet somewhere. Only then would real negotiations begin.

German troops invaded Belgium on 4 August 1914 and Britain entered the war soon after. On 6 October, when King Albert ordered the evacuation of Antwerp, most of the dealers fled to London, leaving everything behind apart from their stock and a few tools. Their arrival massively boosted the diamond trade in Hatton Garden. In the novel, Berman holds on in Antwerp for as long as he can, anxious about leaving his beautiful home behind. The Jewish quarter of the city empties out, the streets are deserted, as are the Bourse and the Diamond Club. In the smaller club known as the Shenkl:

> Bearded young men with worried expressions ran around like scalded cats, stopped at tables, showed each other tiny, rose-cut diamonds, about 100 to the carat, or rough diamonds, which looked like little pieces of greyish washing soda. They weighed them on small scales, wrapped them up again, talked and gestured with their hands, and swore by their wives and children. They tried to make deals, found they couldn't get the price they wanted, closed their cases and ran to the next table.

Kreitman could have been describing a scene in Hatton Garden today such is the timeless quality of the Jewish diamond trade. Eventually, Berman and his family follow the rest of the community to London, where they live for a while as homeless refugees in a Jewish temporary shelter in Shoreditch. As soon as he can Berman dresses himself 'in his smartest clothes in order to make his first visit to Hatton Garden', wearing 'his best frock coat with the silk lapels', a fine woollen overcoat with a velvet collar, brown leather gloves and a black silk umbrella, until he looked like a Jewish banker. He walks through the London streets, 'shrouded in thick black fog', before catching a tram and eventually arriving in Hatton Garden where he makes his way towards 'a grubby, square building, with unpainted walls, blackened slates, a window splashed with mud to more than half its height, and a crumbling, dirty, wet "kosher" sign: this café served as the Bourse. Berman couldn't believe his eyes.'

This fictional account hints that the London Diamond Bourse may have been operating much earlier than first believed, as the novel is set in 1914, although a note at the back of the book states that the Bourse did not in fact open until 1940. As the book was written around this period this seems a likely explanation although I am sure trading took place in similar kosher cafés around Hatton Garden for decades before the Bourse officially opened at Mrs Cohen's.

Harold thought the Diamond Club, for traders in rough stones, had operated from its premises at 87 Hatton Garden from about 1930 but believed it could be earlier.

During my research I came across a brief description of a place called the Diamond Merchants Club in Hatton Garden, which George R. Sims visited in the early 1900s while writing his great work, *Living London*. He described the institution as being located 'behind one of the most prosaic exteriors in this famous street', although he gives no further clue as to the building in which the club is based.

Before I left the Bourse I thanked Harold for his time and the loan of the novel and took a photograph of him sitting at the desk opposite me. 'I look like Godzilla,' he said dramatically, as I showed him the image on the digital screen of my camera. As he waved goodbye, after walking me down to the lift, he said with a wink, 'Don't forget, it might all be nonsense what I have told you – I'm partially senile anyway.'

20

Bleeding Heart Yard

There is a legend – and I give it as such – that this Sir Christopher Hatton married a beautiful gipsy girl, who bewitched him; and the price she had to pay, according to her compact with the Evil One, was her soul, and her body, after a given time. When that arrived, the Devil duly came for her, and seizing her, bore her aloft, and, whilst in the air, he rent her in pieces, and threw her still palpitating heart to the earth. Where it fell was, for years, known as Bleeding Heart Yard.

John Ashton, *The Fleet: Its River, Prison and Marriages*

Arriving early, to speak at a literary conference held at Queen Mary's College on the Mile End Road, I took a walk around the back of the campus, looking for the Old Velho Sephardi Cemetery, which Bill Fishman had told me about. Following the line of a time-worn brick wall, which stood out from the surrounding modern architecture, I soon found the ancient graveyard, the oldest Jewish cemetery in the UK. As crowds of young students walked past on the other side of the wall, making their way to lectures and cafés, I moved slowly around the flat, moss-covered tombs, trying to read the fading Hebrew inscriptions, some of which dated back to the seventeenth century.

Queen Mary's College felt like an appropriate location for me to talk about my previous book, *On Brick Lane*, which includes tales of the former Jewish East End and stories about my own grandparents, who once lived there. In the late 1930s, they had been regular visitors to the college building, when it was known as the People's Palace and housed a free educational and cultural centre for the local poor. By that time most of the Victorian facilities had disappeared but the large ballroom was still intact and well used by the Jewish community for concerts, Yiddish plays and dances.

During my lecture, in a hall next to the old ballroom, I mentioned my Hatton Garden project and, after the event, a smartly dressed older man, with glasses and a trim white beard, approached me and introduced himself as Dr David Parker, a literary historian, who had recently retired as curator of the Dickens Museum in Bloomsbury. He invited me to meet him for lunch at the Bleeding Heart Bistro in Bleeding Heart Yard, located directly behind Hatton Garden, to discuss Dickens and his long association with the area.

A week later, I opened the flimsy wicker gate that leads from Ely Place into the cobbled cul-de-sac of Bleeding Heart Yard and made my way across the courtyard, passing early-twentieth-century warehouses now home to architects, commercial photographers, web designers and jewellery suppliers. Spilling out of the bistro on to the pavement outside were tables and chairs, filled with people drinking, eating and smoking.

Inside, lunchtime service was in full swing: French-speaking waiters, dressed in black with long white aprons, sashayed around crowded tables, pouring wine, pointing out specials on a large blackboard, while swiftly laying out plates of rustic food on to deep-yellow tablecloths decorated with freshly cut flowers. Looking around the brightly painted room, I searched among the diners for Dr Parker, eventually seeing him sitting at a table in the far corner.

The amiable academic was in a good mood, enjoying his retirement; time with the grandchildren, walks in the countryside, holidays abroad. Although he still made regular visits to the Dickens Museum, where he had worked for over twenty years. Based in a Georgian terraced house in Doughty Street, on the fringes of Hatton Garden, the museum is the only one of Dickens's many former homes in London still standing. Dickens lived there from 1837 to 1839, with his wife, Catherine, and the eldest three of their ten children. Catherine's seventeen-year-old sister, Mary, was a constant visitor to that house and tragically died there. 'Dickens was heartbroken by her death,' said Dr Parker. 'A number of characters in Dickens's works seem to have been modelled on Mary, such as Little Nell in *The Old Curiosity Shop*. He finished the *Pickwick Papers* in Doughty Street and wrote *Oliver Twist* and *Nicholas Nickleby* there and the opening of *Barnaby Rudge*.'

Even after decades of working in the building, the thrill of being there on a daily basis never left Dr Parker. He marvelled at being able to touch Dickens's writing chair, handle the great writer's diaries, manuscripts, the porcelain china monkey the author kept on his desk, and other personal artefacts, photographs and relics.

Dr Parker talked at length about Dickens's knowledge of the streets surrounding Hatton Garden, which the writer knew well, having worked as a clerk in a solicitor's office in Holborn, off Gray's Inn Road, at the age of fifteen, before becoming a court reporter, then a journalist. In 1834 he had chambers in Furnival's Inn, which was knocked down and replaced by the Prudential Insurance Building, now a huge office complex near Holborn Circus.

Dr Parker imagined that during this time Dickens would have wandered into Hatton Garden: 'It would have been unlike him not to do so, he wrote about what he knew and explored the streets intensively in and around the places where he lived and worked.' In 1841 Dickens undoubtedly visited the street as Dr Parker told me his sister Letitia and her husband, Henry Austin, were living at no. 87 – a building that kept recurring in my research: as the former home of surgeon John Tauniton in 1821; the house where Sir Moses Montefiore lived in 1824; and the place which later housed the London Diamond Club. The original seventeenth-century building has since been entirely demolished and a modern brick-built block has replaced it, with flats above and two jewellery shops below.

Hatton Garden does feature in Dickens's work, particularly in *Oliver Twist* and *Little Dorrit*, although the street is also mentioned in *Bleak House* as the place where the Jellybys used to live and again when Phil Squod walks a beat 'round Saffron Hill, Hatton Garden, Clerkenwell, Smiffield and there – poor neighbourhood, where they uses up the kettles till they're past mending'. The most well-known

Dickensian Hatton Garden scenes take place in *Oliver Twist*, in the police court at no. 54, where Oliver is brought before the magistrate Mr Fang after being falsely accused of stealing Mr Brownlow's handkerchief. The character of Mr Fang is probably based upon a particularly harsh magistrate called Mr Laing who worked at the Hatton Garden police court from 1836 to 1838.

The police court was actually located at no. 52 and backed on to Hatton Yard. In the archives at the LMA there are plenty of nineteenth-century records documenting the real crimes of those detained at the Hatton Garden Police Office. The most commonly recorded were: rape, pickpocketing, stealing (often handkerchiefs), the possession of counterfeit coins, assault and vagrancy. Most of the names of those arrested were of Irish or Italian origin.

I told Dr Parker I had spoken to someone recently who believed Fagin was based on the Italian *padroni* living in Little Italy, who kept stables of boy pickpockets and beggars. 'When Dickens wrote *Oliver Twist*, there was a famous Jewish fence called Ikey Solomons, based in Spitalfields,' he replied. 'He was arrested, convicted and sentenced to penal transportation to Tasmania. There is widespread conviction that Fagin owes much to Ikey, all the more believable as there was a play called *Van Diemen's Land* (the original European name for the island of Tasmania) featuring Ikey Solomons, that Dickens would have seen. But he was interested in the growing Italian community and the Italian school. He was friendly with many prominent Italian refugees, including Mazzini and Emma Novello, and in 1838 he edited Joseph Grimaldi's memoirs. There are multiple references in his work to barrel organs – played chiefly by Italians – from *Sketches by Boz* to *The Mystery of Edwin Drood*. In *Little Dorrit*, he makes the most carefully crafted Italian character in all of his novels, Giovanni Baptista Cavalletto, who finds lodgings in Bleeding Heart Yard. Dickens seems to have located the fictional yard, within the topography of the novel, more or less where the actual yard is to be found in London.'

We began to talk about the etymology of Bleeding Heart Yard, a place of urban legend, associated with bloody and violent murder and the black arts. Most of the stories about the yard stem from 'The House-Warming!!: A Legend of Bleeding-Heart Yard'; a long, humorous Victorian poem, based on earlier myths and ghost stories, from a collection called *The Ingoldsby Legends* by R. H. Barham (aka Thomas Ingoldsby), first published in *Bentley's Miscellany* from 1837. The poem, set in the 1570s, begins with a description of Sir Christopher Hatton and goes on to describe his relationship with Queen Elizabeth I and his acquisition of Ely Palace. The story moves into the territory of folklore with the introduction of Alice Hatton, née Fanshawe, Sir Christopher's wife, who makes a pact with the Devil; a contract written in her own blood; her soul in return for social and financial standing. The Hattons quickly rise among the ranks in court; Christopher is knighted and soon after becomes Lord Chancellor. On the Eve of St John, the Hattons hold a house-warming party at their newly acquired mansion. The ballroom is packed full of important guests: the Earl of Leicester, William Shakespeare and other great dames, ladies, knights and gentlemen. At midnight, there is a knock at the door: 'a tall *Figurant* – ALL IN BLACK!!' enters and dances so wildly his toe breaks the top of a glass chandelier. 'With horrid black claws, / Like the short, sharp, strong nails of a Polar Bear's paws,' the 'coffee-faced' stranger grasps the hand of Lady Hatton, which becomes red hot and her arm shrivels up. She screams. The pair move around the ballroom at great speed, whirling and twirling past 'the girls in their curls, / And their rouge, and their feathers, and diamonds, and pearls.' Their frenetic performance ends in 'one grand pirouette', which reaches great heights from which they do not come down. A violent storm follows, lightning comes into the ballroom; the guests pour out of the house, 'calling, and bawling'; some dash 'down Holborn-hill into the valley', others do not 'pause to take breath till they get beyond Gray's Inn'. The following day, at Hatton House, the tapestries are blackened and scorched, the crockery all broken and in the roof, 'one very large hole in the shape of a hoof'.

The only trace left of Lady Hatton is a 'large bleeding human heart' found beside a pump in the courtyard of the mansion house.

The wooden handle of the pump is stained with blood and brains, as if someone's head 'with a very hard thump' had been smashed on top of it. The poem claims that sometimes, 'on a moonshiny night', the lady is still seen there, dressed in white, working away on the wooden pump. Different versions have appeared over the years. In one, night wanderers are warned not to use the pump in Bleeding Heart Yard at midnight, as blood will flow from it. In another, the ghost of Lady Elizabeth Hatton appears in the yard, clutching her chest, searching for the heart that had been ripped from her. The moral of the story: Lady Hatton's death is a form of magical retribution from the Church, who were 'robbed' of their property, Ely Palace, by the Hattons. The poem ends with a warning not to visit Bleeding Heart Yard at night, which is described as 'a dark, little, dirty, black, ill-looking square, / With queer people about'.

This fantastical story has become a kind of truth, with fragments of the tale seeping into historical accounts of the place and back again into mythology.

Rehashed many times over on the Internet is another version known as 'The Legend of Bleeding Heart Yard', set some fifty years after the Ingoldsby poem, on 26 January 1626, at Hatton House, on the night of the annual winter ball. The event is hosted by Lady Elizabeth Hatton, the daughter-in-law of the original Sir Christopher Hatton, a wealthy society beauty, who inherited the mansion after the death of Sir Christopher's nephew, William Hatton. During this telling, Lady Hatton spends the night of the ball dancing with a finely dressed, handsome stranger, thought to be the Spanish ambassador. At midnight, he whisks her out of the ballroom into the garden. She is never seen alive again. The next day, her body is found torn limb from limb, with her still-pumping heart lying beside it on the cobblestones of Bleeding Heart Yard. More gruesome tellings have her being ripped to pieces while still alive during the ball in front of her guests, by the Devil himself, who leaves her pumping bleeding heart at the scene.

Dickens discusses the naming of the place at length in *Little Dorrit*:

The opinion of the Yard was divided respecting the derivation of its name. The more practical of its inmates abided by the tradition of a murder; the gentler and more imaginative inhabitants, including the whole of the tender sex, were loyal to the legend of a young lady of former times closely imprisoned in her chamber by a cruel father for remaining true to her own true love, and refusing to marry the suitor he chose for her. The legend related how the young lady used to be seen up at her window behind the bars, murmuring a love-lorn song of which the burden was, 'Bleeding Heart, Bleeding Heart, bleeding away,' until she died. It was objected by the murderous party that this Refrain was notoriously the invention of a tambour-worker, a spinster and romantic, still lodging in the Yard. But, forasmuch as all favourite legends must be associated with the affec-tions, and as many more people fall in love than commit murder – which it may be hoped, howsoever bad we are, will continue until the end of the world to be the dispensation under which we shall live – the Bleeding Heart, Bleeding Heart, bleeding away story, car-ried the day by a great majority. Neither party would listen to the antiquaries who delivered learned lectures in the neighbourhood, showing the Bleeding Heart to have been the heraldic cognisance of the old family to whom the property had once belonged. And, con-sidering that the hour-glass they turned from year to year was filled with the earthiest and coarsest sand, the Bleeding Heart Yarders had reason enough for objecting to be despoiled of the one little golden grain of poetry that sparkled in it.

Thornbury believed the yard to be named after an ancient public house in Greville Street, called the Bleeding Heart, whose sign of a bleeding heart dated back to before the Reformation and repre-sented 'the five sorrowful mysteries of the Rosary – viz., the heart of the Holy Virgin pierced with five swords'. These mythic stories may have arisen after the Reformation, as a way of concealing the Catholic past of the area.

When I asked Dr Parker what he thought, he replied, with typical good humour, 'If there is any truth in the "Legend of Bleeding

Heart Yard" I couldn't say; but local taxi drivers think it is called Bleeding Heart Yard "'cause it's so bleedin' hard to find".'

On the corner of Bleeding Heart Yard and Greville Street today sits the Bleeding Heart Tavern, thought to be on the same site as the above-mentioned pub and the possible model for the place described in *Oliver Twist* as the Three Cripples, the haunt of Bill Sikes and Fagin, 'a low public-house, situated in the filthiest part of Little Saffron Hill; a dark and gloomy den, where a flaring gaslight burnt all day'.

As we sat and finished our meal the owners of the bistro, Robert and Robyn Wilson, came into the restaurant and made their way over to our table, greeting Dr Parker warmly before enthusiastically telling me how he had helped them acquire the premises we were sitting in: 'We were turned down for a licence to this place seven times,' said Robert, a tall, slender, elegant man who spoke with a light Scottish accent, 'mainly due to a single protestor from the Abstinence Society, so I called the Dickens House Museum to see if there was a genuine connection with Bleeding Heart Yard, hoping it might help our case. Dr Parker wrote a lengthy letter to the court, which stated that by opening the wine bar we would be reinventing the yard, which Dickens thought had a hint of ancient greatness about it. The guy from the Abstinence Society was there as always, complaining heavily that now we were trying to make spurious connections to Dickens. The magistrate looked at Dr Parker's letter and said to the man, "I happen to be a member of the Dickens Fellowship and if Dr Parker says there is a genuine connection to Dickens then I'm sure he knows more about it than you; licence granted."'

'We would not be here without the help of Dr Parker,' said Robyn, Robert's beautiful wife and business partner from New Zealand.

'Delighted to have helped,' said David, grinning. 'This place, when it first opened in 1983, became a special secret for those who knew about it. This was a time when the rest of the area was mainly industrial, with manufacturing workshops; there were a few cafés for workers in Hatton Garden but there were no wine bars, this was long before Clerkenwell and Farringdon became fashionable destinations. There was a very enthusiastic, select clientele who would come here, including senior executives who came with attractive young secretaries, a wonderful place for clandestine meetings. Most who heard about it could never find the place; you had to be taken by someone who knew. This area is such a hidden pocket, you have to dig deep to understand the place.'

21

Diamond Dealers

Hatton Garden itself is not more than a mile and a quarter in length but it is safe to say that within that few hundred yards are assembled all the great diamond merchants, the lesser men and the smaller dealers in precious stones. They look much like other businessmen. Only a quick ear for multitudinous languages and an eye for a rich assortment of name plates in office doorways would perceive the presence of the curious and glamorous traffic in diamonds.

John Pudney, *Hatton Garden*

Mr Weissbart is a Hatton Garden diamond dealer and a long-term member of the Bourse, who works from offices on the street. Now in his mid eighties, the small, gentle Orthodox man is a familiar face in the Garden, always dressed smartly in a dark suit, with a black *yarmulke* covering his balding head. I often see him walking along the road, shaking hands with everyone he meets. He is a respected member of the community, who has been supplying stones to the trade for over half a century.

I bumped into him in Hatton Garden recently and told him of my interest in the history of the street. He wanted to make sure I had covered all the stories: the Dickens connection, tales of Bleeding Heart Yard, Sir Christopher Hatton, the River Fleet, the seventeenth-century residential homes, which later became shops. He remembered a time when Hatton Garden had been 'an ordinary shopping street with a smattering of jewellery shops and other businesses connected to the trade, lots of offices, a tobacconist, restaurants, cafés and of course Gamages. After the First World

War Gamages slowly bought up all the houses along that stretch of Hatton Garden and Holborn but there was one house, he refused to sell, so they had to build around it. Eventually it went.' He even remembered my parents' shop when it had been a barber's.

He talked about the diamond industry, tales of dealers out on the streets, stones being strewn across tables in cafés, how relaxed everyone had once been. He talked for some time about the former London Diamond Club: 'It was a very closed place, only for dealers in non-polished, rough; they were nearly all Hasidic, there were offices on the ground floor and the Diamond Club was on the first and second floors. It was a large room, a bit like a cafeteria, with long wooden tables that would seat about twelve people, where dealing took place. Above the Diamond Club there was a synagogue for members and a kosher restaurant. As far as I know it started in the early 1940s when Belgium was invaded, the dealers who managed to escape from Antwerp came to London and started trading, and formed the Diamond Club, that's when the Hasidic traders arrived, others followed, nearly all the members there had family connections to each other. Before the war it was possible to get inside the Club but afterwards things changed: non-members were not permitted: they didn't like young people going in there.

'During the war many polishers and cutters came here from Belgium and taught us their secrets. There was no polishing of diamonds taking place in London before then, apart from maybe one company, based in Ely Place, who have been there since the First World War. At least 500 different diamond workers arrived in Hatton Garden during the war. Diamonds were a huge export then, they didn't need ships to move them – goods worth thousands of pounds could arrive in very small packages. They came from the colonies, from De Beers, who allocated the rough. The diamond business thrived here. Of course many working in the diamond industry were called up during the war, so there was a lot of movement within the factories.'

I asked him how he had come into the business and he began to talk about his early life, which, like that of so many of the older Jew-

ish men I had spoken to in Hatton Garden, had been marred by tragedy. His mother, born in the town of Auschwitz, into a Hasidic rabbinical family, left Poland and settled in East London in the 1920s.

She met his father there and they had a Hasidic wedding in a small *shtiebel* off the Commercial Road. When Mr Weissbart was born a few years later, the family moved to Berlin, but quite soon returned: 'I came to England in 1933,' he told me. 'I was eight years old, my father had been horribly beaten up in Germany, he wanted me to be safe, they couldn't get a visa, I moved in with my grandmother in Hessel Street. I never saw my parents again.' His grandmother had a shop there, selling eggs, butter and cheese. He described Hessel Street as 'a very lively Jewish area. When the war began, after the first air raid, the street emptied and it never became the same again. Of course during the war we had rationing until 1951. Things were very difficult. My grandmother was a widow, she worked hard, she didn't have it easy but she managed to find work for me when I left school. She knew one of the people who started the diamond-polishing factories and she arranged for me to start working there in 1941.'

The factory was located in Woodbridge House, Clerkenwell Green, on the top floor. There were fifty other workers, who were taught the trade by Jewish refugees from Antwerp. 'It was a nice atmosphere, with lots of Dutch and Flemish people; I was one of the few who wasn't Dutch but we mainly communicated in English. Quite a few of those trained after the war built up businesses of their own in diamond polishing. I was such a bad polisher I became a dealer!'

It was wartime when Mr Weissbart started working in the area and there were many air raids at night. He remembers that when he walked to work from the East End he would see firemen trying to put out the fires from the burning buildings. 'No. 32 Hatton Garden was bombed out – just a shell was left. Beside Gamages was another department store, which was completely destroyed. Holborn suffered greatly during the Blitz. Many properties were ruined and many people were killed. The area was aglow with fires at night. More people died in Holborn than any other part of the country.'

During and just before the war, the diamond business boomed in Hatton Garden; after the war, however, many of the polishers and factory owners returned to Antwerp and lots of people, including Mr Weissbart, lost their jobs. He became an independent diamond polisher, which was fine for a while until more of the diamond-polishing industry began to shift to Israel, the Far East, places with lower cost centres, in the 1950s. With the support of others in the community, he began trading in polished goods. The former treasurer of the Bourse helped him greatly: 'He was a lovely person, he used to live near me and drive me to Hatton Garden, we got on well together, he knew I was still a polisher and advised me how to buy, how to become a dealer: I went to Belgium and bought some stones and once he asked me what I had bought and he said he'd give me 2 per cent profit on the lot, apart from the small stones, and that's how I started out, building up the business from scratch.'

He met his Hungarian wife in London. She had moved to England after being liberated from a concentration camp at the age of ten. She came to work in the firm after their first child was born and now his two sons, who are much more Orthodox than he is, run the business, although he still comes in regularly and his wife does the books. 'We are now one of the longest-established diamond firms in the street,' he said proudly. 'We have been in Hatton Garden for

nearly sixty years. We stock diamonds from Israel, Antwerp, India and other places, with and without certificates. We sell emerald-, princess-, oval-, pear- and marquise-cut stones as well as old cuts, Edwardian and Victorian diamonds, which are used for repair work. We also have our own polishers on site. We sell to the retail shops, e-tailers, the trade, jewellers and designers. Members of the Bourse also buy from us. Some dealers joke that at times it is busier in our office than in the Bourse,' he said, smiling.

I remember visiting his office many years ago, when I was working as a runner for my parents. It was a little rickety old room in the back of a building, which you had to reach by cutting across a wobbly staircase and climbing up some other stairs. There appeared to be little security, just a few desks, with a couple of polishers perched at the back. Since then the company have moved to much bigger offices, with very tight security, new equipment and high-tech lighting.

Mr Weissbart invited me to come and see the new office, although I would have to tell him exactly when I was going to visit as only people they know will be admitted inside. Someone else in the trade took me there: the building was impossible to find, in a deliberately hidden location. Getting inside took some time, as I had to pass through a number of security measures: CCTV recognition, questioning, interlocking steel doors. Inside, the place was buzzing: a row of high, white Formica desks faced me as I entered, four Orthodox men, some with black hats, sat on stools, bent over brightly illuminated benches, inspecting stones, talking and trading in Hebrew. A large Hasidic man, with a long grey beard and an ample belly, wearing a black coat and a homburg, was waiting patiently on a chair for a space to free up at the bench. In a niche in the office, two men in blue overcoats stood at machines, visors down, polishing stones. A couple of young female secretaries sat at desks near by piled high with papers, typing away on computers. I found Mr Weissbart around the corner, sitting beside another desk, near to a microwave with a large sign stuck on the front, written in black marker pen on neon card: ONLY KOSHER FOOD IN HERE.

We spoke for some time about his long connection to the Diamond Bourse. He became a member in 1965, after going through a rigorous interview process: 'You have to be interviewed by a panel and be well known in the street, with at least one recommendation and at least one year's trading, to become a member. Your reputation is everything: you must have correct and honest behaviour.' On his resignation in 1980 the former treasurer of the Bourse knocked on Mr Weissbart's door and asked him to take over, so for the next fifteen years he looked after the finances: 'At that time we had nearly 500 members, individual diamond and coloured-stone dealers as well as other jewellery traders. The Bourse was such a bustling place then, with tables where people sat and looked at goods. Brokers would take the goods from the dealers and try and sell to other traders who had offices. Now it's a different business – there are only about 300 members today and only one or two rough-diamond dealers left, who deal in industrial rough not polished rough. Back then it was nearly all Jewish traders. Now members are more ethnically mixed. There are a lot of Muslim and Indian traders. Now the Bourse is a very international place.'

He became vice president of the Bourse for two years, then chairman, and retired from the committee in 1995 at the age of seventy. He is now a well-respected honorary member, part of the old guard, who has worked very hard to achieve the success he has had.

Luckily his great knowledge of the diamond trade has been passed on to his sons.

I wanted to meet with other diamond dealers to see if the tight-knit family set-up I saw at his office was repeated elsewhere. Through the Hatton Garden grapevine I was put in touch with another family-run diamond firm, working in Hatton Garden offices, who are unusual in that they have two women working as dealers in the business.

After the now-familiar security checks I entered a bright, airy office, which was considerably larger than any of the other diamond dealers' premises I had visited before. A slim woman, called Marsha, wearing heavy make-up, a crisp white shirt, black patent stilettos and a peach-coloured business suit, introduced me to the two other people in the room working at computer terminals. One of them was her boss, a Jewish man in his sixties, the other was his daughter, Samantha, another female diamond dealer, about my age, wearing jeans and a green V-necked jumper, who seemed keen to tell me about her experiences.

After graduating as a sculptor at the Slade School of Fine Art, Samantha had been unable to find a job, so ten years ago she began working in the family business. 'Most people in this industry will only employ family because you need to have someone in the business you can trust – an employee could walk off with all your stock. Family ties were my way in. I don't know a single woman working here who hasn't come in through family. Within the Orthodox community years ago, the only way women could work here was if their husbands died and they inherited the business.'

Marsha also entered the diamond industry via family, joining her father's diamond company in Holland thirty years ago. Unusually she started at the bench, beside master craftsmen, learning the arts of cutting and polishing. She cannot remember ever coming across any other women in the workshop at the time, either in Holland or later in London, where she started a diamond distribution company: 'I did all the sorting. We sent most of our stock on to the Far East. It was the days before the Gemological Institute of America began grading stones, so you really had to know what you were doing when you were sorting polished diamonds. I had lots of battles with all the men as they didn't trust women. I had to be firm. I was young, I stood my ground, I didn't think about it too much – it has made me tougher. I take no notice of a lot of things. There are still very few women in the business, which is strange as jewellery and diamonds seem to be such a female item. There are some female designers coming into it, but dealers, very few.'

She recognized it was difficult for women to work in the industry because of the restrictions imposed by the Jewish Orthodox religion, which mean observant Jewish men are not allowed to be alone in a room with a woman who is not their wife, or to shake hands with a woman, making business transactions difficult. 'These problems can be overcome,' said Samantha, 'but the men still like to deal with men. When I started at the Bourse one of the dealers said to me, "You know nothing – you should go and work in a bank." I had been doing this much longer than him; it was insulting. They would say, "Go ask your daddy what the dollar rate is," then I would tell them and they would elbow each other and say things like, "Look, a girl knows what the dollar rate is." They were incredibly sexist towards me at first. Being in the Bourse I watched young boys come into the business and other men would give them advice, help them out straight away, and that did not happen for me until I had been here for at least five years. I had to stand up to them and then, when they realized I knew what I was talking about, eventually I was accepted and taken seriously, but as women working in this business, we have had to prove ourselves twice as much as the men.'

Marsha recognizes the backward attitudes of some of the men she has to deal with but feels it has made her better at what she does: 'I can't have any doubt in my product or my knowledge, or I will be undermined straight away. I have had to be incredibly strong, and if I took offence at what was said to me I would be upset all day long.'

'They will try and trick you or catch you out,' said Samantha, 'try and sell you a cubic or expose you in some way, it is very challenging but I have learned a lot faster because you have to to survive. I visited the Bourse in Tel Aviv a few years ago for the first time and I couldn't believe it: there were so many women in the trade there, strong, respected, powerful businesswomen.'

'There were a few women working in the Bourse in Hatton Garden when I started,' said Marsha. 'Scary Margaret Thatcher types, terrifying, very strong and tough, there are a couple here older than me but no more than that; Samantha is the youngest.'

Sadly both women felt there were fewer rather than more opportunities for women to come into the trade now, not because of gender issues but because the business as a whole has shrunk over the last few years because of the worldwide recession. 'Some family businesses have sold up after not seeing a long-term future in diamonds,' said Marsha. 'People have died off, some went into property, the economic climate is changing everything and people don't spend the money they used to on gifts, bracelets, necklaces. Now most of our business is for diamonds for engagement rings. Hatton Garden used to be the busiest, hubbiest place; you used to walk along the pavement and it was packed full of people coming to buy jewellery but now there are less people around. But there is still a strong sense of a community here, between the Bourse, the workshops, the shops, all aspects of the trade. You get to know everyone in the Garden, chat to people every day, it is an amazing place to work and Hatton Garden is still very much the centre for manufacturing and the biggest cluster of jewellery shops in the country. You can of course buy stuff on the Internet but people like to come to Hatton Garden to have a real experience.'

'People do want to help each other here,' said Samantha. 'You might want to win the deal but relationships are long term, we are part of a community, we all need to support each other.'

We spoke for a while about the Bourse, which they both felt functioned primarily as cheap office space now with great security and facilities. 'Deals do take place there internally but not how they used to,' said Marsha. 'The London Diamond Bourse used to be a place where people showed and traded diamonds but now they are certificated the business has changed. We mainly have to find customers who need them, like the shops on Hatton Garden. In the UK the Bourse seems to be a dying thing, the Antwerp Bourse is much busier but in Tel Aviv it is a very vibrant market, possibly the only real functioning bourse left in the world, the others have ceased to be an exchange any more, because the diamond business has mainly gone to offices.'

Marsha introduced me to another company, who deal in rare and fancy, coloured diamonds, from extensive offices off Hatton Garden. They are not located in the Diamond Bourse building although they are members; and, unusually, they are not a Jewish-run company either. As I waited in the foyer of the office for one of the company directors to finish a phone call, I sat and talked with Angela, the secretary, who has worked for the company for the last twenty-seven years. 'It's like being part of a family working here,' said the lady, who described herself as the only black woman in the Hatton Garden diamond industry. She knows most of the other women working in the business; the saleswomen in the shops, the diamond brokers, some designers, diamond setters, lots of female secretaries like herself, who work hidden away behind closed doors for small family firms, organizing the travel, meetings, business and personal arrangements for their male bosses. About twenty-five years ago she started a secretaries' club, to meet these other women, by putting an advert in a free magazine. 'Four people turned up to the first meeting, seventeen to the next and now there are over fifty of us. We have developed a strong network and we are very supportive of each other, while remaining extremely private about the business of the people we work for. We have many stories between us, some women have had very difficult times here, either being unfairly dismissed or their ideas are taken and they are never rewarded for it, some have sued and there have been issues. Not all bosses are good bosses and you are often working for one family. Although we are highly thought of we are still secretaries and will always be the outsiders.' Angela told me she was happy in her job, the company she works for had been good to her. 'The secretaries represent a different story of Hatton Garden, one few people ever get to see, we keep the whole thing functioning, we deliberately network with each other. Women have a need to do this.'

She spoke for some time about Hatton Garden, the friendly

atmosphere, the glamour, the romance of the street: 'I love working here. It is an exciting trade to be in, handling these incredible
stones. Women will always love diamonds. Some of the most
famous diamonds in the world have been cut and polished here.
Every day is different for me. I visit the workshops where we have
our jewellery made up, I know the people there very well; we have
been going to the same places for a lifetime, the same old boys are
still there. Sometimes I go to meetings, auction evenings, to the
Bourse to collect or deliver goods. I do not trade. Clients may leave
stones with me and I often visit the shops. There are more women
than men working in the shops now, which has changed since I
started working here, and there are more places to go in Hatton
Garden now, it is livelier and security has improved tenfold. I don't
know why there are not more black people working here; there are
many Asian and Indian women here now. Even in the jewellery
magazines you never seem to see black models wearing diamonds,
which of course is strange as they would stand out so much better
on a darker skin.' She picked up a random jewellery magazine and
flicked through it, looking at the models inside to demonstrate her
point. 'Hang on, here is a black model,' she said with surprise,
before realizing it was in fact a white woman whose skin had been
darkened with make-up.

The door behind us opened, and Angela disappeared for a while
into another office. 'He can speak to you now,' she said, 'go through.'
A tall, well-spoken white man, who I imagined to be in his early fif-
ties, wearing an open-necked pink shirt and dark trousers, sat at a
desk in a clean, bright office and introduced himself as Richard
Vainer. On a wall behind him was a large map of the world, beside
him an open safe, stacked with black leather boxes. He explained to
me that his father, Milosh Vainer, who he referred to as 'a legend in
the rough-diamond business', had been a political refugee from an
old aristocratic Czech family: 'He came to London escaping the
Russians, just as the Iron Curtain came down. En route to Canada
to start a new life and complete his law studies he, by chance, while
playing a game of bridge, met Harry Oppenheimer, who at the

time was head of De Beers, the legendary diamond company. My father was then invited into the business, soon becoming in charge of all outside buying for De Beers, not bad for a Czech refugee.

'In 1964 he left, at that time the most senior executive of De Beers to ever do so, and began the family company, which specialized in cutting rough diamonds. With his background in rough diamonds he was subsequently approached to provide valuations to the government of Botswana. This spawned a whole new industry within the diamond business and he was soon providing valuation and consultancy services for many of the major producer countries and mining companies.'

Their business, although still international, is now based in the Garden. Milosh died in 2007 and his sons have since taken over the company. Richard described himself as a diamantaire; being a member of a diamond family, established in the upper echelons of the international diamond world, and a considerable expert in coloured stones. He opened one of the boxes from inside the safe, which was filled with one-, two- and three-carat-plus pinks, blues and yellows. Over the years the family has bought stones from different mines all round the world, building up a collection of some of the most unusual and rare coloured diamonds in existence. Currently very fashionable with celebrities, these coloured diamonds have recently increased in value and business is booming.

'We have an international private clientele who come to us. Most are not British – the society here is not attached to buying high-value items, such as diamonds, for their women to wear. They spend their money on art or a new roof for their country house instead! Other countries and cultures are happily far more enthusiastic.'

He also spoke of the old ways, the handshake, the *mazel*, the traditional values, which he felt were disappearing along with the trust. 'We are very careful who we deal with; we only sell to established clients.'

Their company is one of the last left in the UK to deal in rough diamonds, which are cut and polished at their in-house workshop

by experts, one of whom has been working in the business for over forty years. He explained the process: 'The rough stones will be studied for a long time, to determine the best shape they could be cut into, then a resin mould will be made, which they mark with permanent pen, showing where to make the cuts. After this careful planning stage the rough diamonds are then either cleaved or cut using diamond-tipped saws, which in itself is an incredibly skilled art. Then they are shaped in numerous stages of polishing, starting with the facets being cut on to the diamond; and then the final polishing is performed, which takes a long time, as very fine layers from the surface of the stone are gently worn down by diamond-encrusted polishing wheels. Sadly this workshop is one of the last polishing workshops in the UK; this small family company has polished three of the largest-known diamonds, each over 100 carats!'

He showed me pictures in a book of some famous diamonds, some of which had been cut and polished on the premises, including a large, fancy, yellow octahedral rough diamond, which was cut into a briolette, an elongated pear-shaped cut with triangular facets, one of the oldest diamond cuts in the history of gem-cutting, having first been developed in India at least eight centuries ago. The resulting Vainer Briolette Diamond weighed 116.6 carats and was in 1984 the second-largest briolette-cut diamond in the world. The stone has 192 facets and was certificated by the GIA as having perfect polish and symmetry.

As Marsha had already mentioned, Richard told me there used to be many more individual family diamond firms in Hatton Garden but their numbers had reduced over the last couple of decades 'as sons went off and worked in the City'. The business, he said: 'is now more elderly than it used to be, there are far fewer hands for a diamond to pass through and small businesses like ours are the cracks within the paving stones. We are no longer masters of our own destiny, we just pick up the crumbs left by the big corporations. The diamond business used to be like a big tree with lots of branches and now there are only a few big branches. As rough are sold straight from the mines to the big companies and from there into their own

shops, we are being squeezed out. Luckily for us, we work in a very specialized area, which is how we have survived. I don't know how those dealing in white goods manage to make a profit in the age of the Internet, which has turned white diamonds into a commodity.'

Although a long-standing member of the Bourse, with his background Mr Vainer has never really been involved in the Jewish community or Bourse politics: 'Business does go on there between the backgammon playing, the share dealing and the property speculation, but London is a backwater in the diamond business, sadly, and with the Internet, computers, mobile phones and quick shipping the reason for having the Bourse is fading. I wonder if it will still be here ten years from now.'

22

River of Wells

There had been a time when the foul Fleet of Pope, Gay and Swift
was a clear river, taking its rise in the springs of Caen Wood, and
flowing down through Kentish Town; always turbid on account of its
Fleet current, and given to flooding its banks, for which riotous conduct,
however, much blame was attached to the River of Wells, a branch of
which rose at Holborn Bars and rushed with the force of a torrent
down Oldbourne, or Hilbourne, and swelled the waters of the
northern stream at Oldbourne bridge.

Henry Barton Baker, *Stories of the Streets of London*

John Stow states that the Oldborne rose 'where now the Bars do
stand', ran down to Old Borne Bridge and then into the River of
Wells or Turnmill Brook. The lower course of the River Fleet, as it
passed through Clerkenwell and out into the Thames at Blackfriars,
was often known as the River of Wells, which according to Stow
had been formed by: 'Clerken well and other nearby wels, along
with the Horse Pool in Smithfield' all uniting 'their streams'. William Pinks believed that Holeburne, or 'burne of the hollow', was
the name of the river as it ran through Clerkenwell down to Holborn Bridge and thereafter it was called the Fleet, although other
historians disagree. Walter Thornbury often refers to this section of
the river as the 'Fleet Ditch'.

Thornbury discusses the various names for the River Fleet, which
he calls an 'ill used stream' once 'fresh and fleet', which by the
seventeenth century had become little more than a 'sluggish and
plague breeding sewer'. Eventually the Fleet became impassable

and by the nineteenth century it had been entirely culverted underground. The only visible remains of this once-great waterway, London's largest lost river, are now found near to the ponds at Hampstead Heath and deep beneath the city streets, flowing in the Victorian brick tunnels of Joseph Bazalgette's brilliantly designed sewage system.

Adele Leffman had told me she had visited the Bazalgette sewers in Paris, which she described as 'grand, cathedral-like spaces, with exquisite brickwork and high, vaulted ceilings lit by chandeliers'. She went there to see a classical concert below ground: 'It was extraordinary – there were alcoves housing fascinating artefacts, and a complete absence of any smell.'

I wanted to explore the tunnels below Farringdon Road, to see the subterranean river for myself, but had been told the trip would be too dangerous. 'The Fleet is tidal,' said an official of Thames Water when I telephoned to enquire. 'We cannot risk the public going down there, you'd be wallowing in raw sewage up to your neck and there is a real risk of drowning as water levels rise. The tunnel now functions as a storm drain and if the tide is high you could be completely submerged.'

On the Internet there are accounts of illegal explorations to the underground sewers. Sub-Urban, an anonymous group of psychogeographers, managed a clandestine visit to the submerged river, which they later blogged about online. After months of planning, a small group jumped down a manhole at night and ventured into the murky, rat-infested waters beneath, armed with torches and maps. They described the atmosphere underground as 'heavy' and at points 'unbearable'. Hours of wading through slippery, low tunnels, up to their chests in thick sewage, almost ended in disaster when one of their party fell and was nearly swept away by the fast-flowing water. They posted some beautiful photographs on their website, documenting their adventure; atmospheric images of cavernous chambers and waterlogged brick tunnels flooded by torchlight.

Surfing around for someone with expert historical knowledge of this lost river and its effect on the development of the area around Hatton Garden, I came across the name of Diana Clements, a geologist currently working in the Palaeontology Department of the Natural History Museum who curated an exhibition some years ago called 'Beneath Our Feet: In Search of Lost Rivers', which included a large section on the Fleet. After we communicated by email, Diana invited me to a Palaeontology Open Day at the museum, where she would be exhibiting some fossils, maps and other information about the geology of London, along with a collection of material about her researches into the Fleet.

Passing through the dinosaur galleries, I made my way to the concourse outside the Flett Theatre where Diana had told me to meet her. Sitting on the floor, in front of an exhibit, was a slight woman, wearing a long tartan skirt and a polo-neck jumper, showing some fossils to a school group. A curtain of long brown hair completely obscured her face as she bent double over the ancient rocks on the carpet. I heard her tell the class, in a firm, educated voice, that they were looking at the entombed remains of a tropical plant, over 100 million years old. The children gazed at the woman in wonder as she told stories about a time when the land where London now sits had been submerged under warm seas.

Spread out on a table behind her were examples of the different rocks and strata that lay under the city: the iron-rich pebbly sand called the Bagshot Beds, found on top of Hampstead Heath; the finer, sandier Claygate Beds; and a hard wad of London Clay, extracted from Holloway Road after being deposited there millions of years ago by tropical waters that once covered the city. 'Clay at depth is termed "blue" clay,' I read, 'but turns brown near the surface where it is oxidized.' Next to the golden chunk of clay were examples of the variable sands and clays that make up the Woolwich, Reading and Upnor Beds, and next to them sat a pot of silica – a sample of the geological layer known as the Thanet Sands. A lump of chalk formed from the crushed skeletons of tiny organisms represented the deepest layer under London. Beside this were some flinty-looking stones from the Thames Gravels, extracted from terraces on both sides of the river, remnants of melted glaciers from the Ice Ages.

Fossils from the museum's collections, retrieved from the London Clay, sat behind the rock samples: crabs and other crustaceans, gastropods and bivalves, along with shark's teeth, tropical plants and seeds. In the Regent's Canal Tunnel the vertebrae of a crocodile had been uncovered. A football-sized piece of Lambeth rock, embedded with fossils of shell horizons, lay next to petrified bones pulled from the Thames Gravels: a mammoth's tooth, a bison's jaw, the thigh bone of a Jurassic deer.

Above these were maps showing subdrift contours, buried channels and the tributaries of the Thames. Beside them, a number of other maps plotted the course of the Fleet in blue. Many of them were now familiar to me – the Agas, Rocque, Ogilby and Morgan maps – but there were some I had never seen before including a geological map with the River Fleet cutting through the Thames Gravels, carving out a deep valley, the London Clay exposed. There was also a map from the 1920s, with borehole details, evidence of the abundance of water and springs near the course of the now-underground river. I saw a contemporary survey by Thames Water, detailing the position of the eighteenth- and nineteenth-century sewer pipes, along with the original route of the river and the abandoned subterranean railway platforms. The depths of different pipes and outlets were marked in red ink. The map that interested me the most came from a microfiche at the Camden Archives and depicted a rare illustrative drawing, dated 1638, plotting the sites of the natural springs along the route of the Fleet: Sadler's Well, Clerk's Well, Skinner's Well, Todwell, Radwell and Horsepool in Smithfield.

As I stood examining this drawing Diana came up behind me and introduced herself. The geologist, who was older than she had first appeared squatting on the floor like a young girl, spent some time talking about her job at the museum and her passion for the stories behind London's lost rivers. Pointing to a spot near to the ponds on Hampstead Heath on one of the maps, she showed me the origin of the Fleet, arising from two streams, which she explained had been dammed to form ponds in the eighteenth century. 'The water comes out from the base of the permeable Bagshot Sands, and from between the less permeable Claygate Beds and the impermeable London Clay. When it reaches an impermeable layer, it takes on the line of least resistance and often appears at the surface as a line of springs, which are formed by falling rainwater percolating through the top layer of loose sand. Spring lines are a great aid to the geological mapper, particularly when trying to track the route of hidden water. At Hampstead Heath, if you walk down to the base of the gully, you will be able to see the trickle of water, which eventually becomes the Hampstead branch of the River Fleet, near the ancient Caen Wood. Plants on the route can help you find this spring line. There are usually plenty of water pepper plants and reeds near by and, in springtime, a profusion of yellow buttercups.'

She continued to plot the course of the river on the maps, tracing the faint wobbly blue line as it came out of the ponds before exiting the heath under Highgate Road, where it becomes subterranean. 'The remains of the culverted river continue to flow through the deep valley of Chetwynd Road and then it briefly comes above ground in a pipe, which runs over the railway to Burghley Road, before heading back down into the sewer system again to Kentish Town, King's Cross, Farringdon Road and then finally out into the Thames under Blackfriars Bridge. If you hang over the bridge at low tide, you can sometimes see the remains of the Fleet gushing out of the sewage outflow pipe into the Thames.'

Picking up a large red file off the table, she showed me other images she had gathered over the years about the Fleet. The first, a copy of a 1750 painting by Samuel Scott called *Entrance to the Fleet River*, depicted a place which looked more like Venice than London, with tall sailing barges, three abreast, moving freely from the Thames up the wide and navigable shipping lane of the former river. Stow wrote that the Fleet had once 'been of such breadth and depth, that 10 or 12 ships, with merchandise were able to come up to Holborn bridge together'. By the time he was writing his *Survey of London* in the sixteenth century, however, the river had become impassable to nautical traffic, 'filled with filth of the tanners and such others', and patrolled by pirates. Diana told me: 'Boats used to make their way from the Thames up to the docks by Holborn Bridge or Ludgate Circus, taking coal, wool, rocks and other goods into the city. The names of the streets around that area, like Old Seacoal and Stonecutter lanes, reflect the items that once arrived in the area by way of the Fleet. Archaeological investigations have uncovered the remains of a Roman ship near the mouth of the Fleet, filled with Kentish Ragstone, which they used to construct the wall around the city. This eighteenth-century painting is a highly romanticized impression of the river; in reality, by the time this painting was completed, the Fleet had been reduced to little more than an open sewer.'

An engraving from the seventeenth century showed bathers on grassy slopes beside the former river, resting after a swim in the once-clean waters near Battle Bridge, roughly where King's Cross Station is today. 'It is said that Boudicca fought a battle against the Romans there,' said Diana. 'The tooth of an elephant was found near by, along with a hand-axe, artefacts which were once thought to belong to the Iceni tribe but are in fact much earlier, from the Ice Ages. In the seventeenth century that area became a famous spa and tea garden called Bagnigge Wells, which developed around the natural spring there, whose iron-rich chalybeate waters were believed to have health-giving and medicinal properties.'

A humorous sketch of the bridge over the New Canal at Holborn, dated 1728, printed beside Alexander Pope's satirical poem *The Dunciad*, shows corpse-like naked bathers – a comment on the disease-infested waters of the river. Three bridges spanned the Fleet: one at the foot of Holborn Hill, another at the end of Fleet Street, and a third opposite Bridewell. Pope wrote: 'to where Fleet Ditch with disemboguing streams, Rolls the large tribute of dead dogs to the Thames'.

The New Canal, designed by Christopher Wren, built at great expense, was completed in 1680, with docks and wharves on either side, to allow boats to move between Ludgate Circus and Holborn

Bridge after this section of the river had become impassable. When the canal was being dug out Roman utensils, broken pottery and household goods were discovered buried under the thick mud along with objects from later periods – spearheads, keys, daggers and crucifixes, as well as bones, skulls and broken furniture – the domestic detritus of centuries. The seventeenth-century residents living beside the New Canal continued to throw discarded objects, food and human waste into the water, soon rendering this section of the river unuseable again. In 1737, after a drunken butcher fell into the river and drowned in the gloop, the New Canal was finally arched over and Fleet Market built on top of it, replacing the Old Stocks Market. Rocque's map of 1746 outlines the new market development, with its rows of shops on either side of a pedestrianized street. Diana showed me an eighteenth-century engraving of the market, with the sellers of fish, meat and vegetables gathered beside a central clock tower. The market was not a success however and after decades of neglect it was demolished in 1820 to make way for the new road of Farringdon Street and a smaller market building called Farringdon Market. Henry Mayhew visited in 1851, while conducting research for his extensive work of Victorian journalism, *London Labour and the London Poor*. He spoke to some of the watercress sellers there, girls as young as eight years old, who gathered on the cold stones before dawn with bunches of fresh cresses from the country. Dressed in rags, barefoot and freezing, these children could only hope to earn at most a few pence from their day's hard labour. Mayhew concluded that 'in no place in all London is the virtue of the humblest – both young and old – so conspicuous as amongst the watercress buyers at Farringdon Market'.

Diana also showed me a number of engravings of the notorious Fleet Prison, which stood on the eastern banks of the Fleet near the market site. Erected in 1197, the building burned to the ground several times and was rebuilt, before finally being pulled down in 1846 after being used for 649 years as a prison. Unimaginable pain and suffering were endured there, from torture during the Inquisition to hangings and burnings in the medieval period. During the eighteenth century it became a debtors' prison, where the mad, diseased and violent were locked up together with those who could not pay their bills. Dickens had Mr Pickwick imprisoned there and Plate 7 of Hogarth's series *A Rake's Progress* shows aristocratic gambler Tom Rackwell incarcerated in the Fleet Prison with lunatics after losing all his money during a card game.

Everything at the prison had its price, from the cost of the cells to the food and drink consumed there. Prisoners who could not pay for their keep were allowed to beg at an open grate, which faced the street. Corrupt guards forced new arrivals to pay an additional fee, to avoid being locked up underground in the damp, disease-ridden dungeons known as 'Bartholomew Fair' after the wild annual celebrations that took place in the churchyard of St Bartholomew's Church, mentioned earlier. Noxious gases from the polluted river beside the prison filled the subterranean cells with infected air and most prisoners soon developed 'grievous maladies'. The life expectancy of the poor who entered the Fleet Prison was unsurprisingly short.

During the seventeenth century a strange loophole in the law allowed those who wanted to wed quickly or in secret to do so in the Fleet Prison, where, according to Thornbury, 'degraded clergymen could easily be found among the herd of debtors to perform the ceremony'. Tens of thousands of Fleet marriages took place until the Lord Chancellor passed 'An Act for the better preventing of Clandestine Marriages' in 1753.

An engraving in Diana's file from Thornbury's *Old and New London* showed the Fleet Ditch in 1844, where it ran beside the slums of Saffron Hill. By then the river had become little more than a narrow waterway, with pipes from the crumbling tenements near by pouring household and human waste directly into the water. Thornbury describes it as a 'foul stream' around which were 'gathered a maze of narrow streets, courts and alleys, in which lived the most desperate characters of the metropolis'.

The last images in Diana's folder were photographs from the early 1900s, of workers standing inside the sewers in waders, water up to their knees, holding gas lamps that illuminated the intricate Victorian brickwork of Bazalgette's underground tunnels. I asked Diana if she had ever managed to visit the tunnels herself and she told me she had

not though she would be keen to do so. I then asked her if she would be willing to guide me above ground, mapping the course of the river from Clerkenwell to Holborn, and she generously agreed.

On one of the coldest December days on record we met outside Farringdon Station. Dark clouds, heavy with snow, filled the sky. Diana arrived promptly, dressed in a long black coat and a large Russian-looking fur-trimmed hat. On her back was a rucksack, filled with files, books and maps. Stepping out of the station we made our way towards a billboard attached to the hoarding opposite, erected to protect the gigantic building site below it.

A computer-generated image of the new Crossrail Station showed a steel-and-glass interior, an environmentally friendly green roof and multiple escalators connecting platforms and passengers to Heathrow and Gatwick airports, Maidenhead and Brighton. When finished, the huge new terminus will have over 140 trains an hour passing through it. Farringdon itself will undoubtedly 're-emerge as a destination', as the website for Crossrail vision boasts (fuelling my suspicion that the nearby Smithfield Market is earmarked either for demolition or complete regeneration as some kind of major tourist site).

Crossrail is supported by the Mayor of London and is currently Europe's largest civil-engineering construction project. One of Boris Johnson's wilder ideas is to uncover sections of the buried Fleet for Londoners to use again for recreational purposes: the hidden city revealed. The opening of an ornamental version of the Fleet for tourists is unlikely to happen: 'These underground tunnels are still heavily used as a sewage outlet and storm-relief drains,' said Diana, unfolding a map from her bag. 'This stuff still needs to go somewhere otherwise we would be back to the days of the Big Stink again.'

By peering through a small viewing window in the hoarding, next to a sign saying DANGER DEEP EXCAVATIONS, we could see down to the railway tracks far beneath the level of the street. Diana pointed to a large pipe, which had been temporarily exposed during the building works, and predicted that the Fleet could be accidentally uncovered again, for the first time in over a century, during these developments for Crossrail. I had recently read, in *A Short Guide to the Fleet River* (1955) by Ellic Howe, that in 1862, just before the opening of the Metropolitan Railway from Farringdon to Paddington, the waters in the Fleet sewer undermined the foundations of the railway embankment near Coppice Street in Clerkenwell and the sides caved in, exposing the river.

Diana's map revealed the location of Bazalgette's tunnels, deep underground, carrying the waste of the metropolis away to outfall sewers and treatment works well beyond London. Crossing the Northern High Level, Middle Level and Low Level Northern sewer tunnels were three of London's subterranean rivers: the Westbourne, the Tyburn and the Fleet. She told me: 'The Fleet itself has since been diverted into these sewers, which were built at great heights, to allow for flash flooding. When this happens, the tunnels fill up and the water flows out into the Thames, stopping the city from becoming submerged.'

I asked Diana if she knew anything about the wharf that allegedly once stood here during the time of the Knights Hospitaller, and was believed to have been shared by the priory and St Bartholomew's Hospital, allowing goods and people to be ferried up the Fleet from the Thames. Diana thought the Fleet could only ever have been navigable by boat from Blackfriars to Holborn Bridge but added that there are so few documents in existence from the twelfth century it is impossible to be certain. I loved the idea that the site now being developed as one of the most advanced new railway terminuses in the world had once been a wharf where warrior monks and other passengers alighted into the area, hundreds of years ago, from all over the world. Thornbury believed 'the river was no doubt navigable, ages ago, much further than Holborn Bridge'. Ellic Howe imagined this section of the Fleet had been used in the thirteenth century to bring stones, wine, hay and other supplies up from the Thames to St Bartholomew's and the Fleet Prison.

Before we moved on, Diana directed my gaze up beyond Farringdon Road to the steep incline of Greville Street, noting how the contours of the area, the continuous sloping gradients on either side of the former river, show the deep valley that has been carved out of the Thames Gravels by the Fleet. She asked me to observe the street names in the area, many of which still have an aquatic, herbal or horticultural ring to them and are located near to the original course of the river. Memory traces abound.

Following a similar route to the walk I had taken a few months earlier with Adele, we made our way to the corner of Cowcross and Turnmill streets, where Diana imagined herds of cows and flocks of poultry being driven across the bridge to market. Droves of turkeys and geese once arrived at Smithfield from as far afield as Norfolk and Suffolk, wearing little cloth shoes to protect their delicate webbed feet on the eighty-mile journey.

As we walked along Turnmill Street, Diana read a quote from William Fitzstephen, who described the area in the twelfth century as 'a delightful plain of meadowland, interspersed with flowing streams, on which stand mills, whose clack is very pleasing to the ear'. She told me that a tributary of the Fleet, called Turnmill Brook, once ran alongside Turnmill Street after being especially diverted to turn the mills along the banks of the river.

'After the Dissolution, the mills here were used for other industries,' said Diana, 'which spilled over from the market area.' In Pinks's 1881 *History of Clerkenwell* he mentions an advertisement in the *Daily Courant* of 1741, for a house to let in Bowling Alley, Turnmill Street, 'with a common sewer, with a good stream and current, "that will turn a mill to grind hair-powder or liquorish, and other things"'.

We crossed Clerkenwell Road and stood for a while on the other side, struggling to keep warm against the biting wind. 'Try to imagine,' said Diana, gesturing up towards Clerkenwell Green, and spluttering on the stink from the exhaust fumes spilling out of a bus beside us, 'before the monasteries were dissolved, this whole area was part of the countryside, with open fields bisected by the River Fleet and other small rivulets which used to run into the Fleet and kept these fields well watered. Water was readily available in Clerkenwell, as it permeated through the water-bearing strata of sand and gravel lying on top of London Clay. Its flow was naturally towards the Fleet and on into the Thames. Where this water collected beneath the surface, wells came into use. There is still one of these ancient wells underneath Sadler's Wells Theatre today. It reopened quite recently and the water was bottled as mineral water and sold, although it was brackish and didn't taste good, so the operation soon stopped. However, the water is still used for the hydraulics for the stage and then recycled into the toilets.'

We stopped for a while outside the Clerk's Well in Farringdon Lane, which is thought to pre-date the foundation of the nunnery and the priory in the twelfth century. A geological diagram inside, of a cross section of the London Basin, showed how Clerkenwell sits just above sea level, on a bed of London Clay, with lower levels of chalk and sand beneath.

Diana told me the land surrounding Clerk's Well had been open fields for centuries, mentioned by Fitzstephen in 1174 as a place that 'received throngs of visitors', especially 'students and young men of the city, who head out on summer evenings to take the air'. By the seventeenth century these fields became popular recreational grounds, used primarily for archery, wrestling and other sports. Health spas developed beside the river for the middle classes around

the same time, such as Bagnigge Wells, mentioned earlier. Other stretches of fertile open land in the area, such as Spa Fields towards Islington, were filled with grazing cattle, munching on well-watered grass and producing high-quality milk. Many dairies sprung up in the area, which frequently employed Welsh milkmaids. Coffee houses followed in the eighteenth century, famous for their wonderful cheesecakes and other dairy produce.

Diana told me that the deep valley carved out by the Fleet had created a unique microclimate in the area. The sheltered slopes beside the river were perfect for vineyards, fruit orchards, herb gardens and strawberry, crocus and rose fields, which developed on the western banks of the Fleet, near Hatton Garden. This special climate had probably been responsible for the success of the many herb gardens present in the area during the medieval period. John Gerard, the most famous Elizabethan herbalist, who had a large physic-garden in Holborn in the sixteenth century, noted that the many rare plants he grew there would not flourish anywhere else in London.

Heading past Vine Walk and up the hill to Bowling Green Lane, I began to sense the fresh, verdant valley, filled with an abundance of vegetation and fruits, a place to walk across fields, outside the city, beside the clear, flowing waters of the river.

By the start of the nineteenth century this lush landscape had all but disappeared. The area had been heavily developed, the former fields built upon, the Fleet narrowing to a stinking ditch, choked with filth and sewage. Public outcry at the stench led to its being covered over but the authorities neglected to clean it out first and in 1846 the noxious gases imprisoned within burst it open, causing heavy flooding and the loss of at least five houses.

We continued walking up Farringdon Road to the site of Cold-bath Square where another spring had been converted into a large bathing area in the seventeenth century. The waters there were thought to provide a natural remedy for aches and pains. The Fleet Valley, which for centuries had been a rural idyll, became a place for outcasts and undesirables. Later, Coldbath Fields Prison was built on the same ground. Diana pointed out the irony of the renamed area, which had been a rubbish dump for hundreds of years and a prison and is now called Mount Pleasant.

We strolled past the Mount Pleasant Post Office into Rosebery Avenue, and Diana led me to a bridge that looked down on to War-ner Street, the original route of the river. 'After flowing down from King's Cross Road, the river came along Warner Street, into Ray Street and then down into Farringdon Road.'

A steep set of stairs led down into Warner Street, where we followed the flow of the river, directly into Ray Street. Outside the

Coach and Horses pub, Diana moved to the centre of the road, narrowly avoiding a passing car, and bent over an iron grating. 'Listen,' she said, smiling, 'you can hear the Fleet still rushing underneath here. It is one of the few places along the route of the subterranean river where this can happen.' Bending near to the drain, I could both see the waters of the Fleet flowing below me and hear the sound of the submerged waters whooshing past.

Thornbury mentions excavations that took place in Ray Street in 1855, while the 'great sewer which now conveys the Fleet Ditch' was being built. About thirteen feet below the surface workmen came across paving slabs made of old ragstone, 'quite worn smooth by the footsteps and traffic of a past generation'. Below them was found 'another phase of Old London. Thickly covered with slime were piles of oak, hard and black, which had seemingly been portions of a mill-dam. A few feet below were very old wooden water pipes.'

Avoiding the traffic-choked Farringdon Road, we followed the course of the river along the narrower, parallel street of Saffron Hill. I told Diana about my recent walk there with Tudor, and his stories of the ice-cream sellers who lived in the streets around Little Italy in the nineteenth century. 'The story of ice is also connected to the river,' said Diana, and she told me about the giant wells next to the Regent's Canal, which had once been used to store ice imported from Norway, before the advent of refrigeration. 'This ice was then sold all over London. I expect much of it came here, to Little Italy. One of these huge ice wells, used by Gatti, still exists in the London Canal Museum near to King's Cross Station.'

Walking along Saffron Hill we passed another tiny side street I had not noticed before: Lily Place. I imagined large ponds once stood there, stocked with live fish for the Bishops of Ely Palace to eat on meatless Fridays.

As we crossed Greville Street the level of the street dipped down, lower and lower until we reached the end of the road, which is far below the level of Charterhouse Street above it. Diana imagined we were walking somewhere near the original depth of the Fleet.

Looking up to the office building near the stairs, which houses De Beers, she suddenly noticed the stone slabs that clad the exterior. 'How wonderful,' she said, 'it is covered in Portland Roach.' Taking me by the arm she led me over to examine the holes in the stone, created by dissolved fossils, algae, gastropods, oysters and other bivalves. As we moved up the stairs, looking at the remnants of these 150-million-year-old creatures, it felt as though we were indeed walking along the bottom of the river bed. The photograph taken then of Diana examining this wall, dressed in her long black coat and furry hat, looked exactly like a picture I had taken years before of Hasidic Jews praying beside the Wailing Wall in Jerusalem.

Exiting Saffron Hill on to Charterhouse Street, we walked to the stairwell of the viaduct and climbed it, stopping for a while to admire the huge mural inside, which shows the great Victorian structure being built. On top of the viaduct, looking down towards Smithfield and over the other side of the bridge towards Blackfriars, I closed my eyes. The sound of the traffic rushing underneath became the noise of fast-flowing water.

Diana had enabled me to visualize the former river, to understand its effect on the topography, geology and human settlement that developed beside it, even to hear it again. Now, to complete my journey, I knew I had to find a way underground, to visit the remains of the Fleet for myself.

23

A Family Business

Since the family left Poland in the 1930s, all the Lichtenstein
men have been jewellers, watchmakers or antique dealers.
The business is in our blood.

Mr Lichtenstein

My paternal grandfather first started visiting Hatton Garden in the
late 1930s, when he had his watchmaking and jewellery shop in
Whitechapel – Gedaliah Lichtenstein's. He would come to the
street regularly to buy gold and findings, the separate component
parts needed to make jewellery, along with tools, boxes, tickets,
receipts and other necessities of his business. He was also frequently
in Clerkenwell purchasing watch parts for repairs from Shoots, the
watch- and clock-part suppliers. In later years, when he had scrap to
sell, he would take that to Hatton Garden along with second-hand
jewellery and silverware, which he mainly traded in the cafés. He
must have got to know all the dealers and characters over the years;
I wish I could have spoken with him about it, but he died in 1987,
when I was seventeen.

When my father was a boy he accompanied his father on these
trips sometimes. His recollections are sketchy but there would have
been many of these visits over the years, with him sitting in a back
office somewhere, listening as the men tried to strike a deal. These
expeditions held little interest for him back then. Hatton Garden was
not a strange or mysterious world for my father, but rather something he had been born into. The only detail that struck him as
unusual, looking back, was the number of Hasidic men in full regalia,

talking and dealing on the street. Hatton Garden for him was just a place he'd always known and often visited, somewhere that was always there in dealers' conversations, a part of the landscape of his

life. The one place on the street that did fascinate him was Gamages. His father would often take him there after a buying trip to Hatton Garden as a treat: 'It was a wonderland, full of blokey things like tools, cars, bikes and tents. It had lots of dusty corridors and you just wandered from room to room, a real Aladdin's Palace.'

My father's oldest brother, Henry, 'a natural-born wheeler dealer', started trading in Hatton Garden soon after leaving school. He went into partnership with a talented diamond mounter, and they bought and sold a bit of jewellery, then did some diamond mounting, from a small office somewhere in Hatton Garden. Things went very wrong when Henry's partner started taking trips to Africa and bringing back gold, which he imported illegally: 'He made a lot of money but came a cropper and was sentenced to a lengthy prison term, which he couldn't face.' He committed suicide, which hit my uncle very hard.

My father began to visit Hatton Garden again regularly in the late

1970s when he was antique dealing, 'selling a few pieces up there to other dealers'. I remember accompanying him on one particular trip when I was about ten years old. I was sitting in the office of a second-hand trader; my father was rummaging through a box of stock, picking out the items he was interested in and putting them on the table. I probably looked bored so the dealer asked me if I wanted to see his prize-winning Afghan dog. I crept around to look under his desk, where I saw a large creamy-brown long-haired creature curled up in a ball fast asleep. Presumably in an attempt to rouse the dog the dealer kicked the animal violently, who woke with a start, took one look at me, bared its huge teeth and went for me. Luckily I was wearing a very thick polo-neck Aran jumper, which took the brunt of the attack. The dog ripped a massive hole in my top and I escaped with nothing more than a few scratches and an acute fear of dogs, which has only recently left me.

My mother's first memory of visiting the street was when she went to buy stones for her engagement ring in 1968. Because of my grandfather and my uncles and all their contacts, she was given a number of addresses of small workshops and diamond dealers to look up as she wanted to buy the stones separately, then get the ring made up to her own design. She found it 'exciting to see behind the scenes of these places'. It was a world she had never dreamed existed: 'so strange, so exotic'. Coming from a small Essex village where everyone kept their doors unlocked, the level of security to get into the workshops was unlike anything she had ever experienced before: 'The whole area seemed so foreign. We bought diamonds from one dealer and looked for hours for a black opal, which I wanted for the centre of the ring.' Eventually they found the stone they wanted, lying on a velvet pad in a small cabinet in the back of a tiny old-fashioned shop – a magnificent black opal doublet, which had an amazing array of colours within the stone, priced at five pounds. They had a big, typical 1960s cluster ring made up, which she wore for over twenty years until the black opal cracked. She then had the diamonds removed and reset into two separate rings, one for me and one for my sister.

My mother didn't return to Hatton Garden until my dad got a job there. Then she would visit. She loved going to Leather Lane Market, which she described as 'a fantastic market, with amazing

fashion stalls; it was nearly as good as Petticoat Lane then; the place you would go to get all the latest designs before they came into the shops'. She told me that my Aunty Evelyn, Henry's wife, had a shop there in the 1950s selling ladies' fashions when Henry was working in Hatton Garden as a diamond mounter.

My dad's other brother, Stanley, a larger-than-life character in every way, was the first in the family to start working in the jewellery shops in the street. In the early 1980s, after decades spent working alongside my father and grandfather as an antique dealer, he took a job with Laurence Collins, a friend of my Uncle Henry from Essex, then known as the 'King of Hatton Garden'. Laurence did an apprenticeship as a diamond mounter in Black Lion Yard

before moving on to a bullion business in Hatton Garden, then opening up a number of retail jewellery shops on the street. He built one huge new shop, where Gamages once stood, 'which was all done out in 70s decor; that was his flagship store; then he had a little shop over the road, along with a few others. He did so much in the 70s and 80s to turn Hatton Garden from a place of trade and manufacture to the well-known retail jewellery street it is today.'

My Uncle Stanley managed a small shop for Laurence at the northern end of the street, where his wife, my Aunt Betty, worked as well. She stayed in the Garden for the next twenty years, working as a successful salesperson at various different shops, a familiar presence on the street with her beehive of backcombed blonde hair and bright-blue eye shadow, standing outside the shops, smoking and chatting to everyone. She died of cancer in 2009.

When my father could no longer provide a viable income for his family from the antique business my Uncle Stanley helped him find a job in the Garden, in one of Laurence Collins's shops. After a lifetime spent as his own boss, buying and selling at the markets, dealing, being on the road, my father found it incredibly hard to start working for somebody else. He was forty-eight years old at the time and became a salesman on the shop floor, staying for the next five years, and ending up as manager of the flagship store.

When he first started working there he couldn't imagine how the street could function, with sixty-odd shops in such a small area all selling the same thing, but he quickly realized this was the very reason Hatton Garden was so successful: 'It was the same as any conglomeration of businesses, back then if you wanted a hi-fi you went to Tottenham Court Road, if you wanted a used car you went to Warren Street. The same applied to Hatton Garden; and because Hatton Garden started as a place for the trade only, there was a perception among the public that they were getting a bargain when the shops opened up – a trade deal more than a retail deal – and this was true: Hatton Garden has always been more than competitive with the high street and there is more individuality with the products on sale there along with the potential to buy something handcrafted on site. When Gamages closed down and the Gold Rush started in the early 70s many people came out of the workshops and started opening up retail shops. They saw the business opportunity was there. Shops became like gold dust.'

With the growth of the shops, the workshops and dealers all flourished too. Sadly many of the small spaces above the shops that had been used by individual artisans in the trade as workshops were sold off and turned into flats. 'For a period of time Camden Council allowed change of usage but this has since been stopped and the council have decided to preserve the area as a jewellery quarter. Without this Hatton Garden would not have survived. The future is positive for the street as long as this policy does not change.'

Over the years my father spent working in the street he got to know many of the characters in the area, like Dave Harris and Mitzy, both of whom he was terribly fond of, along with Ron Meadows, a rep who worked from a shop on Farringdon Road selling boxes and display material for the jewellery shops: 'He was a real old woman, who would chat for hours with everybody, he knew everyone, everything that was going on. One day I was talking to him and he told me Mr Carlo, a jeweller who had a few businesses on the street, had a shop for sale.'

Carlo was an Italian immigrant, a tailor by trade, who came to London after the war. He worked in Savile Row for a while, before opening up a small tailoring shop in Leather Lane, which moved to Greville Street in the early 1960s. Many of his customers were in the jewellery business and gradually he got to know a bit more about it. He moved the tailoring business to the back of the shop and started to put some imitation jewellery in the shop window, along with the suits, shirts, umbrellas and watches he sold. Many Italians living in nearby Back Hill would come into the shop and ask him if he stocked any real jewellery, so he started to buy from suppliers close by: gold St Christophers and other pieces that would appeal to that community. In 1969 he gave up tailoring and turned the shop into a proper jewellery store. There were few other retail jewellers in the area at the time, so the shop did well, and he expanded into a larger premises on the corner of Greville Street in 1977. Then about twenty years ago he bought another shop on Hatton Garden as well, which he later put up for sale.

My father went to see Mr Carlo as soon as he heard the shop was coming on the market and asked how much he wanted for the business. 'He told me a figure, a vast amount of money, and I made him an offer, pretty close, and we shook hands: we had done the deal. I walked out of his shop thinking: how am I going to get hold of the money for the shop and the stock? I went to see my accountant and, at that time, 1989, the banks were lending freely. The accountant put together a business plan, with projections, cash-flow forecasts, other required details, and we put it in a nice leather-bound folder and started hawking it round the banks. We got chucked out of the first two but the third one said yes and lent us the money.

'The amazing thing about Mr Carlo was that he was such a gentleman. When it became known I was buying the shop, other people came to him and said, "Well, how much did you let it go for?" and they offered him substantially more. This happened on a number of occasions, but he said, "No, I have shaken hands, it is a done deal."'

Moved on hearing my father recount this tale, I recognized it as a version of a Hatton Garden story I had now heard several times before, all of which involved *chutzpah*, a bit of *mazel*, support and insider knowledge from others in the community and the understanding that your word is your bond. If you renege on a deal in Hatton Garden you are finished; no one will work with you again.

It must have been terrifying for my parents, taking on a loan so far above and beyond the value of their property. If things had gone wrong it would have meant bankruptcy. We had one week from the time we got the keys to when the shop was to open. I came back from university to help, hitching down from Sheffield

with my boyfriend of the time; my sister was there as well, my parents were too nervous to employ anyone else in case the business failed.

We all worked long hours, cleaning out the dusty display cabinets, rushing around to different suppliers, fetching boxes, bags, labels, stands, tickets and all the jewellery needed to fill the large windows. The stock was mainly on approval from suppliers, meaning we did not have to pay for it up front – but if it sold the suppliers took a bigger cut of the profit. Many people helped us out. They trusted my dad, they knew him from the street, knew his father and brothers. It is unlikely anyone opening up a new business in Hatton Garden who wasn't known would have been helped in this way.

I remember spending hours during that frantic week writing out by hand the price labels for the jewellery and diamond rings in the window, in gold pen on shield-shaped tickets. As I placed these tickets in the boxes in the window I would watch the activity on the street. In the late 1980s most of the shops had *schleppers*, who would stand outside the arcades, much like the waiters do now outside the curry houses on Brick Lane, trying to entice people inside. The street was buzzing with people, talking on the pavements, stopping to shake hands; the place had the atmosphere of a small village rather than a street in Central London.

During that first week I spent at the shop, I visited many different workshops and suppliers. I remember dropping something off with some diamond dealers, who were all extremely Orthodox, Hasidic, dressed from another era, speaking a forgotten language, bent over low tables examining diamonds. I stood beside the open door; they could not look at me directly or shake my hand – but we managed.

My parents made a great team. My father had the experience of working in the area and had always been a brilliant salesman. My mother, once a fashion buyer for a large department store in Southend, had a good eye and chose the right stock for the times, which back then included a lot of big gold jewellery: choker necklaces, bangles and large dangly earrings. My father was still dealing in antique jewellery then, which they also put in the window, along with the modern wedding and engagement rings they sold.

I remember the excitement of the first Saturday we opened the shop, the whole family in place, nervously waiting for customers to arrive. Even I sold a diamond ring that first day. It was thrilling. Back then business was easier for everyone: the yuppies were still around and the City boys would come in with wads of cash; you could sell them anything. The main customers though, then and today, were young couples looking for diamond engagement rings. My mother told me that: 'In the 80s they used to come in and choose the ring that the woman really loved, whereas now they come in and pick the stone they can afford that has the best certificate. They didn't used care if the diamond was a D colour or an H colour; now there is total concern.'

My mother, who is a very sociable person, knew all the suppliers and dealers. 'They became our friends, we knew about their families, their kids. Walking from one end of the street to the other took a long time; going on an errand you would meet so many people on the way it could take hours.' For the first few months both of my parents worked seven days a week, before gradually taking on more employees. The street had always been open on a Sunday: the shops there received special dispensation before the Sunday-trading laws as most of the businesses had originally been Jewish-run, much like the markets in East London.

One of their first members of staff was a seventeen-year-old girl called Tracey, from Poplar. She told me when she came to the street to work as a jewellery salesperson she thought it was 'a posh, classy, glamorous place that was very mysterious'. She learned the trade through watching others – 'how to display, how to sell and talk to people, then you progress with your own style'. She was taught how to sort diamonds by someone taking her under their wing: 'There wasn't no fanciness about it; they just spent time with me and showed me how to do it. You have to be willing to be quiet and learn and listen, get people to talk to you and tell you what they know. I've learned this way, I never went to college or nothing like that; this is the traditional way of learning this trade.'

Tracey got to know all the 'old boys in the workshops', who adored her. Over the years she has been working there she has noticed that 'most of the workshops have gone; people have died; there are no apprenticeships left; when the last of the old ones go, their secrets will die with them'.

Journalists working in nearby Fleet Street used to come to the shop, along with doctors and lawyers and even the odd celebrity. Jeremy Clarkson bought his engagement ring from my parents, and when Patsy Kensit got engaged to Liam Gallagher they came in together and bought a ring from my father, made in 22-carat gold. My father advised them against it, as the gold would be very soft and might bend. A few weeks later they came back. The ring had somehow been squashed flat – another one was made up in eighteen-carat gold, which is far more durable. Most of their customers were middle-class couples living within the M25 (along with the odd lord and aristocrat). On Sundays, lots of East Enders would come to Hatton Garden.

My mother loves selling wedding and engagement rings to couples: 'It is a landmark experience and if you can add to that experience then it feels wonderful. When we sell an engagement ring to a couple we say congratulations and we are often the first people to know, we share in their joy.' Over the years they have witnessed many emotional scenes inside their shop. Sometimes people weep and cry, nervous men often come in alone to choose a ring and tell their stories about the romantic places they have chosen to propose in: on a mountain, in a gondola, up the Eiffel Tower.

One Saturday my father was in the shop serving customers when a Dutchman entered with a parcel wrapped in paper under his arm. My dad thought he might have some silver or jewellery to sell but when he unwrapped the package he produced a nineteenth-century glass bottle. Embossed on the side were the words 'Rowland & Son, Kalydor Warehouse, Hatton Garden'. The man had found the bottle on a spoil tip outside the city where he lived in Holland; it was his hobby to find old bottles, jars and pottery and then to visit the premises, wherever it was in the world, where they had been made. My father tried to buy the bottle from him, offering a high price, but he refused to sell it. As far as the Dutchman was concerned, he had completed his project simply by making the journey with the bottle.

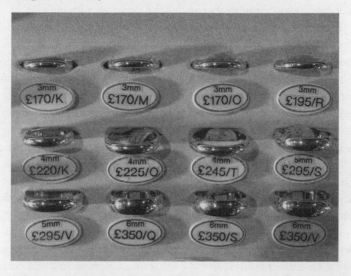

I knew the shop had once been the home of A. Rowland & Sons, Chemists and Perfumers, from at least 1840 (which is when post office records begin), who manufactured and sold, among other products, Macassar hair oil and Kalydor, a Victorian skin ointment cure oil, based on almond oil, which claimed to be 'a never-failing specific for all cutaneous deformities'. I found an old advertisement for these two products in the back of an 1859 Chapman & Hall edition of Charles Dickens's *A Tale of Two Cities*.

VISITORS TO THE SEA-SIDE, AND OTHERS

Exposed to the scorching rays of the Sun, and heated particles of Dust, will find ROWLAND'S KALYDOR A MOST REFRESHING PREPARATION For the COMPLEXION, dispelling the Cloud of Languor and Relaxation, allaying all Heat and Irritability, and immediately affording the pleasing sensation attending restored elasticity and healthful state of the Skin.

Freckles, Tan, Spots, Pimples, Flushes, and Discoloration fly before its application, and give place to delicate clearness, with the glow of beauty and of bloom. In cases of sunburn, and stings of insects, its virtues have long been acknowledged. Price 4s. 6d. and 8s. 6d. per Bottle.

The heat of summer also frequently communicates a dryness to the Hair, and a tendency to fall off, which may be completely obviated by the use of ROWLAND'S MACASSAR OIL, a delightfully fragrant and transparent preparation, and as an invigorator and beautifier of the Hair.

My father remembers antimacassars, linen doilies that covered the back of armchairs, to stop hair oil leaking on to the furniture.

I was given a Victorian etching of Rowland's Macassar and Kalydor warehouse by the former landlord of the building, who I went to visit in his home in Golders Green. He once owned a lot of property in Hatton Garden, which he has since sold on. He told me he misses the Garden: 'I had a lot of friends there. When they were in trouble, being forced out of the building due to higher rents, I tried to buy the building back to help them. What do I want, to be the richest man in the cemetery?' He did much to preserve the character of Hatton Garden when big businesses were trying to push out the independent jewellery shops and small workshops above them. He told me a story about an old man who rented a workshop from him and couldn't pay his rent: 'I went to him, to try and shame him, and said, "What, you want me to treat you like a charity case?" and he said, "Yes please." That was the last rent he ever paid.' He spoke with sadness about some of the long-standing tenants of shops on Hatton Garden, like Jo Ullmann, who 'formed part of the ambience of the place and added flavour and prestige to Hatton Garden and was turfed out of his premises for money's sake'.

He remembered some of the historic Georgian buildings on the street, with beautiful façades and staircases, 'being left to go to rack and ruin, so they were beyond saving and then demolished'.

My parents' shop is in a Grade II listed building, constructed in 1906; the original seventeenth-century house must have been pulled down to make way for it. In later years the shop became a chemist's and a barber's before becoming a jewellery shop some time in the 1980s.

My parents retired from the business some years ago and for the last eight years my husband, Adam, has been managing the shop for them. He enjoys working in the area, which he sees as 'a historic part of old London; wandering around the side streets is always surprising, the little workshops full of craftspeople, and the tiny alleyways and cobbled courtyards you might come across, which seem to be from another era'.

After working in retail since leaving school, Adam was a natural choice to take over the running of the family business. He likes meeting the many different members of the public who come into the shop and has come to love the products he sells. My parents taught him the basics of the trade and he has learned more over the years from others in the business, particularly about diamonds, which fascinate him: 'They are beautiful, they have so much life in them, which you just do not get from any other stone. Nothing on earth sparkles and holds light like a well-cut polished diamond. They are magical stones.'

24

Virtual Drift

American writer Henry David Thoreau extolled going forth in the
world to experience its bounty and characteristics through the simple
act of walking. Thoreau avoided highways, choosing instead to
wander with indirectness in order to understand the spiritual
possibilities of the landscape: 'Two or three hours' walking will
carry me to as strange a country as I expect . . .'

http://www.maryflanagan.com/borders

I came across Mary Flanagan's work for the first time in the autumn
of 2010 at the 'Small World Fair Exhibition'[1] in Southend-on-Sea,
which explored, through a collection of artworks and curiosities,
how the world has become shaped by technology. Mary's piece, a
video installation called *Perfect City*, included a computer-generated
recreation of Songdo, the international new metropolis currently
being built by various corporations in South Korea. Besuited characters, created using SIM City software, meandered aimlessly
around the featureless urban streetscapes of her virtual version of
this allegedly utopian city.

The young professor from New York, a self-confessed techno
geek, spoke energetically about her work after the exhibition. An
internationally renowned digital-media artist, Mary has written
extensively about feminism and cyberspace, and she also directs a

---

1   Curated by the artist Simon Poulter, October–November 2010, and held at
Chalkwell Hall, the Southend Headquarters of the arts organization Metal (www.
metalculture.com).

laboratory, Tiltfactor, which develops and examines computer and Web-based games and play, while investigating radical issues and ideas. She learned most of her software programming skills working at a lab producing educational CD ROMs, where she recreated historical landscapes to allow users to explore virtual worlds in different ways. 'You could read data, listen to stories, take pictures, write in a journal. Working in this way taught me how to have multiple perspectives on a place and to create different ways of telling stories.'

Her current work, the [borders] project, consists of video documentation of a series of virtual walks she has taken through reconstructed sites from the past in popular, shared, online, multi-user worlds. She spends days walking around the perimeters of strange, rendered landscapes – Mayan temples, Egyptian pyramids, Eleanor of Aquitaine's lands and Native American villages – wandering along invisible boundaries, her route often becoming blocked by rocks, stones or other obstacles. Sometimes she is forced underwater or pushed teetering at the edge of different realities. She describes these virtual border-walks as 'psychogeographic drifts', a way of 'surveying boundaries and divisions, alongside exploring notions of historic recreation and property ownership in virtual worlds'. Her walks are purely experiential; roaming without purpose through imagined landscapes, where she becomes drawn into the seductive beauty of the digital image, often finding herself lost. She showed me a glitch in the programming, a seam under a rock, where she could see through to another world: 'Theoretically I shouldn't be able to explore like this but occasional holes appear in the landscapes, a break, where the whole materiality of these imagined worlds becomes challenged.' It made me think back to the time I had spent looking at the GIS system at MOLA, when maps broke apart, a rip in the seam of time, a portal moment.

Fascinated by Mary's work, particularly after hearing her talk about having a psychogeographic response to places she experiences only in cyberspace, I invited the *flâneur* of the Internet to take a virtual walk with me around the perimeter of the area known as the Garden today. I was curious to hear her impressions and responses to a place she would visit only virtually, and intrigued to see whether she would be able to pick up on any traces of the past, any stories or memories still embedded in that landscape, which exists in a part of London she has never been to before, either remotely or in reality.

The idea was to conduct the walk using Street View, the mapping tool. Over the last few years Google has sent an army of vans, rigged with cameras and satellite positioning gear, out to most Western cities to take panoramic photographs of the streets, including buildings, street furniture, traffic and people, which are then synched to its three-dimensional mapping service and layered with other annotated details, labels and images. The resulting visual map, like all maps, tells only a partial truth about a place; access to some streets and buildings has been denied, certain information is erased or blurred and other details are just left out altogether.

Undoubtedly controversial, with all its complex privacy issues, Street View is also truly magical. Particularly when you experience it for the first time, as it gives a sense of an almost godlike power of being able to explore and view anywhere in the world, be it only remotely.

We began our journey by opening Google Earth on Mary's laptop. A rotating blue globe appeared on her screen, surrounded by black sky and sparkling stars. A white circle, like the target site viewed through a rifle, sat high above New York, pulsating. 'As you can see,' said Mary, laughing, 'my computer is very American-centric. I want to start here though, with this satellite view, and then just zoom across to London, as you really feel like you are flying if you use the program in this way.'

Using her mouse, she spun the virtual world around, travelling at great speed across oceans until she reached the UK. She stopped above the green pixelated canvas of southern England. The faint uneven outline of the Thames became increasingly visible as we flew down towards the capital. Pop-ups appeared during our descent; images of tourist sites: Westminster, Big Ben, Buckingham

Palace. Landing on top of Westminster Bridge, I asked Mary to follow the course of the river east, towards Blackfriars. As her cursor rolled over small green-and-yellow squares in the water, white text spewed out as we passed by – 'ding dong, London Eye, eclipse, shining light over Hungerford Bridge, Oxo, St Paul's by night, Thames Riverside'. 'Found it,' said Mary, pleased, as she reached Blackfriars Bridge. '"Friars" – will I find monks here?'

Mary moved her cursor up Farringdon Street, towards Holborn Viaduct, following the wide, straight road north from the river. 'What's this, a hole?' she asked, as she floated over the gigantic, white, rectangular shape of Smithfield Meat Market, which from the air looks like a void among the rooftops and city streets that surround it.

Hovering above the area, looking at the aerial landscape of that part of the city, without any instruction from me, Mary naturally found her own starting point for our walk. 'It seems like this is important,' she said, moving straight over the circular shape of Holborn Circus. 'Oh, is that Seven Dials?' she asked, as she zoomed down towards the roundabout, which from that perspective, with the six roads converging off it, looked something like the star shape of the Seven Dials junction in Covent Garden (Seven Dials, with its pillar of sundials in the centre, sits on the site of a medieval abbey and a hospital for lepers, much as Holborn Circus seems to mark the location of the ancient priory of the Bishops of Ely, who gave alms to the sick).

Seeing the shape of Holborn Circus from above made me think about my recent researches in the maps reading room of the British Library, where I had studied Sir Christopher Wren's original hand-drawn plans for rebuilding the city after the Great Fire. A notable astronomer, geometer and cosmologist as well as an architect, Wren had designed his utopian city on a series of formulaic grid patterns, with wide boulevards like in Paris, linked to each other by a series of huge octagon-shaped piazzas, which resembled stars, or the diagram on a compass. The largest of these piazzas had been drawn directly below the street of Hatton Garden, in the location of Holborn Circus today. In Wren's re-imagined London, this piazza is the single largest open space, stretching from the southern end of Hatton Garden right down towards Blackfriars. In the centre of the piazza would have stood the Templar Church, one of London's most ancient and mysterious buildings. It is as if Wren saw the connections between the stories of Hatton Garden, the Ely Bishops, the Knights Templar, Blackfriars and the river. At the bottom of Wren's map he had written:

> the whole city terminates at Tower Hill, but before it descends into the valley where the great sewer [Fleet] runs; it opens into a round piazza, the centre of eight ways, where at one station we see 1. straightforward quite through the city, 2. obliquely towards the right hand, to the beginning of the quay from Bridewell dock to the tower obliquely on the left to Smithfield and straight on the right to the thames and V. straight on the left to Hatten Street and Clarkenwell and straight backwards towards Temple Bar.

Instinctively, after landing on Holborn Circus, Mary picked up her iPhone from the table and began flicking through some photographs she had taken the day before at the British Museum, where she became obsessed with the astronomical instruments on display. She showed me a series of images she had taken of brass instruments. 'This notion of clocks and clockwork, these mechanisms and mechanical ways of representing and counting metaphysical things fascinate me,' said Mary. 'Mechanical instruments are just machines that try to measure our experience of the world in some systemic way, so they are always going to be faulty.' She showed me pictures of telescopes, mechanical clocks and barometers and a rolling ball clock by Sir William Congreve – a beautiful, complex brass machine, which measured time by a ball rolling on an inclined plane. Looking Congreve up later online, I found out the British inventor and artillerist lived for some time at the Middle Temple in Garden Court, which on Wren's map would have been directly connected to Hatton Garden. While there Congreve developed the first military rocket in 1808, which helped another inventor, Sir Miriam Maxim, come up with the idea for his automatic machine gun at the other end of Hatton Garden in the 1880s – as if the story of war somehow bookends Hatton Garden.

Astonished to see Mary showing me images of the type of artefacts made by the first artisans to arrive in the area, the seventeenth-century Huguenot makers of clocks, who produced astronomical and fine-precision instruments, I had to interject and tell her that within the first few minutes of our walk, she had picked up on traces of the area's industrial, monastic and geographic past. She had also landed on the exact spot where Negretti & Zambra ran their shop, selling mechanical, astronomical and scientific instruments.

'I'm going to take a look around,' said Mary, as her hands flew expertly over the keyboard. She opened up another window on her screen, Google Maps, which allows users to view street-level imagery. After she typed in the address for Hatton Garden a linear, Ordnance Survey-style map appeared, with the star shape of Holborn Circus clearly visible at the southern end of the street. Plucking a virtual avatar from the tool bar to the left Mary placed herself in the centre of Holborn Circus. Immediately, a panoramic, almost three-dimensional, photographic image appeared in front of us of the busy roundabout frozen in a static landscape.

The virtual Mary stood precariously in front of a taxi near the middle of the roundabout. An opaque white circle marked her position on the map. By moving the circle on to a part of the photographic image and pulling the mouse around she could quickly explore. She noted Sainsbury's, the church of St Andrew's, the red, castle-like structure of the old Prudential Building, and the statue in the centre of the roundabout. 'Let's see who is being lauded here,' she said, moving her avatar up towards the bronze man on horseback, doffing his hat. 'Oh, Prince Albert, beloved husband of Queen Victoria.' Instrumental in the abolishment of slavery, the progressive prince encouraged Victorian road developments, including the building of Holborn Viaduct.

Navigating back down to street level, Mary passed a couple of diamond-ring symbols hanging in the air: 'Getting close to the jewellery quarter, I expect.' She read from the pop-up text as she moved over the ring symbols: '"Beverly Hills, London", a classy neighbourhood, possibly, or one that is trying to be; oh, "Celestial Diamonds", that seems to relate back to the mechanical clock and astronomical devices somehow.' Double-clicking on top of the roundabout, the image warped and stretched and Mary found herself in the middle of Hatton Garden itself with many floating symbols of diamond rings suspended along the centre of the street.

'I see modernization here,' she said, as she flew around, 'many people walking past and an abundance of diamond and jewel shops. The street seems to be divided into the old and the new, it appears somewhat reinvented with this giant 1970s-looking block on the south side and some beautiful old buildings on the north side. It looks like a historic place, but split in half. What interests me the most about the image of the street is the way these trees seem to bend over towards the older side of the street, creating a vortex or time tunnel of sorts,' she said, pointing with her cursor towards the row of sycamore trees embedded into the pavement.

Her avatar floated skywards as Mary explored the architecture above shop level. She found the plaque above Mazzini's old school but the text was too blurred to read. She looked at the mouldings around the windows of the buildings, the intricate sculptural frieze above the shops at nos 19–21. 'The view from Street View is slightly elevated from the normal eyeline of street level, as the images are taken from cameras strapped to the top of a van, meaning that the details of the architecture above the shops comes more sharply into focus, making you more conscious of what is going on above you when you explore a place in this way, more than you would be if you were actually walking around.'

After climbing to the top of the buildings, nosing in windows, spotting a few signs for offices and workshops, Mary returned to street level, her avatar resting on a store called Alchemy: 'This place is rich in many senses: gold, alchemy, gardens, dials, diamonds, blood, friars.' She thought the street looked 'boutiquey, upscale, clean, anonymous'. She imagined it to be located near to the central business district, as there were many people in suits walking around. Noting the lack of places to eat, she said, 'there seems to be nothing here but jewellery shops, represented by floating diamond rings, like a procession of jewels along the street'. As she moved back into the centre of the road, the words 'Diamonds Are Forever' popped up in bright white text.

She read out the names of the shops she passed: Pronuptia, Antony Gray, Abiba, then Hirschfield's, the first overtly Jewish name. 'I know, this was or is a Jewish business area, but now that history seems whitewashed, hidden to the casual observer,' said Mary. 'If you visit the diamond district in New York it is very obviously a Jewish space. Hatton Garden to me looks like somewhere that wants to reflect a more old-fashioned, historic British identity. I imagine the area to be very empty at night.'

Mary tried to enter the dark interior of one of the shops on the street but was bounced out, finding her avatar back in the middle of

the road. She explained we could access only the parts of the map where the white circle appeared on the screen, which marks out the places the cameras on top of the vans have been able to document. The interior spaces, the narrow alleyways, the small backstreets and pedestrianized areas are inaccessible because the vehicles are too wide to enter. 'You have to imagine yourself to be the size of an elephant,' said Mary, 'when you are wandering around on Street View.'

We passed other annotated signs: 'The King of Diamonds', 'Cultured Pearl', 'Hatton Garden Metals'. About halfway up the street, she stopped outside a huge new office development, in the recently renovated Johnson Building, once the headquarters of the oldest business in the street, Johnson Matthey, now the offices of Grey, one of London's biggest advertising agencies, as mentioned before.

Directly opposite Grey is the oldest building on the street, St Andrew's Church Charity School, which dates back to 1687 and is thought to have been designed by Sir Christopher Wren as a church, before later becoming a school. Mary became fascinated by the eighteenth-century statues in two niches above the doorway of blue-coated children, a boy and a girl, which had been placed there when the building was a charity school. Attempting to find out the current usage of the building she tried to look inside but the doors were closed. All she discovered was an OFFICES FOR RENT sign attached to the exterior. In the large domed windows the only thing she could see was a reflection of the advertising agency opposite.

Further up the street, she stopped again at a red-brick Victorian block called Colonial Buildings, which she expected to be 'another sort of new media company, because of the frosted windows, which stop computer screens getting the glare from the light outside and stop people eyeballing the technology inside as they walk past'.

She sensed commerce had changed the street but imagined, from the remaining Georgian houses, that people once lived there. As she moved around she noticed many FOR LET signs on the shops and workshops, and surmised that the makers were moving out of the area and new media companies were moving in. 'It's a story hap-

pening in every Western city,' she said, 'in cool areas like this, with warehouse-type buildings, near to the centre. The architects and media companies come in, the artisans move out as rents soar, you can see all the signs of this shift here.'

Near the Clerkenwell end of the street she reached Hatton Wall and started looking around for any remains of an ancient perimeter. She noted the street names near by – Saffron Hill, Herbal Hill, Vine Hill – and searched for an orchard or walled garden of sorts.

Moving around speedily, her face set in deep concentration, fingers flying over the keyboard, Mary reminded me of my two young boys at home exploring the alien landscapes of their Xbox games. She told me it is possible to hook up the computer to a games controller and play the city as a game using Street View.

As it turned sharply, a black cab morphed into a strange lozenge-shaped ghoul in the road, resembling a shadowy monk running past in a dark robe. Unable to access Hatton Wall Mary took a detour around the block, up Clerkenwell Road, and began looking for a well, a spring, water. She imagined clerks, holy people, walking the area.

On Clerkenwell Road she stopped outside the boarded-up building of Terroni's Delicatessen and the recently closed-down Italian restaurant Casa Italiana. 'At last, we have a sense of some ethnicity here,' she said, aware she had found the remnants of an Italian quarter. She spent some time exploring the beautiful exterior of the Italian Church, which sits wedged tightly between the restaurant next door and a Georgian house. Floating near the entranceway was a tiny thumbnail image of the church, with the word 'Panoramio' attached. When she clicked on the box some tourist shots of the interior appeared along the top of the screen with some other general London photographs. Another box linked directly to a Wikipedia page about the church, where Mary read more about the building.

Moving further along Clerkenwell Road she noted the many new buildings and wondered if the area had been heavily bombed or if parts of Little Italy had been ripped down, as they have been in New York. She stopped near a health club and became fascinated with the signage for the sushi bar next door: a gigantic image of schoolgirls' legs, in knee-high socks and tartan skirts, which filled the windows. 'This seems to hark back to the many Italian Catholic girls who would have walked these streets,' said Mary.

Opposite, on the corner of Clerkenwell Road and Farringdon Road, was a grey office building, housing some sort of eco-consultancy. On the ground floor, near street level, were the words 'Techno, Techno' in red vinyl, a visual echo of the more recent club culture that emerged in Clerkenwell. Reflected in the window of that building was a mirror image of St James Church in Clerkenwell along with some of the other Georgian buildings near Clerkenwell Green, looking like an oil painting of a time past. 'Here is Griffin House,' said Mary as we passed a large building, which seemed to her to hint at a hidden mythology in the area; and in the middle of the road was the name Prospero, a memory-trace of Shakespeare, who both wrote about and visited the area. Clicking on the link uncovered a recruitment agency that had adopted the name and was now based on Farringdon Road.

As Mary moved around the streets, buildings compressed and bent, vehicles warped and fragmented, abstract words appeared on the screen: 'Revolving Doors', 'Relish Creative', 'Vine Street Bridge'. She manoeuvred her way on to the yellow cross at the junction of Clerkenwell and Farringdon roads and, quite suddenly, took her hands off the keyboard and made a loud wooshing noise while gesturing forwards with her hands, mimicking the flow of water, as if she was so tapped into the past story of the place she could sense the flow of the Fleet, still moving beneath Farringdon Road. 'Interesting,' she said with a raised eyebrow, as I told her about the lost river; 'this road does still feel tubular, more like a wind tunnel than a river now, although there is a sense of a valley, of being bounded somehow, particularly by this monstrous castle-like structure,' she added, pointing to the gigantic grey-and-maroon modernist building housing the accountancy firm Merrill Lynch, which she felt formed a sort of aggressive city boundary. 'It's so forbidding, there is nowhere to enter, this high wall guides you downwards, it feels like the edge of something.'

Moving along Farringdon Road, Mary imagined architects might have appropriated the loft spaces above the shops and businesses, as they have been doing in similar buildings in the business district of New York. We passed Telescope House and a place called the Aquarium, 'possible references to a watery, seafaring past'. Landing on a Gothic-looking Victorian building on the corner of Farringdon Road and Greville Street she admired the architectural features, before continuing along the course of the former river. As we hit the junction of Charterhouse Street, Mary moved up into the market, immediately recognizing the gigantic site as the white void she had seen from above. The words 'Trunk Animation' floated, briefly, above an icon for a bicycle painted on the road as we moved past. 'Sounds like another new media company,' she said, as we wandered through the vast complex.

Making comparison to the Meatpacking District of New York, as we moved around virtually, Mary told me much of that area has recently been either demolished or redeveloped. Later, researching online, I discovered many of the buildings in Smithfield have only just been saved from demolition, thanks to the hard work of conservationist groups such as English Heritage who have been battling with developers keen to knock the whole thing down and replace it with office blocks and retail outlets. After several campaigns, Grade II listed building protection has been secured on parts of the market. Other sections, sadly, have already been destroyed to make way for London's new Crossrail development.

Cutting right through the market, on East Poultry Avenue, Mary moved her avatar down Smithfield Street, passing the ruinous-looking brick building where Iain Sinclair had described having a wild, drunken afternoon with Peter Ackroyd. At the end of this road she turned left, back on to Farringdon Road, immediately spotting the spectacular red iron structure of Holborn Viaduct. 'I see it now,' she said: 'a bridge without a river.'

Using her avatar she managed to jump like a superhero on to the top of the viaduct where she spent some time examining the four bronze statues situated there: the winged lion, and the Grecian women representing Fine Art, Commerce and Agriculture. 'They seem like guardians at the gates of a new zone,' she said, as we continued along the viaduct. We passed City Temple, with its resonances of a historic, crusader past. She tried to enter Ely Place but the gates were closed, access was denied.

Back at Holborn Circus again, I asked her to sum up her impressions of the area. 'Regeneration is happening. It feels like the City is leaking into that place, changing it from an area that was once filled with hustle and bustle, animals and street life, when the market and the river had been the dominant features. It doesn't look like it can go back; there is no place for people to live there any more.' Before logging off, she turned a full circle in the centre of Holborn Circus and noted the only patch of green space we had passed on our tour; the last remnant of a garden, sunk below the level of the street, beside the ancient church of St Andrew's.

Cities retain fragments of their histories and it did not surprise me that Mary, an intuitive artist, had managed to glimpse much of the story of Hatton Garden and its environs, within an hour, after only virtually visiting the place once. She seemed to be able both to physically tap into the past while acutely observing the contemporary story of the street and its probable future.

25

Full Circle

I find Hatton Garden magical, all the different workshops and suppliers,
all the old-fashioned little businesses mixing with the new places like
Platform. You see a doorway on the street and you have no idea that
behind it there is a maze of workshops, filled with experts in their trade,
people who have spent a lifetime training in certain niche areas of the
industry, engraving, mounting, setting, it is a really hidden world
operating behind the scenes. I feel privileged to be a part of it.

Mandana Oskoui, jewellery designer

The window display of Holts Lapidary Showroom on Hatton Garden is based on a fissure in a rock with floating white pads filled with
rough-hewn coloured crystals, corals and large uncut precious
stones alongside gemstone jewellery. Inside, the shop floor has been
laid out in a circular design, edged by brightly lit glass-topped cabinets, packed with pearls, trays of precious beads, jade, sapphire and
ruby stones among other valuable gems and items of jewellery.
Tall, standing cabinets with rocks, cut into slices, exhibited like porcelain plates, sit beside fossils and artefacts made from very rare
materials such as Blue John and onyx. Situated on the floor, near the
entrance, is a gigantic black rock, which has been sliced in half to
reveal a profusion of luminous-violet amethyst crystals inside. Holts
looks more like a gallery in the Natural History Museum than just
another jewellery shop on the street.

Mr Holt senior, a refugee from Vienna, opened his first shop in
1948 in the former Gamages building, specializing in rocks and precious gems. The art of lapidary, popular in Victorian times, had

nearly disappeared in London by then. He learned how to cut the rocks himself – he even built his own machinery from used eyeglass lenses because there was nothing available to buy then. 'You can historically trace the resurrection of stonecutting in this country to my father,' said his son, Jason, a smart young former lawyer, who is now co-director of the business. 'Lapidary is a very niche area, a real art form, we are the last major stonecutters in the UK now, most of the business has gone overseas.'

I followed Jason downstairs for a tour of Holts's workshops, expecting to see another dark and cramped underground space, filled with elderly craftsmen at work. Instead I walked into a bright, clean, expansive modern room in the basement of the building. Jason led me over to the newest section of the workshop, where designers were working at computer terminals with CAD, computer-aided design, which provides a technology service for jewellers. He showed me a digitally generated image of a cut ruby, which would later be carved by 3D lasers. 'We are also experimenting with new mediums,' said Jason, 'for example, we have a new software business that uses unseen technology to allow you to visualize yourself wearing a piece of jewellery in real time, so if you are at home with a webcam you can click on to the ring and see yourself wearing the ring on your finger. We are deliberately embracing rather than running away from this new technology, while making sure our designers have also been trained in traditional techniques first.'

We entered a large polishing room, filled with machines used to shape, mould and polish stones in traditional ways. He showed me a blue lapis vase being made there by one of their craftsmen. I met another of the lapidaries at work, grinding down sapphire, one of a handful of people in the country able to do this. He told me he carries out a lot of work for Cartier, restoring antique boxes. Stranger commissions have included working on restored Neolithic archaeological finds and making small replica objects out of precious stone for a well-known contemporary artist.

As we walked around the workshop, talking to various different craftspeople, Jason told me when he started in the business ten years ago he noticed most of the old-fashioned apprenticeships had died off and that the majority of quality handcrafted jewellery was being made in the Far East. A DTI report in 1999 stated that within a decade, unless something was done, traditional jewellery-manufacturing skills would vanish from the UK. These statistics inspired Jason to establish an Academy of Jewellery; a not-for-profit organization providing hands-on training by industry experts for young people wanting to learn the trade. The school started in the Holts basement and has expanded into a large warehouse building just off Hatton Garden, offering over sixty different courses, covering all aspects of the trade, to over 1,000 students a year. The latest social enterprise launched by the Academy is called Platform, a showroom where young British contemporary designers can sell their work.

Situated in Greville Street, opposite Bleeding Heart Yard, the large corner premises has floor-to-ceiling glass windows, filled with plinths displaying minimalist modern jewellery. As I looked in the window my eye was immediately drawn to a collection by Amy Keeper, which looked as if it had been inspired by Victorian and Georgian pieces. Using the shape of traditional cameos and pendants, Keeper had etched photos on to glass and metal backgrounds, adding engraved handwritten text, details from old postcards. Nostalgic and modern elements combined, reminiscent of the type of artefacts I was making as a sculpture student. All the other contemporary work on display was also of an extremely high quality, made from a wide range of materials including gold, silver, plastics, enamels, jade, diamonds and pearls.

Sitting on a cerise chaise longue in the back of the shop, I set up my recording equipment and waited for my interviewee, a young jewellery designer called Catherine Zoraida. An attractive woman, with long dark hair, wearing tight leather trousers, a floaty top and sky-high heels, came into the shop shortly afterwards, carrying a heavy black briefcase containing samples of her work; delicate, tactile pieces of gold jewellery, cast from ephemeral, natural objects: a seahorse, the skin of a lychee, the wing of a moth, a broken shell. Other pieces included a dragonfly pendant with ash leaves as wings and an apple twig as a body – a mythical gold creature from a fairy tale.

'The inspiration for this collection comes from a desire to fix decaying, disappearing things,' said Catherine, in a strong Scottish accent, and went on to tell me she had been adopted at the age of two from Colombia and then grew up in Edinburgh, knowing little about her heritage. Recently she returned to Colombia and discovered she had been left at a bus stop as a baby. She managed to find the woman she had been handed to and went to visit the bus stop, 'which felt somehow very important'.

Catherine studied jewellery design in Scotland before being taken on by the celebrated British jewellery designer Theo Fenell, who had his first jewellery workshop in Hatton Garden but is now based in Fulham. 'His craftspeople were all men, incredibly skilled,' she said. 'The oldest man there was in his late seventies and he taught the younger ones, they had all completed an old-fashioned apprenticeship. At art school we had all been women on the course. The design studio at Theo Fenell's was all women too.'

She moved on to work with Simon Harris, making costume jewellery for fashion designers such as Vivienne Westwood, Matthew Williamson: 'a great chance to learn how to adapt to different designers' visions and styles. It was very fast-paced, we had model makers in house but the designs were produced in places like Thailand. I worked with CAD there, learning how to make 3D models on the computer. We could send our designs through to the 3D printer, which would create a perfect 3D wax model, so you can see and adapt your designs very quickly using this technology. CAD is such an amazing tool, allowing designers to build up or carve away minute details in wax, stone or metal, on a much smaller scale than a human hand is capable of. CAD is very new and controversial in the jewellery trade. I am pleased to have been trained in this and in traditional ways.'

Now a successful young independent designer in her own right

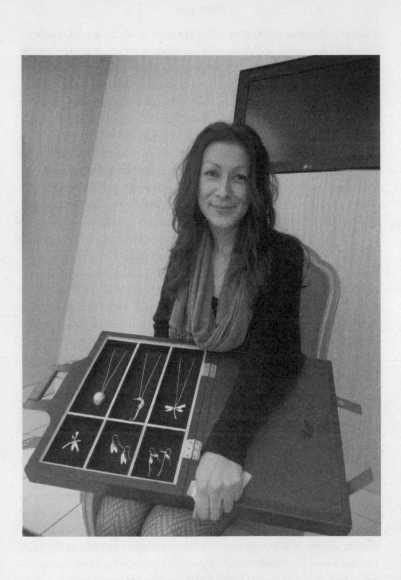

Catherine comes to Hatton Garden every week as she has built up many relationships with people who work there in all aspects of the trade. She visits different workshops, picking things up, dropping things off, getting things made, calling on diamond setters, casters, polishers, engravers, platers and mounters based in and around the street: 'All the suppliers are there whether it is bullion or gemstones, packaging or displays. Everything is so close together, Hatton Garden is still absolutely the centre of the jewellery industry and essential for young designers like myself.'

She started showing her work at Platform after going to the Academy to take a two-day course on promoting her first collection, where she learned how to display and market her work. She enthused for some time about the place, seeing the venture as 'a great opportunity to be showing and potentially selling work to the wider public alongside the best up-and-coming new generation of designers'.

The Academy seemed to be embracing many of the early values of the master craftsmen who first came to Hatton Garden and helped establish the jewellery trade there; focusing on training, attention to craft and learning the skills of setting, mounting, polishing and designing but reinterpreting them in a modern way.

I had recently noticed a couple of large arcades near the Clerkenwell end of the street, which also seemed to hark back in some ways to the very early days of Hatton Garden as a jewellery quarter, with people trading openly across counters, just like they used to in the streets and the kosher cafés before the First World War.

'The big difference is these new jewellery emporiums are not for the trade only. The general public are encouraged to go there to barter and haggle like dealers. Since the credit crunch more of these places are opening up in the Garden. The price for scrap gold is currently comparatively much higher than it was even back in the gold rush of the 1970s. Empty shops have been converted into Manhattan-style jewellery exchanges filled with multiple small market-style units, where traders from across the globe exchange scrap gold for cash, as well as buying and selling antique and modern jewellery, watches, gold coins, loose diamonds, charm bracelets, imported goods, anything they can make a return on.

A cacophony of languages confronts you when you enter these places: Chinese, Yiddish, Urdu, Hebrew, Tamil – with dealers busily striking deals and encouraging potential punters over to their counters: 'Please, miss, you want to sell gold, instant cash for your pre-owned jewellery, best price here.' The pressurized banter in these places reminded me of walking around the Arab market in Jerusalem's Old City. Customers are hassled and cajoled and haggling is an expected part of the exchange.

Many of Hatton Garden's small dealers who used to operate behind closed doors have seized the opportunity and rented a counter in one of these open arcades. Pakistani, Burmese, Indian and Sri Lankan traders have come to London specially to work there, subletting individual booths, specializing in imported goods from their homelands. In the front of one of these emporiums, a row of Sri Lankan dealers sells sapphire stones and jewellery, paying some of the highest rents in the street to have the prime position near to the door, which they trade from aggressively, trying to entice customers over to their counters the minute they enter the building.

In the same emporium, which used to house a Barclays Bank and the London Diamond Bourse, a Chinese-run booth specializes in imperial jade jewellery and freshwater pearls. Near to them an Orthodox bewigged woman sells diamonds. Behind her an Israeli man has a unit filled with gold and silver goods. Many newcomers to the street have also started trading there – the former rules of the Garden do not apply. All the dealers in the arcades have scales for weighing out scrap jewellery and gold. They buy directly off the public and then take the goods down the road to bullion refiners like Pressman's to be melted down.

As they work in such close proximity it is a hard environment to stand out in. Good ideas are stolen, dealers need to be selling more cheaply than their neighbours to survive. The intensely competitive atmosphere and market-style layout creates its own kind of energy, a world away from the gentle vibe in the rest of the shops on the street.

I spent some time speaking with an elderly Jewish man and his daughter, who have worked in the Garden for decades and began renting a booth in one of the arcades a few years ago. He enjoyed the buzzy atmosphere, which reminded him of similar places in New York, Turkey and Tel Aviv. Surrounding his counter was a number of photographs of couples who had bought their engagement rings from him. 'I like to capture this official moment in people's lives, the exact point in time when their world changes for ever. Look at the colour in her cheeks,' he said, pointing to a picture of a young woman in a red top, smiling broadly. 'We have met so many different personalities, from bank managers to very poor people wanting to get married, who come in here with their money saved up in pound coins to buy a ring. I've heard lots of interesting stories.'

We spoke about the international group of people working in these arcades and he told me they all get on well enough. 'Many of the Asian people renting booths working here are very religious like us. Right now it is Ramadan so we commiserate with them about not being able to eat, just like they commiserate with us when it is Yom Kippur.' Although there is a very multicultural mix of cultures in these large indoor markets, the majority are still Jewish. On the lower-ground floor of the largest emporium on the street, a Keddassia dairy vegetarian sandwich bar has recently opened, the only restaurant on the street to offer kosher food. There is also a vending machine selling kosher snacks.

He told me there is a special room set aside downstairs for the Orthodox Jewish traders to pray in and another area in the building where religious Muslim dealers lay out their prayer mats throughout the day. A few minutes later a young man, wearing a suit and a large black hat, came up to him and asked, 'Are you *davening*, Mincha? We need to make up a *minyan*.' This happens every day, someone will go around the arcade looking for the required quorum of ten Jewish adults needed for afternoon prayers.

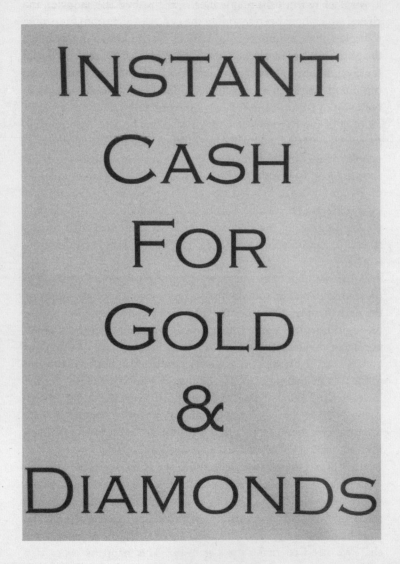

Another recent feature downstairs in this building is tables and chairs, which have been set out in the centre of the room for people to broker deals and openly trade stones and goods from, much like the trading floor I had seen at the Diamond Bourse. It was as if that building, which once housed an earlier version of the Bourse on the first floor, had revolved full circle – Hatton Garden turned inside out.

26

Subterranea

Even as recently as the nineteenth century Ludgate Circus was
shunned by vagrants as a place where rough sleepers could be
dragged down into the sewers, where a monstrous contingent of pigs
roamed; now blind, hairless and white due to centuries of inbreeding in
the darkness of the subterranean network of catacombs beneath Fleet
Street and Farringdon. And more recently, it was alleged that in 1993
two workers doing overtime in the closed tunnels south of Farringdon
tube station disappeared in unexplained circumstances.

Nao Wakarimasen, 'Bladud: The Making of a Tyrant',
from *King Bladud and His Reign of Blood*

The topography around the Hatton Garden area has been physically and geographically altered a great deal over the centuries and
now functions at two different levels: above and below. A warren of
underground tunnels exists around the medieval priories, cells and
subsurface passageways can be found below the prisons of Clerkenwell and disused nineteenth-century railway tunnels sit beneath
Smithfield Market.

Stories circulate about a network of tunnels underneath Hatton
Garden connecting Ely Palace with Ye Olde Mitre and Bleeding Heart
Yard. Under the old seventeenth-century houses on the street, there
are many goldsmiths and jewellery workshops, along with suppliers
of precious metals, stones, gems and even diamond dealers, who all
operate from spaces beneath the shops. I recently visited a cavernous
vault, dripping with gold chains hanging from the ceiling. Against the
walls were cabinets, piled high with nine- and eighteen-carat white,

yellow and rose-gold chains, necklaces and bracelets. These highly secure underground windowless rooms are often run by Orthodox dealers, whose valuable goods are sealed inside heavy safes, with doors as thick as two bricks, made from solid steel.

The largest subterranean public spaces in the area (apart from tube platforms and tunnels) are the London Silver Vaults, situated near to Hatton Garden on Chancery Lane. Built in 1876 as a safety-deposit facility for wealthy individuals to store valuable items, the underground storerooms soon filled up with silverware. Over time the owners of these spaces began trading from there, opening up small showrooms, which gradually expanded into a gigantic hidden silver market. There are over thirty shops there today, selling the largest collection of fine antique silver in the world, along with other jewellery and precious goods. Many of the shops have been handed down from generation to generation. Expert dealers, repairers, makers of silver goods and general silver specialists are now based in this unique shopping centre, beneath London's streets, which seems to mirror the street of gold and diamonds, somehow, just around the corner in Hatton Garden.

Near Holborn tube station there are other subsurface spaces; miles of unused underground lines, along with a hidden fifth platform. Underneath Chancery Lane tube station a vast, deep-level shelter was constructed in the 1940s, to protect Londoners from air raids, with a capacity to hold over 10,000 people, '200 feet beneath the traffic-jammed thoroughfare of High Holborn'. Lit by electric lights and lined with bunks, the shelter was never used by the general public. Instead the twelve miles of tunnels became a top-secret government bunker and communications centre. During the Second World War 'thousands of Government executives would have retired [there] to carry on the battle in the event of invasion or super air raids' (*Evening Standard*, 10 January 1946). Over 500 tons of public records that had been evacuated to the country during the war were temporarily stored there in the late 1940s. The shelter was given to the General Post Office in 1949 and became known as Kingsway or TZK (Trunk Zone Exchange Kingsway), a telephone exchange, which was later run by BT and contained thousands of trunk lines, connecting London with telephone lines all over the UK, along with the hot line between America and Russia, used during the Cold War after the Cuban missile crisis. In 1956 Kingsway became the termination point for the first transatlantic telephone cable. Hundreds of people worked there in the 1950s, 1960s and 1970s, moving around the network of underground tunnels on bicycles. They had their own canteens, bars, a shop, a cinema and a billiard room. The place operated like its own secret underground city before closing in 1979. In 2008 the tunnels were sold to an unnamed buyer.

Deeper underground is a labyrinthine network of brick-lined sewer tunnels, as mentioned earlier, designed by Bazalgette and built in the Victorian era: fluid, watery channels, containing the remains of the River Fleet. Desperate to get down to the sewers myself, I pestered Thames Water for over a year, eventually getting through to the right person in the Press Department who agreed to try to take me on their next journalist visit. I was reminded again of the dangers of visiting these sewers: 'Organizing a trip down to the Fleet sewers is a logistical ordeal; they are the most dangerous sewers to visit, as they are tidal and the hardest to get down to. The flushers have to stop their day jobs, bring a load of kit in their van and park up on the busiest parts of town. So the best we can suggest is you piggybacking on a visit with one or two others,' said the official I spoke to.

A few weeks later a date was fixed, weather permitting. 'If there is any water at all gushing down the drains on the road above, it will be too dangerous to go down as the chance of the storm drain flooding will be extremely high,' I was told.

As the day drew nearer, my curiosity became edged with fear, partly because of my natural aversion to dark underground spaces liable to flooding and partly due to a mild concern about what might be down there. Rats of course came to mind along with other, stranger, mythical creatures. Iain Sinclair told me a story about wild albino pigs, who lived in underground cells beside the

Fleet, grossly fat, munching on the bones of the dead. Thornbury mentions pigsties on the slimy riverbanks in the time of Cromwell; and Henry Barton Baker describes 'grunters' who roamed around beside the 'ditch of Stygian blackness', and 'fattened on putrid garbage'.

A story I came across on the Internet called *King Bladud and His Reign of Blood*, by Nao Wakarimasen, describes a time over 2,000 years ago when London was known as New Troy and ruled by King Lud, who leaves a memory-echo in Ludgate Circus and Ludgate Hill. Bladud, Lud's son, contracted leprosy and was banished outside the city walls where he became a pig herder on the banks of the Fleet, tending to huge beasts, the size of wild boars, as strong and ferocious as Rottweilers. The pigs gained a taste for human flesh and attacked and killed anyone who came near until King Lud drove 'Bladud and his ghastly swine' far from the area, although rumours remain that the giant flesh-eating pigs still wander around in the remains of the Fleet.

In Neil Gaiman's fantasy novel *Neverwhere*, set in 'London Below', the 'Great Beast of London' is a bull that ran into the Fleet before it was enclosed, vanishing into the underground tunnels below, growing fat off the sewage; which may be based on a true story reported on 24 August 1736 in the *Gentleman's Magazine*: 'A fatter boar was hardly ever seen, than one taken up this day coming out of Fleet Ditch into the Thames. It proved to be a butcher's, near Smithfield Bars, who had missed him five months, all which time he had been in the common sewer, and was improved in price from ten shillings to two guineas.'

The very real dangers of exploring the sewage tunnels containing the Fleet were documented in 1851 by J. W. Archer in his *Vestiges of Old London*:

> many persons enter at low tide, armed with sticks to defend themselves from rats, as well as for the purpose 'of sounding on their perilous way' among the slimy shallows; and carrying a lantern to light the dreary passage, they wander for miles under the crowded

streets in search of such waifs as are carried there from above. A more dismal pursuit can scarcely be conceived; so near to the great concourse of London streets that the rolling of the numerous vehicles incessantly thundering overhead, and even the voices of wayfarers, are heard, where, here and there, a grating admits a glimmer of the light of day; yet so utterly cut off from all communion with the busy world above, so lonely in the very heart of the great and populous city, that of the thousands who pass along, not one is even conscious of the proximity of the wretched wanderer creeping in noisome darkness and peril beneath his very feet. A source of momentary destruction ever lurking in these gloomy regions exists in the gases, which generate in their confined and putrefying atmosphere, and sometimes explode with a force sufficient to dislodge the very masonry; or which, taking light from the contact of the lantern, might envelop the miserable intruder in sudden flame. Many venturers have been struck down in such a dismal pilgrimage, to be heard of no more; may have fallen suddenly choked, sunk bodily in the treacherous slime, become a prey to swarms of voracious rats, or have been overwhelmed by a sudden increase of the polluted stream.

Another nineteenth-century explorer of the sewers, a Mr Crosby, visited the tunnels while gathering material for a book about the history of the Fleet Valley on 28 July 1840: 'the tide flowed in so fast from the Thames to Fleet Bridge, that myself and Bridgewater were obliged to fly. It reached the hip, and we got somewhat wet before arriving at Holborn Bridge, quite safe, but much exhausted in splashing through the water in our heavy boots.'

I awoke at dawn on the day of the arranged visit, to a cold, dry December morning. The heavy snow that had recently fallen had just about melted away from the London pavements but patches of black ice still covered the ground. A few dirty piles of slush sat against the kerb of the Embankment as I made my way from Temple tube station towards Blackfriars Bridge for eight o'clock. The rest of the party coming on the expedition was standing beside two large white vans parked up outside Unilever House when I arrived. I waved to Diana, the geologist, who was joining me, along with a photographer, a blogger and someone from the PR Department of Thames Water. Next to Diana was a tall man, wearing khaki waterproof dungarees, a vest and a white helmet. A crowd of about ten men stood near by, dressed in workers' clothes and luminous-yellow jackets with the Thames Water logo printed on the back, all there to assist us on our journey. Bright-orange cones blocked off part of the road and a plastic yellow fence surrounded an open manhole cover on the pavement opposite, which I presumed we would be venturing down later. The person from Thames Water I had spoken to had not been exaggerating when he told me how difficult and costly it was to arrange a visit to the sewers.

A man with the stature of a knight introduced himself as Rob Smith, Thames Water's Chief Sewer Flusher and the person who would guide us underground. We followed him into the back of one of the vans, where he showed us a map of the sewers, pointing out the section of the Fleet we would be visiting, stretching from Blackfriars up towards Holborn Viaduct. Rob explained we had to move quickly; we had only a brief window of time before the tidal waters below reached the roof of the storm drain.

A former oyster dredgeman from Essex, Rob started his career on the cockling boats in Leigh-on-Sea, and has been a sewer flusher for the past twenty-five years: a working life ruled by tides. Clearly passionate about his job, the cheery sixty-year-old described a great camaraderie between himself and his co-workers: 'Our lives literally depend on each other, and of course there is the humour, which is more than necessary in a job like this,' he said, roaring with laughter, slapping his young apprentice Daniel Brackeley firmly on the back.

After signing the necessary waiver forms, we changed into disposable white plastic suits, thigh-high waders with steel soles, hard hats, two pairs of gloves, one latex, the other thick rubber, and colourful harnesses, so if we fell in there would be something to grab us by. Rob placed a heavy gas monitor around the neck of each one

of us, to detect any noxious gases or low oxygen levels, and another weighty lozenge-shape bag over our shoulders, containing a ten-minute saver set with a full-face mask and an oxygen cylinder, 'just in case you get separated from the group'.

Walking outside into the bright, crisp morning, I saw a number of other Thames Water staff around the manhole, lowering ropes, testing equipment. Standing beside the dark void in the pavement, I strained to hear Rob's health-and-safety talk over the noise of the traffic, buses, car horns and loud drilling near by: 'If your monitor starts to beep erratically and the lights are flashing it means the environment below is deteriorating and we will come out sharpish!' he shouted, before descending into the blackness down a slippery vertical ladder, dripping with dark, wet matter. He quickly disappeared from sight. I followed nervously behind, with a rope clipped on to the back of my harness to ensure I did not fall. After a few minutes I reached the bottom of the ladder and stepped warily off into a thick black squelchy substance, a few inches deep.

Rob's voice echoed along a passageway behind me, telling me to move towards him so the rest of the group could come down. Turning around in the narrow space, I found myself in a red-brick arched corridor, just a little wider than shoulder width. I started walking forward into the darkness, the sound of the sirens and the traffic above fading away until all I could hear was the constant 'bleep bleep' of the gas monitor around my neck along with the noise of my short, sharp breathing, amplified by the headphones I was wearing, which were attached to the recording equipment I had strapped to my body. Adjusting the torch on my helmet, attempting to illuminate the corridor in front of me, I began to see the perfectly intact brickwork of Bazalgette's sewers as I walked out of time, through Victorian London.

At the end of the tunnel we turned right into the Blackfriars penstock chamber, a small, square, brick room, containing huge rusty iron cogs used to lower a large gate into the sewers below. Rob pointed out the water flowing beneath the slimy metal platform we were standing on, the low level-one sewer, which runs along the Embankment. Behind us was a dark void, lined with black metal, an old chute used for shovelling snow from the street above.

I stood still, trying to catch my breath, to calm my rising claustrophobia, to adjust to the extreme environment. I inhaled deeply; the smell was familiar, damp, stale, moss-like, ancient, better than I had expected. The air temperature was tepid, at times almost hot; a few feet above us the pavements were still covered in ice.

Rob led us from the low level-one junction, down ever-steeper and ever-more-slippery ladders, the excrement from the soles of our boots rubbing off on to the rungs as we went down. Wandering

through many low-ceilinged narrow tunnels, we moved deeper and deeper underground. 'Watch your step – it's a bit thick here,' Rob called out from the darkness in front of us. Soon we passed a sign on the wall for the Fleet Main Line. We were getting closer.

Walking across Victorian flagstones, we reached a junction, where two tunnels converged into a sharp point. We continued down some stone steps, holding tightly on to a metal handrail, to avoid falling over on the greasy marble underfoot, before moving into another low-ceilinged and very narrow corridor. A large piece of dark, slimy, petrified wood sat on the surface; in front of us the floor was covered in thick black sewage, which reached above our ankles. In one of the tunnels Danny stopped and picked up a huge, gluey-white lump: 'This is a fat berg, made from cooking oil and grease,' he said, breaking apart with his hands the lump, which was the consistency of shiny dough with a filling of human hair and baby wipes. 'I've just spent three months underneath Leicester Square, clearing 1,000 cubic metres of fat from a blocked sewer,' said Danny. 'It was the size of nine double-decker buses. We cleared it with shovels and jet-engine machinery, the last bit we really struggled with, directly underneath the square; we had to get a contractor in with a sort of tunnelling machine, with a giant kind of drill bit on the end and he used that to cut through it. Then it was flushed through the system to Beckton with lots of extra water and eventually burned in incinerators. It comes from all the restaurants tipping oil down the sink, always a lot worse after Christmas.' I noticed Diana's left boot was covered in a thick white substance, which looked like squashed polystyrene, but thought it better to say nothing.

We twisted and turned our way along many more dark brick alleyways, grateful for our kit and our competent guides. Finally we stepped on to another metal gangway, which cut across a large, vaulted chamber. 'Is that all of us, or have we lost someone?' shouted Rob cheerily, over the noise of the rushing water below. As we gathered tightly together on the platform in the cave-like space, the yellow stock brick ceiling above was temporarily lit by the beams of light from our helmets as we looked around. Dark shadows moved across the walls – Victorian ghouls, Dr Dee – many images came to mind. The roof of the chamber dripped with a sticky liquid and small white balls were stuck to the surface – more fat globules. A fossilized pair of tights hung from a stone column above us, with bits of hair, shells and loo roll attached, like a fisherman's net. Behind us were two huge rust-covered metal sluice gates, gigantic steel flaps, the size of houses, hinged from above, ready to swing open into the Thames if the storm drain floods.

Our steel-lined boots echoed on the metal platform, resounding around the cavernous space, as we precariously moved around. Diana's headlight shone on to my previously white suit, which was covered in black skid marks by then. Either side of the Victorian gangway, there were sharp drops down to the swirling waters beneath. Before descending the last ladder, which would take me straight into the Fleet itself, I tried to wipe some of the slime off my gloves to get a firmer grip on the slippery rungs. The flushers had already gone down and were standing in the water below, encouraging me to follow.

Shaking slightly, I arrived at the bottom and took my first step into

the murky, muddy waters of the former river, trying to find my footing on the curved brick floor, thick with silty river mud. Freezing water pressed tightly against my waders, quickly moving up towards my thighs, the cold seeping through the thick rubber. Wobbling in the darkness, I felt a firm hand grab my arm and saw Rob beside me, smiling. Moving around the chamber carefully, my heavy boots glued to the river bed as if I were walking across the moon, I made my way towards the entrance of a long circular tunnel in front of us, which led up to the viaduct. To enter the tunnel you needed to step over a high wooden dam and Rob explained the waters were already too deep there for us to go any further as the tide was rising steadily. He moved into the fast-flowing waters, checking the tunnels for leaks. It was too dangerous for us to follow. Standing firm in a torrent of water, Rob told us: 'If you lose your footing here, the next stop is Abbey Mill Pumping Station. Further up this tunnel there are iron rings attached to the walls, which we think were used for tying up boats when this part of the Fleet was an open canal.'

The smell down there, on the bottom of the Fleet, as low as it is humanly possible to be in London, was different from that in the narrow tunnels above; a familiar odour of salt and estuary mud mixed with something less pleasant, watered-down sewage – the stink of old London.

We stood in silence for some time in the water of the vast chamber, the most dreamlike space I have ever encountered, admiring the incredibly beautiful brickwork, listening to the sound of the rushing water, the clanking of the giant flaps behind us gently swaying open as the river pushed past. A deep rumbling noise came from overhead, as a tube train passed high above. I asked Rob if any animals were able to live down there: 'Nothing apart from a few rats, some crabs, we see a lot of dead rats floating about, drowned when the waters rise, then of course there are the crocodiles,' he said grinning, 'but we chain them up when we get visitors.' He laughed when I mentioned albino pigs lurking in the tunnels and wild bulls but he did say that over the years all the flushers had found something strange down there: bones, rings, guns, even a live hand grenade. Rob had never seen a ghost but others had, in Wick Lane: 'He is called Egbert and wanders around sometimes.'

Exhilarated to be finally standing in the lost river I had now spent so long researching, I spoke enthusiastically about being there to one of the other flushers, who was equally gripped by the place even after decades of working there daily. 'It's like Narnia down here!' he shouted, over the immense noise of the rushing waters. 'If you go further up river, towards Hampstead, the brickwork is immaculate, like it was done yesterday, all done by hand, amazing workmanship. I just love this job. It is never busy down here, not like London, you can walk to Hampstead, Oxford Street, Buckingham Palace, anywhere you want to go, and no one will stop you, there is not one traffic light, you can walk for miles. It's a magical place.'

Not like London. It wasn't. We were physically underneath the city but had entered a different realm, there was nothing in that space apart from ourselves to suggest we were in the twenty-first century. I had managed to achieve something, if only for a few brief moments, which I had been trying to do since I started this project: to peel back the veil of time, to glimpse a moment of the past, to walk in a landscape from a bygone era.

Standing at the bottom of the River Fleet, liquid history, I thought back up, above ground, to Hatton Garden and the stories I had uncovered. After years of researching, crossing the same territory repeatedly, listening and gathering memories, whispers, shards, weaving together fragmentary histories, trying to understand the multiple transitions of the area, I felt that with Hatton Garden, a place so rich in memory-traces, lost landscapes and sacred architecture, I had only just begun to scratch the surface.

Acknowledgements

This book has taken over five years to research and produce and would not have been possible without the help of countless individuals, institutions and private companies. Firstly I would like to thank my editor, Simon Prosser at Hamish Hamilton, for his patience with me again, for allowing me the time and space to complete this project. That thanks extends to Anna Kelly and Anna Ridley from Hamish Hamilton along with Sarah Coward, who has so carefully copy-edited this book. A special thanks also to Iain Sinclair, Chris Schuler and Fiona Perrin, for their invaluable editorial advice and support throughout. I would also like to thank my parents and husband, who have helped in countless ways, with contacts in Hatton Garden, smoothing the way for me, enabling me to access places and people that would not have been possible without their introductions. Many thanks also to my agent, John Parker, for his continued support.

There are many other individuals who have generously shared their stories with me, often taking time out of their busy work schedules to do so. For this I am extremely grateful to: Adriana; Alma (and her daughter, Emma); Tudor Allen; Verusca Calabria; Nigel Cave; Jon Chandler; Adrian Chiappa and the Chiappa family; Diana Clements; Angela Crick; Alan Dein; Mary Flanagan; Iain Godwin, Director of Corporate Communications at Johnson Matthey; Dave and Essie Harris; Gareth Harris; Adam Hasan; Jason Holt and Mr Holt senior; John (the bartender at Ye Olde Mitre); Harold Karton; Henry, Stanley, Antony, Betty, Nancy and James Laurence; Adele Leffman; Martin Macmillan; Marsha; Ron Meadows; Michael (the jewellery repairer), Frederick Mitziman (brother of Isadore 'Mitzy' Mitziman); Ralph Mokades; Mandana Oskoui; Dr David Parker; Jeffery Pinkus; Samantha; Tracey; Dennis Smith; Joseph, Andrew and Amelia Ullmann; Richard Vainer; Stephen

Acknowledgements

Watts; Mr Weissbart; David Williams; Pamela Willis; Robert and Robyn Wilson; and Catherine Zoraida.

A special thanks to Jan Pimblett at the London Metropolitan Archives, for all her help and support throughout this project, and to the rest of the archival staff at LMA too, in particular Jeremy Smith (the maps expert formerly from the Guildhall Library) for both their help with my research and allowing me generous usage of material from their collection in this book. This special thanks extends to Tudor Allen, Chief Archivist at Camden Local Studies and Archives Centre, based in Holborn Local Library, and the rest of the staff there for their continuous support and help and for the use of many images from their collections. A very special thanks also to Johnson Matthey for allowing me to look at their internal history of the company, written by former employees, which was extremely helpful. A huge thank-you to Rob Smith and Daniel Brackeley (sewer flushers for Thames Water) and the rest of the Thames Water team, who made that extraordinary trip under London possible. A special thanks also to the experts who have guided me around the area, sharing their knowledge for this project: Adele Leffman, Tudor Allen and Diana Clements in particular; and thank you to photographer and filmmaker James Price, for taking the journey both above and below ground, for documenting my explorations on the River Fleet and kindly allowing me to use those images in this book. Special thanks also to both Sean Rowlands and Vikki Skinner for their help with obtaining permissions for images and text.

There are many institutions, organizations and private companies who have supported this project in many ways; they include: Artangel, Arts Club, Bleeding Heart Bistro, British Library, British Museum, Camden Local Studies and Archives Centre, Carlo's Jewellers, Clerkenwell Tales Bookshop, De Beers, Dickens Museum, Guildhall Library, Holborn Library, Holts Academy of Jewellery, International Magic Shop, Islington Local History Centre, Johnson Matthey, London Diamond Bourse, London Metropolitan Archives, London Topographical Society, Marx Memorial Library, Metal, Museum of London, Museum of London Archaeological Department, Natural History Museum, National Archives, Ye Olde Mitre Pub, Platform, Queen Mary's College, St Bartholomew's Church, St Etheldreda Church, Smith & Harris Goldsmiths and Silversmiths, and Thames Water.

Because of the many security issues associated with Hatton Garden some names and details have been altered within this text to protect people's identities. Unless otherwise stated the stories included here are from people who have willingly agreed to take part in this project, and are as true as time, memory and artistic interpretation will allow.

Text and Illustrations Permissions

Text

While all efforts have been made to trace the copyright owners of all extracts of published works it has not always been possible to do so and the author apologizes for any omissions. In particular I am very grateful to Howard Marryat and Una Broadbent, whose *Romance of Hatton Garden* (London: James Cornish & Sons, 1930) I have quoted from and used as a major resource throughout this project. Despite extensive efforts to contact the authors and publishers of this long out-of-print book I have been unable to do so. This is also the case with Ellic Howe's *A Short Guide to the Fleet River* (London: T. C. Thompson & Son Ltd, London, 1955).

Many thanks to the following for their kind permission to use extracts from their work: David Higham Associates for the use of John Pudney's *Hatton Garden* (London: Chiswick Press, 1950); Solo Syndication for the quote from the *Evening Standard* (10 January 1946); Hazel Forsyth, the curator of the Tudor Gallery at the Museum of London, for extracts from exhibition panels (originally sourced from Andrea Trevisano's description of London, *c.* 1498, published in *A Relation: or rather A True Account of the Island of England* (London: Camden Society, 1847); David Paul Press for extracts from *Diamonds* by Esther Kreitman, translated by Heather Valencia (London: David Paul Press, 2010); and Crease & Weaken Press for the extract from *Bladud: The Making of a Tyrant* by Nao Wakarimasen (from a pamphlet published in 2002 by the Archaeological Society of Bath).

Illustrations

All pictures are copyright of Rachel Lichtenstein except where otherwise noted in the List of Illustrations. All effort has been made to contact copyright holders of images. Apologies for any omissions.

Many thanks to the following for their kind permission to reproduce these images:

Verusca Calibra, p. 205; Camden Local Studies & Archives Centre, pp. 18, 77, 128, 132, 163, 181, 206; Emanuel's family, p. 94; Islington Local History Centre, p. 195; James Laurence, pp. 275, 276, 279; London Metropolitan Archives, pp. xviii, 12, 13, 16, 39, 44, 48, 50, 52, 61, 85, 102, 105, 125, 135, 136, 140, 148, 166, 169, 178, 237, 238, 240; Frederick Mitziman, p. 119; Museum of London, p. 104; Eileen Nicholls's family, p. 194; James Price, pp. 262, 263, 264, 270, 272, 322, 323, 325, 326, 328, 329, 331; Ullmann family, p. 74; and the V&A, pp. 109, 114.

The author has tried unsuccessfully to contact the copyright holders of the images on pp. 26, 108, 110, 141, 142, 165, 267.

Glossary

baccala: dish of salted cod (Italian)

bar mitzvah: ceremony for a Jewish boy on his thirteenth birthday (Hebrew)

chutzpah: cheek, spunk, audacity (Yiddish)

davening: praying (Yiddish)

frummers: religious Orthodox Jews (Yiddish)

ganufs: old thieves, crooks (Yiddish)

kosher: conforming to Jewish dietary laws (Hebrew)

Hasidic: ultra-Orthodox Jewish sect, originating in eighteenth-century Poland (Yiddish)

latkes: potato pancakes (Yiddish)

mazel: luck (Yiddish)

mazel und broche (also *mazl un brokhe*): luck and blessing (Yiddish)

mensch (plural *menschen*): person of great integrity and honour

mezuzah: small container of verses from Deuteronomy fixed to Jewish doorposts (Hebrew)

mikvah: ritual bath of pure rainwater used for immersion in Jewish purification ceremonies (Hebrew)

mincah: daily afternoon prayers in Judaism (Hebrew)

minyan: required quorum of ten Jewish adults needed for afternoon prayers (Hebrew)

Ostjuden: Eastern Jews (German)

padrone: person who exploitatively employs or finds work for immigrants (Italian)

schleppers: from the term *schlep*, meaning 'to drag'. Roughly translated (in the context used in this book) as someone who brings customers off the street into a shop (Yiddish)

schlemiel: slang for a fool or unlucky person (Yiddish)

shtetl: small village with a Jewish community in Eastern Europe (Yiddish) *shtiebel*: small house of prayer (Yiddish)

tefillin: leather boxes with straps, used in Jewish prayer by men, containing biblical verses; also called phylacteries (Hebrew)

yarmulke: skullcap worn by observant Jewish men (Yiddish)

yeshiva: school for rabbinical and Talmudic studies (Hebrew)

yiddishe: Jewish, Yiddish

yontif : Jewish holiday or festival (Yiddish)

Select Bibliography

Arthur St John Adcock (ed.), *Wonderful London*, 3 vols (London: Amalgamated Press, 1926/7)

Tudor Allen, *The Story of London's Italian Quarter* (London: Camden Local Studies and Archive Centre, 2008)

J. W. Archer, *Vestiges of Old London* (London: David Bogue, 1851)

John Ashton, *The Fleet: Its River, Prison and Marriages* (London: T. Fisher Unwin, 1888)

R. H. Barham (aka Thomas Ingoldsby), *The Ingoldsby Legends* (London: Bentley, 1879)

Caroline Barron, with Penelope Hunting and Jane Roscoe, *The Parish of St Andrew, Holborn* (London: The Diamond Trading Company Ltd, 1979)

Henry Barton Baker, *Stories of the Streets of London* (London: Chapman and Hall, 1899)

John Carter, *Views of Ancient Buildings*, Vol. I (London, 1786)

Helena Chew and Martin Weinbaum (eds), *The London Eyre of 1244* (London: London Record Society, 1970)

S. Denford and D. Hellings, *Streets of Old Holborn* (London: Camden History Society, 1999)

Charles Dickens, *Barnaby Rudge* (London: 1841)

——, *Bleak House* (London: 1852–3)

——, *Little Dorrit* (London: Bradbury and Evans, 1857)

——, *Oliver Twist* (London: Richard Bentley, 1838)

Edward Jay Epstein, *The Rise and Fall of Diamonds: The Shattering of a Brilliant Illusion* (New York: Simon & Schuster, 1982)

G. J. Evans, *An Illustrated Account of St Bartholomew's Priory Church, Smithfield* (London: Normanus, 1874)

John Evelyn, *Memoirs illustrative of the life and writings of John Evelyn, comprising his diary, from the year 1641 to 1705–6, and a selection of his familiar letters* (London: Henry Colburn, 1818)

William Fitzstephen, *A Description of London* (London, c. 1174)

Geoffrey Fletcher, *The London Nobody Knows* (Harmondsworth: Penguin Books, 1970)

Jean Froissart, *Des Chroniques*, 4 vols (Paris: Antoine Vérard, c. 1498)

Thomas Fuller, *The History of the Worthies of England* (London: T. Tegg, 1840)

Neil Gaiman, *Neverwhere* (London: Penguin Books & BBC Books, 1997)

John Gay, *Trivia: or, The Art of Walking the Streets of London* (London: Bernard Lintott, 1716)

Mary Dorothy George, *London Life in the XVIIIth Century* (London: Kegan Paul & Co., 1925)

Francis Grose, *The Antiquities of England and Wales* (London: S. Hooper, 1772)

Henry A. Harben, *A Dictionary of London* (London: Herbert Jenkins Ltd, 1918)

Ellic Howe, *A Short Guide to the Fleet River* (London: T. C. Thompson & Son Ltd, 1955)

Michael Howell and Peter Ford, *The True History of the 'Elephant Man'* (Harmondsworth: Penguin Books, 1980)

Esther Kreitman, *Diamonds* (trs. Heather Valencia) (London: David Paul Books, 2010; orig. pub. 1944)

Louise Lamprey, *In the Days of the Guild* (London: G. G. Harrap & Co., 1918)

John Lehmann, *Holborn: An Historical Portrait of a London Borough* (London: Macmillan, 1970)

Mary Lobel, *The City of London: From Prehistoric Times to c. 1520* (Oxford University Press: International Commission for the History of Towns, British Committee of Historic Towns, 1989–99)

William Maitland, *The History of London from Its Foundation to the Present Time*, 2 vols (London: J. Wilkie, 1772)

Francis Marlowe, *The Hatton Garden Mystery* (London: Arthur Gray, 1935)

Howard Marryat and Una Broadbent, *The Romance of Hatton Garden* (London: John Cornish & Sons, 1930)

T. J. Maslen, *Suggestions for the Improvement of Our Towns and Houses* (London: Smith, Elder & Co., 1843)

Henry Mayhew, *London Labour and the London Poor*, Vol. 1 (London: Woodfall, 1851)

Michael Moorcock, *London Bone* (London: Scribner, 2001)

——, *Mother London* (London: Scribner, 2000)

Henry Morley, *Memoirs of Bartholomew's Priory Church* (London: Chapman and Hall, 1859)

John Noorthouck, *A New History of London: Including Westminster and Southwark*, Book 2, 'Farringdon Ward Without' (London, 1773)

Samuel Pepys, *Diary and Correspondence of Samuel Pepys* (London: Frederick Warne & Co., 1879)

William J. Pinks, *The History of Clerkenwell* (London: Charles Herbert, 1881)

Alexander Pope, *The Dunciad* (1728)

John Pudney, *Hatton Garden* (London: Chiswick Press, *c.* 1950)

Ann Loreille Saunders (ed.), *London Topographical Record*, Vol. XXV, publication no. 132 (1985) (VI. 'The Survey of Hatton Garden in 1694 by Abraham Arlidge' by Penelope Hunting)

George R. Sims, *Living London*, 3 vols (London: Cassell & Company Ltd, 1901–1903)

Iain Sinclair, *White Chappell, Scarlet Tracings* (London: Vintage, 1995)

John Thomas Smith, *An Antiquarian Ramble in the Streets of London* (London: Richard Bentley, 1846)

John Stow, *A Survey of London* (London: J. Wolfe, 1598)

John Strype, *A Survey of the Cities of London and Westminster* (London, 1720)

Richard Tames, *Clerkenwell and Finsbury Past* (London: Historical Publications, 1999)

Christopher Thomas, et al, *Excavations at the Priory and Hospital of St Mary Spital, London* (London: Museum of London Archaeology Service, 1997)

Walter Thornbury, *Old and New London*, Vols I–II (London: Cassell & Company Ltd, 1879)

Ben Weinreb and Christopher Hibbert (eds), *The London Encyclopaedia* (London: Macmillan, 1995)

Sarah Wise, *The Italian Boy: Murder and Grave-Robbery in 1830s London* (London: Jonathan Cape, 2004)

Virginia Woolf, *A Room of One's Own* (London: L. & V. Woolf, 1929)

Websites

www.ancestry.co.uk

www.catherinezoraida.com

www.cityoflondon.gov.uk/lma

www.collage.cityoflondon.gov.uk/

http://www.davidpaulbooks.com/diamonds.shtml

www.debeers.com

http://diamondgeezer.blogspot.com/

www.dickensmuseum.com/

www.field-studies.co.uk

www.googlestreetview.com

http://www.hattongardenjewellerywcck.com/history.htm

http://www.hatton-garden.net/heritage4.html

http://www.hidden-london.com/littleitaly.html

www.history.ac.uk/gh/

http://www.holtsgems.com/

www.islington.gov.uk/heritage

http://libcom.org/library/reds-green-short-tour-clerkenwell-radicalism

http://lndn.blogspot.com/2005_08_01_lndn_archive.html

www.maryflanagan.com

www.matthey.com

www.movinghere.org.uk

http://www.museumoflondon.org.uk/

www.nationalarchives.gov.uk

http://www.platformjewellery.com/

http://shop.slowlydownward.com/FleetStreetStore/fleetpigs.html

www.smithandharris.com

http://www.spartacus.schoolnet.co.uk/LONfair.htm

http://www.subbrit.org.uk/rsg/sites/k/kingsway/index1a.html

http://www.thesilvervaults.com/

http://www.tudorplace.com.ar/Bios/ChristopherHatton.htm

http://www.webhistoryofengland.com/?p=139

www.wikipedia.com

Maps & Surveys

Ralph Agas, *Civitas Londinium: London in the Reign of Queen Elizabeth* (London, *c.* 1570)

Abraham Arlidge, *The Survey of Hatton Garden* (London: London Topographical Society, 1983)

Charles Booth, *Descriptive Map of London Poverty* (London: Edward Stanford, 1889)

Fairthorne and Newcourt, *Survey of London*, 1658

Mary Lobel and W. H. Johns (eds), *The British Atlas of Historic Towns*, Vol. III (Oxford: Oxford University Press, 1989)

John Ogilby and William Morgan, *Survey of the City of London* (on a scale of 100 feet to the inch), completed in 1676

Adrian Prockter and Robert Taylor (eds), *A to Z of Elizabethan London* (London: London Topographical Society, 1979)

John Rocque, *An Exact Survey of the Citys of London, Westminster . . . and the country near ten miles round* (London, 1746)

THE **DIAMOND STREET** APP

The Diamond Street App takes you on a walk in and around the jewellery quarter of Hatton Garden.

Using content from the book along with specially developed rich media, sound-scapes and interactive features, this app allows you to either go on a real guided tour around the area or follow a virtual version from the comfort of your armchair.

As users move within the boundaries of the original Hatton Garden estate, they are immersed in the atmosphere, history and stories of specific locations by GPS-activated sounds, images, film and text.

Part new media experience, part walking tour, this location-based app is a fusion of text, event, documentary film, image, play and real time experience.

It is the perfect companion to the book and offers a new and deeper way to engage with the story of this fascinating area.

The Diamond Street App is free to download in the itunes app store from June 2013.

www.diamondstreetapp.com